Vengeance of the Allies: A World War 2 Novel

Ethan Watts

Published by Ethan Watts, 2021.

This is a work of fiction. Similarities to real people, places, or events are entirely coincidental.

VENGEANCE OF THE ALLIES: A WORLD WAR 2 NOVEL

First edition. August 9, 2021.

Written by Ethan Watts.

This book is dedicated to my beautiful wife, may you always be an inspiration to me. A special shout out to Chris, David, Natalie, Brittanie, and Jess, for all your hard work in helping me realize my dream.

PREFACE

THE SECOND WORLD WAR was easily and single-handedly the most destructive and defining conflict of the 20th century. It also brought to light the very worst humanity had to offer and affected the lives of millions of people all over the world.

While this is a work of fiction, there are many elements of this story that are based on actual places and some real-life characters. This story is in no way meant to desecrate their memory but is meant to honor the sacrifice they and many others had to make. There are many stories told about the heroism of Allied soldiers, but none with predominantly Canadian characters. There is a widely held belief that Canada truly came of age as a nation during the Second World War, and contributed greatly to the Allied victory. From the shores of Dieppe to the D-Day invasion at the beachhead at Juno to finally the liberation of Holland and the continent of Europe, Canada's fathers, brothers, and sons sacrificed their lives for the freedom of the Western world.

My grandfather was a navigator in the RCAF, and my great uncle was a soldier in the Canadian Army, and this novel is an homage to them and all those who fought for Canada and all the Allied nations for the cause of freedom. I encourage you to go and look up Canada's role in WW2 and learn about the challenges that faced the greatest generation of Canadian citizens.

—E. WATTS

CHAPTER ONE

IT WAS TURNING INTO a very slow night.

Patrice took his cloth and wiped down the top of the chipped, old wooden bar. There were only a few customers left, wallowing in their miseries it seemed. His bar, *Le Rose Noire* or *The Black Rose* to those across the channel, was looking every bit its age. Located on a simple side street off the promenade, it was walking distance to the ocean and had been known as a fixture in the Marseille lifestyle. Back then, it had oozed old-world charm, with its handcrafted furniture and bespoke booths for intimate conversations. It was a place to be and a place to be seen. He looked around the room, seeing the decay in the auburn stained chairs and tables, the distressed cracks in the black leather that covered the seats of the few booths dotted around the room. It may not be the diamond that sparkled so brightly, but what did sparkle were the memories.

He vividly recalled the birthday parties, anniversary celebrations, birth announcements that were celebrated with such vigor. There was even a particular retirement party for a local dock worker that lasted well into the early morning hours, forcing Patrice into a lengthy conversation with the gendarmes. But those paled in comparison to the celebration that was held at the ending of the Great War. Patrice had not been able to serve, due to an accident he had as a boy, which left the strength of his right arm severely reduced. He had helped in any way he could, and when the final shot rang out on November 11, he had made sure to open his establishment to all returning countrymen. The smiles and the laughter on those men's faces as they felt peace for the first time in many years was something Patrice would never forget.

Sadly, some twenty-five years on, the only smiles and laughter from soldiers in this bar were coming from the large corner table.

And they were not French.

One of the soldiers seated at the table waved at Patrice, calling for a refill on his cognac. Sighing, Patrice obliged him.

"Barkeepppp..." slurred the German soldier, in his native language. His voice had a high-pitched lilting tone to it, no doubt made worse by the alcohol. *Such a waste of good cognac*, Patrice thought to himself.

"Tell me, as we have a little wager going..." He paused again, stifling a little laugh. His compatriots at the table also snickered under their breath.

Patrice grabbed a few empty glasses off the table, trying desperately to hide his annoyance. "What is it, *Oberleutnant*?

"Whyyy...is this place such a shithole?" At the end of the question, the table burst into riotous laughter. Patrice smiled, even though he didn't want to. He looked down at the man who'd spoken to him. Strands of almost opaque blonde hair draped across his face. He could not have been older than twenty. His cheeks, already rosy from drinking, were now a bright crimson from laughing. Patrice felt like throwing up.

"Begging the *Oberleutnant's* pardon..." Patrice was interrupted by the German tugging on his sleeve.

"Rissmiller."

"I'm sorry?"

"That is my name—Rissmiller. But, please, continue Barkeep..." Rissmiller grandly waved his hand.

Patrice hesitated, then continued.

"Begging the *Oberleutnant* Rissmiller's pardon, but the occupation has left us with very little..."

Again, Patrice was interrupted by Rissmiller.

"I'vvve heard enough, Barkeep." Removing a fold of money from his pocket, he peeled off two bills and laid them on the table. One of the other soldiers quickly gobbled them up.

"As you can see, I lost." He made a pantomime sad face, punctuated by his fingers pulling the sides of his mouth downwards. "You seeee...I told them it was because you had a mistress!" He chuckled to himself. Peeling off another two bills from his stack, he put them in Patrice's palm and enclosed it with both of his hands. "For God's sake, Barkeep, go buy some better chairs. These are very wobbly!"

At that, Rissmiller pretended to fall back, and the whole table burst into laughter again. Patrice pretended to laugh as well, bowed his head, and returned to the comfort of behind the bar. He threw down the money, stifling the anger that was rising inside him. *Disgusting pigs, these Germans.*

He ducked below the bar to grab a few more bottles for stock when he heard the main door swing open; it was then that any hopes that Patrice had of closing up were dashed.

Stepping into the bar, and taking a long look around was another group of German soldiers. The lead German, removed his leather coat, revealing a crisp uniform dotted with patches and medals. Patrice had no idea what each one meant, but he assumed he was an officer of some sort. If the old wooden beams holding up the bar ceiling had been a bit lower, Patrice mused, the man would've had to duck under them just to get to a table.

Patrice had begun to re-stock, placing the liquor bottles on the slanted shelves, but out of the corner of his eye, he saw the new officer and his entourage make their way to the other group. What ensued next surprised even him even further.

The large officer approached Rissmiller, whose friends had seen him coming and stood at attention. With his back turned and senses no doubt dulled by the cognac, he was slow to notice his surroundings. The officer, seemingly impatient, picked up the red-faced Rissmiller and proceeded to verbally berate him. Patrice was no stranger to this, he had to have many similar conversations with inebriated customers in the past. He just didn't expect this to come from another German.

After a few more words between the two, the conversation began to get more animated until Patrice saw the large German raise his hand, and browbeat Rissmiller into submission like an insolent dog. The yelps of pain as the large German's open palm struck Rissmiller's face hastened the exit of the last few remaining non-German patrons that inhabited the bar. While he enjoyed what he was witnessing, a small sense of dread began to creep into the back of his mind. The size and demeanor of this new German, coupled with the display of brute force, began to sober Patrice's thoughts.

The large German shouted, "*AUS! [OUT!]*"

Rissmiller, by now cowering on the floor, held his hands up in a pitiful defense. His friends, their faces in shock at what had just occurred, grabbed the bruised and battered *Oberleutnant* from the bar's floor. Nodding curtly at Patrice, they made their way to the exit. Three of the new party shared a joke it seemed, and two sat down at the table. The larger German, fresh from his accosting, came over to the bar, while a fourth leaned against the back wall.

He sat down, tossing his hat and slowly removing his black gloves. He ran a hand through his dark brown hair and looked up at Patrice. Sizing him up, Patrice believed the German was easily over six feet. He barely fit on the stool. However, that wasn't the main feature that drew Patrice's eye. He tried not to stare, but the scar that stretched from his right cheek down to his neck was hard not to notice. One of the other soldiers standing a few feet back, had his machine gun slung around his shoulder, his eyes watching every movement. Trying not to show his unease, Patrice felt a bead of sweat roll down the side of his head.

"My apologies...?"

The German paused, waiting for Patrice to respond.

"Patrice."

"My apologies, Patrice, for the conduct of the *Oberleutnant*. As a German Army officer, he should conduct himself in a manner that is more... becoming."

Patrice shrugged his shoulders. "It is no trouble. Would you like something to drink?"

The German brushed off Patrice's question, waving his hand around at the surroundings. "This... establishment, it is popular with the German officers, no?"

The question caught Patrice a little by surprise. It was true, there were Germans soldiers in and out of here on a daily basis. Maybe this hulking German was new in town.

"Yes, we do serve lots of soldiers. I am told that we are one of the only places that serve schnapps nearby."

Patrice was desperately trying to keep the conversation light, but he couldn't help but stare at the soldier leaning against the wall.

The large German, seeing Patrice's gaze leave his face and fixate on the gun, smiled and said, "Don't worry about the Corporal back there, one can never be too careful these days. Now, that is interesting about the schnapps! My officers and I will have a couple of schnapps and then we will be on our way." The man's voice chilled Patrice's blood immediately. The tone of his voice, while seemingly calm, had a strong undercurrent of subtle menace to it. The large German grabbed his hat and gloves, heading back to join his men. Patrice removed four small crystal glasses, giving them a quick wash from the tap. Grabbing a half-filled bottle from the shelves behind him, he filled the glasses and took them to the Germans. They clinked their glasses and sat conversing in their native tongue. Patrice went back to wiping down the bar and stacking some more of the glasses. All the while, he kept one eye on the night's last patrons. Patrice was sure he had not seen them around the bar before. *Could they be part of some new unit coming into town?* The flashes on their uniform were different from the men that usually came in here. He had to find out more information, so he poured another four glasses of schnapps and wandered over to the table.

Placing them in the center, he said, "Here you go gentlemen, compliments of the house."

The large German took one of the glasses, raising it in a toast. While the other soldiers clinked together, he just held his glass in front of him. As Patrice stood there, the large German's eyes never left him. Patrice smiled and did his best to look non-threatening. As he walked back to the bar, he could feel the German's eyes still on him.

He finished stacking a few cases of wine, and as was a tradition every night, Patrice poured himself a small glass. It was his treat for making it through another day. He had come to cherish it. Sipping it slowly, he watched the new set of Germans chat politely as they drank the last round of schnapps.

Patrice checked his watch. Closing time. He began to get the bar ready for closing and took off his apron as he made his way over to the Germans.

"I am sorry, my friends, but I have to close up for the night. I will be back here tomorrow at noon if you'd like to come back then." Patrice said as he gathered up the empty glasses from the table.

The massive German with the scar running down his face stood, brushing some dust from his uniform. While his comrades also stood, he responded to Patrice. "Of course, barkeep, we are keeping you from your duties. I must say, our friends were wrong about the decor, but they were correct about the schnapps. Ah, but I'm keeping you. We will be on our way."

He grabbed his long leather jacket and remaining uniform accessories. The rest of the men shuffled past, gave some sort of thanks in German, and headed towards the door.

Patrice waited until they had left, then shuffled some of the chairs, turned off the lights, and went out into the night air. He turned the key in the semi-rusted lock, heard the familiar click, and started walking down the block. He was lucky, he only lived a few blocks away, in a small two-bedroom apartment. Not completely sure why he did it, Patrice lingered outside the bar, staring back through the darkened window. Just like the glass of wine, he did it every night. He supposed he wanted to forget the struggle that he and his fellow countrymen had endured, day after day. Perhaps it was to also remember happier times when the lyrics of *La Marseillaise*, not *Deutschlandied* were sung with such gusto and passion by all those present. However, at this very moment, it was just an empty window to a now empty bar.

The smell of the salt from the sea touched his nose, carried on the warm breeze that signaled the spring and summer months. The street lights flickered along the cobblestone streets, casting dancing shadows along the many shop windows. The large plane trees, with chalk-colored trunks, dotted the median at regular intervals. The rustle of their recently sprouted leaves mixed with the distant chiming of a church bell, tolling the top of the hour. He remembered running down this bustling sidewalk as a young boy, touching the green and purple window coverings along the way. Then he would stop at *Monsieur* Rideau's bakery, the smell of fresh baking bread and pastries wafting in every direction, enticing passersby in. Sadly, the bakery sat boarded up, as did most of the block's stores, save for the bar. *Monsieur* Rideau and his family had gone, fleeing from the threat of danger in this old city. His mind started to wander back to the second group of Germans that had come in that evening. He had never seen their uniform type before, but to be honest, Patrice saw so many on a nightly basis, they all blurred into one.

As he rounded the corner and walked up the block to his building, he fumbled in his pocket for his cigarettes. If he timed it right, he could smoke one and be done in time to head up the stairs. Placing the cigarette between his lips, he reached for his lighter, not paying attention to his surroundings for a moment.

Suddenly, a bright white light shone out from the alley, temporarily blinding him. He put his hand up to shield his eyes hoping to get a glimpse of the light source.

Then he heard a voice, somewhere behind the light, one that he had heard earlier that night.

"Ahhhh, where are my manners barkeep, let me get that for you." The German officer from earlier stepped out from the shadows and came over to Patrice. The lighter, barely visible in the man's large gloved hand, sparked as he lit the cigarette for Patrice, and then proceeded to light one of his own.

"How insulting of me, calling you barkeep, when we should be exchanging names. I, for instance, am *Sturmbannführer* Maximillian Vahlen. And you, you are Patrice Robillard."

His voice had a purpose, little inflection. The way in which he spoke belied a modicum of charm. Patrice began to sweat profusely. "How... how do you know my name?" His hands were shaking, and there was a slight crack in his voice.

"Oh, I know a great many things. I, for instance, know that a man of your name owns a lovely little bar in a certain district of Marseille. I also know that this bar is frequented by many German officers stationed here and that there are... some suspicious events that need explanation. But that will come in time, I'm sure of it."

At the end of the sentence, Vahlen took a long drag of his cigarette and came closer to Patrice.

"Now, get in the car. This is not a request."

Patrice gulped. It felt like his stomach might try to escape through his mouth. He hoped the cigarette would calm his nerves a bit, but it did not. Vahlen waved his hand and two more German soldiers appeared, each armed with a machine gun.

"Come, Patrice, you have given us the hospitality of your establishment. It is now time for us to return the favor."

Vahlen smiled, and put his hand on Patrice's shoulder, ushering him towards the car. For a moment, he considered making a run for it but knew they would cut him down before he reached safety. The open car door was dark, and fear crept over Patrice like an ocean wave. He had heard stories, stories of people being taken by the Gestapo or the *SS*, and then never being heard from again.

He got in, reluctantly, and as the car pulled out, Patrice's thoughts turned towards his wife and child, and lastly to his beloved bar. Perhaps, when he looked at it earlier tonight, it really was been for the last time.

The car drove down a few back alleys and came out onto *Avenue Du Prado*, pulling up in front of a large stone building. Patrice recognized it as the Marseille police headquarters, and as the guards sitting next to Patrice exited the car, he was soon made to exit it with them. Going up the crumbling stone stairs, past the large double doors, the station opened into a massive lobby. Patrice noticed the two marble stone pillars immediately, standing guard at the base of the wide staircase that led to a darkened second level. On his left, a varnished wooden banister cordoned off a bullpen of desks, currently vacant and devoid of sound. To his right was a thick auburn receiving desk that seemed to stretch all the way to the roof, currently manned by a sleepy-looking *gendarme*, who gave a brief nod as the Germans pushed Patrice along before returning to his late evening haze. The floor, patterned in alternating black and white tiles, echoed their footsteps in the cavernous room.

"There... now move!" shouted the soldier behind Patrice. The man was pointing to the left of the stairwell, down a softly lit hall. Patrice obliged, and one of the soldiers stepped in front of him, opening the white door, which led to a descending spiral staircase. At the bottom, a long hall opened, with metal doors on either side. They were now in some lower level of the station. The bright colors of the upstairs were replaced with bland, gray walls, and the smell of dampness was all around, which made the air slightly thick. The light came from a few uncovered naked bulbs, dangling from the ceiling. All of this would've shaken Patrice, however, there was something else that was garnering his attention.

It was the cacophony of human misery that rang out, from everywhere.

Whimpers and cries for help, coupled with general sobbing assaulted Patrice as the guards led him down the corridor. The voices, both male and female it seemed, were dripping with despair and desperation. Patrice could barely walk; he was shaking so nervously. His vision had tunneled.

Finally, the guards stopped in front of a thick metal door. They opened it, and the loud scrape of it echoed in the hall. Patrice looked in, seeing a small wooden table, with four chairs neatly stacked around. A low shaded lamp hung from the ceiling. The guards, impatient at his dawdling, shoved him into the room. The loud scrape of the heavy door, followed by the clank of the bolt locking it shut, drove home the point to Patrice the type of situation he was in.

Many horrible thoughts raced through his head. *Why were they doing this? Would he see his family again?* At this last thought, he lost himself over to his grief.

Last summer, he had taken his wife, Yvonne, and their young daughter, Esmée, to the beach, not far from the Old Port district. The sun had been shining brightly, and it was Esmée's first time down by the ocean. Oh, how she frolicked about in her little bathing suit, running back and forth from the rising tide. The look of joy on his wife's face, how in that shared perfect moment, they had known true happiness. No strife of occupation, no threat of death hanging over them. That memory seemed like something out of a motion picture, compared with the grim surroundings he currently occupied. He let the emotion wash over him and started to weep.

The door flew open, forcing him to look up.

A German officer entered, who was much skinnier, with carefully slicked back golden blonde hair. He was quite odd-looking, with a sharp nose and beady eyes. He had a languid pace about him, neither hurrying nor traipsing, but his rangy legs quickly made up the distance from the door to the table.

He sat down across from Patrice, placing a small folder down. After him, the large German, Vahlen, came in and shut the door. He stood near the back of the room, ominously so, staring only at Patrice. The German at the table took out a pack of cigarettes, and slid it over to Patrice, gesturing for him to take one.

After watching Patrice light the cigarette, he spoke: "Good evening, Mr. Robillard." The German opened the file folder on the table and started to leaf through the papers. "This conversation of ours can go one of two ways, so I urge you to make your choices wisely. I am *Hauptsturmführer* Eberhard Teicher. I would very much like to see you give us what we are looking for and spare yourself future... *trouble*. Now, I will ask you some questions, and in turn, you will give us some answers." Teicher closed the file folder in front of him and interlaced his spindly fingers on the table.

Patrice nodded solemnly before Teicher continued.

"Two months ago, there was an assassination of an *SS* officer, Ludwig Kampfer. The person who committed this horrible crime has not been found. But... we have some clues. And one of those clues... is you."

Patrice shook his head, trying to avoid the gaze of the man across from him. Teicher unclasped his hands, opened the folder again, gently turned a few more pages, and continued to speak.

"We found a few officers that said he frequented your establishment, quite a lot from what it says here. We also know he was ambushed and killed not long after leaving your establishment. That makes you our number one priority, Mr. Robillard. Now, if you confess, we can make sure that your family is spared from being shipped to a prison camp."

Patrice started panicking and began a rambling statement, almost pleading with the them. "Lots of Germans frequent my bar, that doesn't mean I shot this... this Kampfer. Besides, I was working that night, many people saw me... I'm not a violent man!"

"ENOUGH!" shouted Vahlen, as he came away from the wall, walking over and standing behind Patrice. He lifted Patrice from the chair and held him up by his collar against the wall, leaning in close. "If there is one thing I cannot stand, it's LIARS! Even if you did not pull the trigger yourself, you know who did. Talk, and I will promise to make your death quick." Vahlen's eyes narrowed as he stared at Patrice. The strength of the Germans' grip was tangible. Patrice felt he could crush him at any moment.

"I swear to you, sir, on my wife and daughter, I did not do anything."

That statement seemed to catch Vahlen off-guard, and he lowered Patrice back to the ground.

"You swear, do you?" Vahlen paced back towards the door, where he turned back. A wicked grin had come across his face. "On your wife and daughter?"

He opened the door and shouted something in German, then waved with his hand. There was a brief silence that came over the room. Then, the unmistakable clicking of boots and shoes on concrete. The sounds got closer, and closer until they reached the entrance.

"PATRICE!"

The familiarity of the voice sent a chill down Patrice's spine. *Yvonne.*

She looked distraught, as to be expected. Her shoulder-length auburn hair, normally tied up, hung loosely at the back. Her bright yellow dress looked rumpled, and a bit of her lipstick was smeared at the corner of her mouth. The eyeliner on her lovely round face had started to run. *What had these beasts done to her?*

"Papa, papa!"

Esmée. The sound of her panicked voice broke Patrice's heart. Not much older than seven, she clung to her mother's hand in her little white dress. He wanted to run to her, and scoop her up in his arms. Something was beginning to replace the fear and dismay in Patrice's heart.

It was rage.

Vahlen said something else in German to the guards, then shut the door.

"Now, Patrice, you were going to swear on these ladies' lives that you know nothing about the death of Kampfer?" Vahlen pushed Yvonne and Esmée further into the cell, towards the far wall.

"Patrice, what are they saying? I don't understand..." Yvonne was practically pleading to him.

"For the last time, sir, I swear I know nothing of this Kampfer!" Patrice cried, turning towards Yvonne. They locked eyes, Patrice mouthing the words "I'm sorry."

Again, another lengthy silence. Vahlen sighed, then looked at Teicher. The men nodded.

Suddenly, Teicher came around the table, grabbing hold of Patrice by the arms. "What... what are you doing?" Patrice shouted.

"Putting the right amount of pressure," responded Vahlen, going over towards Yvonne. With a swift motion, he brushed aside Esmée, knocking her to the ground while simultaneously grasping Yvonne by the throat with both hands. He held her against the wall, choking her.

Despite the pleas from Patrice, and the shouts of their seven-year-old daughter, he did not stop. Patrice watched in horror as a twisted grimace came over the man. He recognized it, from that day on the beach.

Pure joy.

Patrice struggled against Teicher's hold, and try all he might, he couldn't prevent what was happening. He watched in horror as Yvonne's eyes started to roll into the back of her head. She flailed wildly, her lungs desperate for air. Her arms struck the side of Vahlen's, but they were as thick as steel beams, her efforts bouncing off without effect.

Just when all seemed lost, that Patrice would witness the horror of his wife murdered in front of his and his daughter's eyes, the door to their right burst open.

"*Sturmbannführer Vahlen*! Unhand that woman. This interview is over!"

Patrice turned towards the door, to see where the voice was coming from. He was greeted by a man, early fifties by his guess, his hair closely cut, but clearly with grey at the temples. His face was round, his nose flat, but red, probably caused by excess drink. His white dress shirt, which held back a small belly, was partially buttoned, covered slightly with black suspenders that held up his ashen uniform pants. He couldn't quite place it, but he had seen the man's face before. He had been to the bar, of that Patrice was sure.

Incredulous at the recent events, he turned back towards Yvonne and watched as she fell to the floor, gasping for air and clutching her throat with her hand. Esmée was off to the left of her, sobbing.

"Patrice, you and your wife and child are free to go. Take them, and leave... now!" The mystery German gestured to the corridor, and Patrice didn't think twice. He struggled out from Teicher's grip and raced over to Yvonne. Cradling her in his arms, he grabbed for Esmée's small hand, which trembled in his clutch. He placed Yvonne around his shoulder and they moved towards the door. Vahlen stood not far away, seething. Patrice could practically see the fire in the man's eyes. *Bastard*, Patrice thought.

Once they reached the door, Patrice said to the German, "Thank you."

The man said nothing but continued to point. Patrice exited the room, and it immediately felt as if someone had removed a stone slab from his chest. Yvonne was coughing profusely, but he refused to stop, for fear that they would come for them again. He used all his strength and helped her down the hall, past some surprised-looking guards, up the spiral stairwell, and finally through the opulent lobby and then outside into the night.

Once they were a block away, Patrice collapsed next to the side of a sandstone building. As Yvonne struggled to regain her breath, he held Esmée close to his chest. All three huddled like that for some time, before heading back home.

———◆———

BACK DOWN IN THE CELLAR of the police station, Vahlen and Teicher were confronted with a very stern-faced Colonel Thomas Grassl. They had heard he was the commanding officer of the *Wehrmacht* units stationed in Marseille and the surrounding areas. Vahlen had met him earlier in the day, after he and his unit had arrived from Germany. A career Army officer, Vahlen had found out his family background traced back to the Prussian military, and every generation of his family had served in the military for Germany in one way or the other. There were also rumors that he wasn't an ardent Nazi, but they were only that—rumors. Not quite as tall as Vahlen, he nevertheless cut a commanding presence.

Once Patrice and his family had left, Colonel Grassl had begun his questioning of Vahlen and Teicher. "Major, I don't pretend to understand your methods. I know the *SS* is skilled in dealing with the Resistance, and that you were assigned here to find the killer of that murdered *SS* officer. However, I feel that choking a man's wife in front of him and his daughter is grotesque, especially when the man is innocent."

"Oh, is that so, Colonel Grassl?" Vahlen retorted, letting the insolence drip from his voice. "Don't forget, it was our officer that was assassinated, and my orders come from Himmler directly to find those responsible."

"I know, *Sturmbannführer*, I am simply saying..."started Grassl, but he couldn't continue as Vahlen spoke up.

"When I want the Army's help, I'll ask for it. We have it on good authority that that man you just let go did it himself or knows who did. And as for my methods, it's not up to you to dictate how I conduct my business!"

"Oh, but it is, Major. Did you not accost *Oberleutnant* Rissmiller earlier tonight for his conduct?"

Vahlen was silent. *That's what must have drawn the Colonel down here*, he thought, *so late in the evening*.

Grassl continued. "I thought as much. I know you're Himmler's favorite lapdog, Vahlen, but that doesn't give you the right to challenge my men, or go around torturing the citizens of this town for your enjoyment. You want to create more danger for the units here?"

Grassl let the question hang in the air, but didn't give Vahlen enough time to answer.

"I can say for certain that he did not shoot *Hauptsturmführer* Kampfer, and I can also say that he most likely does not know who killed him. I assure you."

"Well, if you are so informed, Colonel, maybe I'll just send a message to Himmler myself that we are not needed here because you have things well under control." Vahlen snorted with derision. "Tell me, how do you know this?" he continued to chide Grassl.

"It's simple, *Herr* Vahlen. The night Kampfer was shot, I was hosting a party for my officers, and we were at that man's establishment. He catered dinner for us, and he did not leave. I can assure you, Major, we did not see anything out of the ordinary that night."

Vahlen and Teicher shared a look but did not say anything.

"It's your decision gentlemen, but there will be many a disappointed soldier if you shut down their favorite drinking establishment." At that statement, Colonel Grassl turned to leave.

"Let me remind you, Major, that this is an *SS* operation. We will make the final decision, with or without your consent. Remember this as well, Kampfer was a family friend of the *Reichsführer*, so he has taken a deep personal interest in this mission. When you speak to me, consider that you are speaking directly to him."

Colonel Grassl nodded his head curtly and left without saying a further word to either man.

"Thank you for your time, Colonel." said *Hauptsturmführer* Teicher, moving towards *Sturmbannführer* Vahlen. "What now, Major?"

"Something is going on here, I can feel it. I want you to get yourself immersed into it, Eberhard, as you usually do."

Teicher smiled and nodded. "What do you want to do about the bartender, sir?"

Vahlen braced himself against the wall, deep in thought. "I doubt the good Colonel would lie to us about that party, but Mr. Robillard does know something. Have Weiss talk to the local Gestapo and tell them to keep an eye on him. If they object, tell them they can expect a visit from me.

"As you wish, Major."

"And have them keep an eye on Colonel Grassl, as well," said Vahlen, acknowledging a salute from his subordinate as he left.

———— ◉ ————

A FEW HOURS LATER, still shaken from the nights' events, Patrice stood next to his small sink, filling a small glass of water. Grabbing a cloth, he dampened it, watching his hands shake uncontrollably as the water washed over them.

Taking a deep breath to calm his rapidly beating heart, he reflected on the fact he was still alive, and he was home.

The apartment, just a few blocks away from the bar, which allowed Patrice to walk to work every day, was nothing special. The walls, painted in a pale mustard color by the previous owner, had started to peel in certain spots. The floorboards, once shiny and polished, were now dented and damaged. The kitchen was especially horrid, cramped, and confined. It barely had enough room to hold the charred stove, which was offset to the sink, stained brown by rust. The icebox door was barely hanging on, and Patrice had fixed it multiple times.

He sighed. Despite all of this, it was the best thing he could ever see, right at this moment.

Carrying the items down the narrow hall, he passed Esmée's room. Hearing no sounds, he continued towards the main room. No doubt she was sleeping soundly. There was something to be said about the innocence of youth.

Reaching the end of the hall, it opened to the biggest room in the apartment— the living room. Yvonne, her neck still flush from where Vahlen had choked her, lay strewn on their green velvet couch. He placed the cloth across the top of her forehead, and gently put the cup on the coffee table. Her hand reached out and grabbed Patrice's, lightly squeezing it.

Across from the table, a weathered dark brown leather chat sat with its footstool, which Patrice headed for. Strategically placed to take advantage of a roaring fire, should there be one from the nearby hearth, the chair seemed to envelop Patrice as he collapsed with exhaustion.

Without a shadow of a doubt, he thought he would be executed. He thought back to what the Germans had said—that he had committed the murder of this *SS* officer, that he was responsible.

How did they even get his name?

Patrice racked his brain trying to figure out what had happened.

"Patrice?"

He came up empty.

"Patrice?"

It was Yvonne. She was still lying prone, her voice raspy.

"Don't speak, my darling. You must rest."

Ignoring his advice, she started to sit up. "I will survive, my loving husband. How... what happened tonight? Why did the Germans come after you?"

Patrice scratched the back of his head, shrugging his shoulders. "I don't know! I didn't even know about this German officer that was killed!"

Yvonne took her hand, feeling around the red marks on her neck. She winced as she touched one of the finger marks. "I was so worried. When you didn't come home, I thought you might be dead. I thought that I would never see you again. Then came a knock at the door. I thought it was you. They said we just had to come in for a little chat..."

Yvonne tailed off as tears streamed down her face. Patrice got up to comfort her, but she waved him away.

"I knew it. All those Germans in the bar, every night. I knew one day it would come back on us."

Patrice ignored her comment and sat back in the chair. He thought back to earlier when the skinnier German... what was his name... Teicher, had started the interrogation. He had said that the German who had been killed drank in Patrice's bar the very night he died. More thoughts started to form, and his face started to grimace. Yvonne must have noticed, as she spoke up.

"Patrice... are you alright?"

The question snapped him out of his thoughts. "What? Oh yes, I am fine. Just idle thoughts."

Checking his watch, he rose from the chair and made his way towards his wife. "Come, my dear. Let's go to bed."

She nodded in agreement and outstretched her hand.

Patrice helped her up, and they both walked back through the kitchen and made their way to the bedroom. It was time to get some well-deserved rest.

The next day, Patrice awoke before Yvonne, leaving her sleeping away in bed. He went to the kitchen to fix himself a cup of coffee. Putting the cup to his lips, he tasted the watery bitterness that sufficed for coffee in this occupation. He was still rattled by the previous night's events and now there was the gnawing thought in the back of his mind that wouldn't go away. A high-ranking German officer, killed on the night he happened to be drinking at the Black Rose. He could understand the German's interest in himself, and Patrice had resolved last night, before he fell asleep, that he needed some answers. And he knew the exact spot to get them.

Walking over to the phone, he set the cup of coffee down and began dialing. Once the operator came on, Patrice said, "Doctor Moreault's office," and the call got put through to a sprightly sounding voice of the receptionist. After a little small-talk, which Patrice tolerated, he requested an emergency appointment, today.

She acquiesced, and he hung up the phone. His appointment would leave him just enough time to finish his coffee.

Heading back into his kitchen, he happened to look out the window and down onto the street. A man was standing there, not far from the entrance to his apartment building, dressed in a suit and hat. He was smoking and looking off into the distance. Patrice instantly got a chill. *Were the Gestapo or the SS watching him? Was that a German agent down there?* His mind raced, and he quickly shut the blinds and went back to finishing his coffee. *You're just being paranoid*, he told himself.

He always knew that danger could lurk around every corner, he understood that when he and Yvonne had decided not to leave the city after the Germans took over. But now the threat had almost taken his life and that of his wife and child. The rules of the game had changed. And there was one person who just might know how it was possible this all came about.

Patrice went back to the bedroom, dressed, and went to kiss Yvonne goodbye. She was still asleep, and as he bent down to kiss her forehead, she stirred a bit and grabbed his hand. Groggily, she said to him "Where are you off to?"

"The doctor. I want to ask him if he has anything for your neck."

At the mention of her neck, she involuntary grabbed for it. It was still tender. Patrice's temper boiled below the surface.

He composed himself, kissed her hand, and he and Yvonne bid their farewells. He made his way to the hall and down the stairs to the street. Once he exited the building, he stopped and lit a cigarette, much like the man he saw earlier do, who was nowhere to be seen. He sauntered over to the light post and leaned against it, taking in the surroundings. He took a good, long look around to see if he noticed anything out of the ordinary. There were a few people out for a morning stroll, the usual bustle of car traffic, but nothing that stood out. So far so good. Taking one last drag from his cigarette, he dropped it on the pavement, stubbed it out, and began to walk down the block. In the end, he took a sharp right and walked briskly down the street, weaving in and out of the people walking the opposite way. At the next intersection, he waited for a couple of cars to go by and then moved across, ducking into a drug store for a few moments.

As he milled around the store, he kept a close eye out the front windows to see if the man he had seen earlier from his kitchen was there.

But he was nowhere, inside or outside the store.

Satisfied as best as he could be that he wasn't being followed, he headed back out onto the street and continued on his journey to the office. The streets were starting to bustle a little more, which helped Patrice blend into the crowd. After a few more blocks, he arrived at his destination. It was an unremarkable stone building; a simple gold plate with stenciled black lettering hung outside the door, *Francois Moreault, MD.*

Walking up to the chipped and dilapidated stairs, he reached the indoor stairwell, which smelt like a mixture of lead paint and spiced tobacco. The reception was cramped, and the few patrons that occupied it no doubt felt the same. Its tiled floor was uneven in spots and the small glazed windows, one of which was open, brought in the noise from the street. The patients were a diverse group: a haggard-looking mother, her son cloyingly pawing at her, she seemingly oblivious to him; an elderly couple, their hands embraced, the weight of the world upon their shoulders.

A lovely girl, no doubt the voice he'd spoken to on the phone this morning, sat behind the reception desk. She wore a flowered dress, her black hair done up with many ruffles and curls, which matched her shadowed eyes and puffed-up red lips. Patrice imagined she was a hit with the local gentlemen. And the Germans.

Patrice walked to the desk, catching her eye before speaking quietly. "Mr. Patrice Robillard. To see... the doctor."

She looked at him with the general malaise she had for most of the patients. Then, Patrice could see the recognition in her face at the mention of his name. She sat up straighter and nodded her head. "Good morning, Mr. Robillard, the... doctor is expecting you. Right this way."

She got up from the desk and led him down the hall to one of the doctor's examination rooms. Patrice followed closely behind, and once they stopped at Examination Room Three, she opened the door and Patrice sat down.

If the reception was cramped, it was positively palatial compared to the examination room. The smell of must lingered in the air, and Patrice was glad he wasn't actually here for any medical reason. He checked his watch, again. *Where was this man?*

Suddenly, there was a curt knock at the door.

"Come in," Patrice said, sitting down on the examination chair.

A man, clad in a white full-length coat, entered quickly and shut the door. Walking with a slight limp, he was in his late forties, with jet black hair, cut angularly, and broad shoulders. He cut a striking pose. The thick black beard, trimmed sharply around the cheeks, managed not to obscure facial features that would appeal to the fairer sex. It had been almost six months since Patricc had last seen Franck Chabert, and the man looked like he hadn't aged a day.

"Good morning... Doctor." Patrice's voice dripped with sarcasm, at which Franck chuckled.

"Looks good, no? It makes this cover all the more convincing. Thankfully, the good Doctor Moreault is the same size as me."

Franck walked over to the chair, removed the coat, and draped it on the back. Coming around, he was now facing Patrice. "So, my old friend. To what do I owe this... unexpected visit?"

Franck offered Patrice a cigarette, which the latter greatly accepted. Once lit, he proceeded to give Franck a rundown of the previous nights' events, including what had happened with Yvonne.

"*Mon Dieu! [My God!]*" exclaimed Franck, clapping his hands together. "You are lucky to be alive. The Gestapo do not let many go from their crooked grip. I would know."

"This is no joke, Franck. This wasn't some interview with the gendarmes. They came after me! They came to my home. They attacked Yvonne right in front of me!"

Franck lit his cigarette, then limped over to Patrice, coming in close. He left the cigarette dangling and placed both his hands on Patrice's shoulders. "I know, my friend. I know. But, you're alive, and you came to me, which is good."

"I need to know why, *mon ami.* As the local leader of the Resistance cell for this area, I figured you might know why this is happening to me."

A former soldier in the French Army, coupled with training from the Special Operations Executive, made Franck one of the most feared and ruthless men in Marseille.

Patrice's face saddened. "I... just don't understand it. Why did they pick me? I'm not involved with the Resistance... "

Franck took a long drag from his cigarette. He ashed to the floor, something Patrice thought happened more often than not in this place.

"True... but you do provide us information, do you not, from time to time?"

Patrice nodded.

"It is possible they found out you're giving information to us, but I doubt it. Tell me more about last night, that will help me understand a bit more."

"I've told you everything I know, I swear!"

Franck shook his head and scratched his beard. "There must be more. The Army don't usually just go..."

Patrice interrupted Franck, "I... don't think it was the Army. These soldiers, they came into the bar right before closing, had some drinks, and then once I locked up, they were waiting for me on my walk home. I think they were *SS*."

"*SS*, are you sure?"

"Yes, I saw the flashes on their uniforms. They took me to the police station, and as I said, they asked me again and again about the killing of some *SS* officer."

Franck nodded, snapping his fingers together, then turned away from Patrice.

"What... what is it, Franck?"

Franck hesitated, avoiding Patrice's gaze.

"You know, don't you? You know why they came after me... TELL ME!"

Franck turned back, holding up his hands.

"I thought we might cause a little stir with that assassination, but I swear I did not think they would come down on us so hard so quickly. Especially on you. You must understand, Patrice, we never meant for any harm to come to you."

Patrice stood up, starting to breathe heavier. "So you knew? You knew there was the possibility and you said nothing to me?"

The men were now standing face to face. Patrice's fists had started to ball.

"Patrice... forgive me, this was meant to be done discretely..."

"Well, it didn't work! Did you do it, did you kill this *SS* officer?"

Franck looked to the ceiling, exasperated. "No, it was—someone else. Someone outside of Marseille. It's the truth, I swear."

After a few more tense moments, Patrice relaxed his hands. Both men stepped away from each other.

"I want to say something, Patrice. Didn't you come to me, some months ago, complaining about the Germans, wanting to do something?"

Patrice said nothing, his anger coursing through him.

"What did you think we were going to do, push them down on the street and make funny faces at them?"

Franck took a long, deep breath. His face felt like it was on fire.

"I suppose, Franck, that I did do that. But watching them almost choke the life out of your wife has a way of changing things. I realize now I'm not cut out for this cloak and dagger business."

"What are you saying?" Franck was starting to get pensive.

"I'm saying... I want out. I won't be able to give you information, any longer. I hope you understand."

Patrice got up from his seat and made his way towards the door. Before he could leave, he felt Franck's hand on his shoulder.

"Wait... no need to be hasty. I'm sorry I didn't tell you about our plans, but your bar is our best source of intelligence about the Germans right now..."

Patrice held up his hand, gesturing for Franck to stop. "My decision is final. I don't want Esmée growing up without a father."

Franck put his hands on his hips, clearly unhappy. Through gritted teeth, he said, "Fine, if that's what you want."

Patrice sighed and turned around. He grabbed the doorknob just as Franck spoke again.

"One last thing before you go?"

Patrice stopped, still slightly mad, but nodded his head.

"Tell me about these new Germans. Give me something."

"Fine. I can tell you this, they were cruel, vicious men, the worst I have ever met. There was a skinny one, who seemed intelligent but menacing. The brute with the scar was probably the worst."

Before he opened the door, Franck turned to Patrice, furrowing his brow. "What did you say about the large *SS* man?"

Patrice shrugged off the question until he saw the stern look on Franck's face. "The commanding officer, he was charming when I spoke with him at the bar, but then frighteningly violent in the interrogation room. He's the one that choked Yvonne. He had a large scar, stretching from his cheek down to his neck."

Franck limped over as fast as he could and grabbed Patrice by the shoulders. "Are you sure? This skinny officer, was he a tall, spindly man, gaunt features and long fingers, blonde hair?"

Patrice thought for a moment, going back to his interrogation. "Yes, he was the man I spoke with. Teicher, I think he said his name was."

"And the large German... did he tell you his name? Remember damn it, did he tell you his name?"

"Yes, yes he did. Vahlen. Maximillian Vahlen."

Franck looked down and was lost in thought. *No, it wasn't possible. Vahlen. Here, now.* He had to get to a radio straight away.

"Am I free to go?" Patrice asked, moving preemptively towards the door.

"Yes, my apologies." Franck waved Patrice away, hunching over the examination chair now, his breath heavy and labored. The door opened and closed, leaving Franck alone in the tiny room.

So, Vahlen, that vicious bastard, was in Marseille. A solemn look came over him, and his fist clenched into a tight ball. The radio set was back at his apartment, hidden away under a loose floorboard in his bedroom. He would need to wait till the evening, as the Germans would no doubt have their signal finders out and about, looking for Resistance transmissions.

Vahlen. Franck could scarcely believe the news himself, or his luck. Four long years, he had waited for a sighting, a scrap of information, anything really, of this man. And now he was here.

Major Webb in London must be notified. There was little time to waste if they were going to act.

———◉———

A RAY OF LIGHT SHONE through the window, blanketing Major Theodore Webb, forcing him awake. Both his administrative duties, coupled with his oversight of some rather troublesome late-night missions on the continent, had demanded much of his time. Due to this, he had taken to sleeping in his office at headquarters in London recently. He also had the habit of indulging his taste for scotch, and it was just as easy to sleep it off in his office. He groggily rubbed his eyes and stretched. The couch, which was by no means as comfortable as his bed, did the job. However, it also left his back in a state of tightness. He stood, bending backward and trying to work out the kink. Unable to, for the time being, he looked down to the coffee table where his cigarettes and his half-drunk bottle of whiskey lay. He picked up the bottle and took a large swig, wincing as it went down. He dragged himself to the small sink in the far corner of his office. After splashing some cold water on his face, he looked in the small mirror and stared. It had been some time since he had slept a full night, and it was starting to show. Webb ran a hand over his sallow face, examining the wrinkles that seemed to appear faster each day.

He had been working in 'Churchill's Secret Army' or the Special Operations Executive going on four years now. His ability to communicate effectively and find the best way to get through a problem brought Theo to the attention of his superiors. He was quickly plucked from the Army and shifted into the SOE. As part of the Army, he had fought in France at the beginning of the war, with the British Expeditionary Force. As the German Army advanced, and the surrender of France became inevitable, Theo became adept at making sure that nothing of use in his area fell into German hands. These skills, along with his aptitude to understand some French, set him up as a perfect agent trainer within the Executive. He had trained many of the Resistance members right here on Baker Street and had been recognized as someone who 'got the job done' no matter what.

Webb wandered down the hall, no doubt frightening the few staffers that milled about as he nursed his hangover. His head pounding, he needed more coffee and something to eat. The cafeteria at Baker Street was crude, but there was always something to eat... usually. Sometimes, if they were lucky, they were even able to get a good sausage now and then, which Webb treasured.

Grabbing a cup from the rack, Webb poured himself a cup of black coffee and made his way over to get some eggs and toast. Sitting at the nearest table, he munched away and tried to take his mind off the dull pain pulsating through his skull. A few other stragglers had started to arrive, and Theo recognized one of them. Lieutenant Percival Martin was quite lanky, slightly taller than average height. Webb was told that Martin rowed crew at Cambridge before the war, but in addition to his athletic achievements, he was also academically sharp. Younger than Webb by a few years, he was the perfect complement to the way Webb conducted his training which was why he had made him his staff officer. Martin noticed him, smiled, and shook his head as he strode over to the table. "Good morning, sir, long night?" Martin waited for the answer by going and getting a cup of coffee.

"None of your business, Lieutenant. You are on a need-to-know basis and you don't need to know," replied Webb, with a wry smile creeping across his face.

Lieutenant Martin tossed a couple of aspirin on the table in response to that comment and watched Webb gobble them up.

"You're up quite early Lieutenant. What brings you in?" Webb said, washing the aspirin down with a gulp of coffee.

"There was something that came in through the wire last night, and the boys left it on my desk. Said you'll want to see it right away."

Theo Webb furrowed his brow. It was not often that wires from the field were passed to him, as he didn't actively run agents. That Lieutenant Martin had come in so early and had been searching for Webb only piqued his interest further.

"Not sure what this message is all about my dear boy, but let's go find out. I think I've had enough here to cut through this hangover," said Webb.

The two men grabbed their coffees and started back up from the basement towards Webb's office. The early morning sun had started to crest on the sky, and as they climbed the stairs, more and more people moved about. Despite the war entering what many thought was its final phase, there was still much work to be done. The Allied forces were going to land in Normandy sometime in the next few months or so, or so the rumors said. More importantly, the cultivation of resistance networks in France and the rest of the occupied countries was vital.

They reached Webb's office and as he went to collapse on his couch, Lieutenant Martin continued on to retrieve the wire sheet from his own office. Coming back, he laid the wire down on the table next to Webb and lit a cigarette. "The boys figured 'TW' was you, so they called me. I couldn't find the codename '*Eager Patriot*' in any of your files. I figured it went back to your days in France, so I told the boys it was nothing to be concerned about." Martin finished, sitting across from Webb.

Webb sat up and scanned the paper:

Eager Patriot for TW
Sighting of V
Confirmed location
Request contact and support

His head still cloudy from last night's drinks, Webb sat back and let the message sink in. Then the gravity of the words struck him. He looked back down and read the words again. The German with the scar. *Vahlen*.

At last, he had shown himself. Webb had to tread lightly. He didn't want to raise any suspicion. "Shut the door, Lieutenant. This information can't leave this room." Martin stubbed his cigarette and got up to shut the door. Once he sat back down, he lit up another and waited for Webb to speak.

"A few years back, in 1940, I was with the British Expeditionary Force. We were pulling back as the Germans had started to overrun France. As you know, when my unit and I retreated, I was trapped behind enemy lines and was on the run. Unable to get back to Allied lines, I made the decision to hide out in a crude field hospital till I could come up with a plan. It was there I met a French soldier." Webb paused and seemed to stare off into the abyss. Martin went to say something when Webb started back up again. "He became the first agent I trained back here in London, given the codename Eager Patriot. He's a good man. He wouldn't have messaged me directly unless it was vitally important."

Lieutenant Martin nodded and sat forward. His knowledge of his senior officer's time in France before coming to SOE was very limited, so this was very interesting.

Webb picked up the paper and tapped it with his index finger. "This message here is his way of saying to me... that he has found him."

"Found who?" asked Martin.

"We call him the scarred German. Maximillian Vahlen. He's a Major in the *SS*. I have heard for the last few years he's been hunting down Resistance members all over Europe. But... he's finally shown himself in France. I don't want to understate this, Lieutenant, his capture would be a windfall of intelligence."

"I see. So, this '*Eager Patriot*' fellow, he's hoping that you'll help him with what? Turning him to our side?" queried Lieutenant Martin.

Webb sat forward and patted Martin on the knee. "Not quite. I doubt he'll give up the information willingly. He was a brilliant tactician, so no doubt the Jerries have him in France helping them shore up the Atlantic Wall."

"Alright then, what's our next move?"

"Nothing we can do now, as I know the Germans monitor the wireless traffic during the day, but we can reconvene later this evening and hopefully get some more information from our friend here. In the meantime, Lieutenant, I'm going to see if I can catch up on some sleep. Come wake me in a few more hours."

Webb watched as Martin acquiesced and headed out of the office.

He laid back down on his couch and found his thoughts turning towards that night back in 1940. What he had told Martin about meeting *Eager Patriot*, otherwise known as Franck Chabert, in France had been true. They had met on the run, at a crude field hospital in the French countryside. But all those details about Vahlen being an intelligence windfall and helping plan the defense of the Atlantic Wall, well, that was all just smoke.

There was only one thing that giant German was good at—hunting, torturing, and murdering anyone and everyone that crossed his path.

He had tried for four years to suppress those memories of what he saw at the hospital, of what Vahlen had done. Even with drink, they had become too much to bear. It was hard to forget her smile, the way she had touched his arm. He reached for the scotch bottle and took another big swig. A few more quick gulps and he closed his eyes, hoping that the brown liquid had washed away those wrenching shards of memory, the carnage imposed on that house's occupants by Vahlen and his men, while Webb watched helplessly. He desperately wanted them to go away forever, and finally, he was being presented with a chance for that to happen.

Revenge.

It would not be easy, and it would require Webb to go outside the normal channels, but for this man, for what he'd done and probably was still doing, Webb would gladly take that risk.

Webb would see to it that Vahlen had everything he'd doled out revisited back upon him. And nothing would stop him from doing it.

This thought gave him a tiny bit of comfort as he willed his eyes to close for what he hoped was a nightmare-free rest.

AS PROMISED, MARTIN returned to wake Webb, and the men proceeded about their day. The war continued, and there was much to prepare for the invasion of Europe so Webb helped to oversee the efforts. There were always missions on the go, and questions to be answered. However, he found that his mind kept drifting back to the wire that had been sent the previous night. While he feigned interest in whatever task he was accomplishing, he was also busy formulating plans. No doubt, Franck would have some of the details sorted, but if he was asking for help then it must be that Vahlen was not alone. Webb had resigned himself to the fact many years ago that he would never see Vahlen again, but he could never forget his face. While he contemplated those thoughts, he noticed a figure at the door, followed by a sharp knock. "Come in," he commanded.

"Is this a good time, sir?" replied a familiar voice.

"I've always got time for you, Captain."

Captain Tom Ellis smiled and pushed through the door. A few years younger than Webb, he was highly regarded around the SOE as an incredibly intelligent officer. Average height and average build, if you were to look at him in a group of people you would not be able to pick him out. It was a great skill to have in the spy business, as any agent would tell you. Where Tom did stand out, however, was in his keen intellect. He had an almost encyclopedic knowledge on a variety of topics and could talk at length on a great many things. Before the war, he had been a university professor, but once hostilities had broken out, he found his way to first the armed forces and then the SOE. The government had wanted to accumulate as many brilliant people as possible, and Captain Ellis fit the bill. "Drink?" Webb said, pouring some scotch into a glass and placing it on the desk.

"You always were a good host, Major," said Ellis, taking a long pull from the glass. "Well, it's your meeting, what did you need?"

"I wanted to pick your brain about something, Captain. And... I'd appreciate it if we kept this conversation off the record."

Ellis had been working in the SO3 section, which dealt mainly with research. It wasn't often he was asked these types of questions, but it was a clandestine organization after all. Looking over his wire-rimmed glasses at Major Webb, Ellis replied, "Of course, Major. It seems I'm at your mercy, sir, ask away."

"Without boring you with too much detail, I'm looking at putting together an operation, something that could get fairly messy, and I'm going to need some boys who aren't afraid of trouble. Now, you keep records of all these kinds of things. I'm looking for your opinion on who is the best of the best out there."

"I see, well, what kind of mission are we talking about?"

"Seek and Capture type, limited action if possible."

"I see. Well, if I knew where the mission was to take place, I might be able to..."

Webb shook his head slowly and refilled Ellis's empty glass. "It's better if you didn't know, Tom, for both of us."

Ellis took the glass and nodded his head in silence. He sat there for a few minutes before speaking again. "Well, Major, it would seem you posit quite the problem. If I had to hazard an opinion, there is one group that I've heard of. They have seen some action in Italy, and I think they have the skills that would be highly valuable to your... mission."

Webb interlaced his fingers and sat back in the chair, seemingly deep in thought. "Sounds promising, Captain. Alright, give me their information."

Ellis took a scrap of paper and pencil from Webb's desk and scribbled down a few scant words. Once done, he handed the paper to Webb. As the Major looked it over, Ellis continued, "I think you'll be quite happy, sir. The Germans are bloody well terrified of these boys."

Webb perked up at this statement by Captain Ellis. In his experience, there weren't many things the Germans feared, and if this unit was as good as Ellis professed them to be, then that would be more than adequate for him. Webb gave Ellis his thanks and the Captain excused himself and headed on his way. Before leaving, Webb made sure again that Ellis understood to forget their conversation.

The rest of the day proceeded without any real events. After doing some consulting, Webb slipped back to his office to have a small nap before the evening festivities. No doubt, Franck would be waiting for his communication and time was of the essence. He would grab a quick bite to eat in a few hours and then head down to the signals room. He'd left instructions for Lieutenant Martin to wake him in a few hours.

Shortly after nine in the evening, Lieutenant Martin, Major Webb, and a young Private by the name of Jones arrived in the signals room. Webb waited patiently while the Private found the frequency. Once located, he picked up the microphone and called out:

"*Eager Patriot, Eager Patriot*, do you read me over?"

Silence.

"*Eager Patriot, Eager Patriot*, this is *TW,* do you read me over? I repeat, this is *TW*, over"

A slight crackle from the static, but otherwise no other sound was heard.

The men patiently waited, and then a heavily accented voice came through the headset. Private Jones tuned some dials to clear up the interference, and the voice became clearer.

"*TW*, we read you loud and clear, this is *Eager Patriot*, over."

Webb stepped in and took the microphone. "What is the target's status, over?"

"Target sighted but not confirmed. Location is Marseille, does our agreement still stand? Over."

Webb thought long and hard. There were too many ears to go into much detail. He needed a one hundred percent guarantee before putting things in motion. But that was unlikely at this juncture. Before Webb could respond, *Eager Patriot* responded back. "We will track and advise, but will need outside assistance, does our agreement still stand, over?"

Webb was put in a tough position. He had to make a choice, or potentially lose a chance at getting Vahlen. He picked up the microphone. "Affirmative, we will need a three-day window to assist."

"Roger that *TW.* Will keep you updated. *Eager Patriot* out."

The transmission ceased, and Webb and Martin offered their thanks to Private Jones, then told him to have any messages from *Eager Patriot* marked as urgent and deliver them to Major Webb's office. He was a young lad, easy to please, and no doubt happy not to be stationed near the front lines. He agreed pretty quickly. Webb and Martin then sauntered back to the Major's office. On their way, Martin piped up, "What did he mean by agreement, sir?"

Webb chuckled a little, "It's in reference to what we had agreed on back in France. Just a mutual understanding to look out for each other's... interests."

The Lieutenant nodded, but his face turned what Webb could only describe as perplexed. The men said their goodbyes, and Webb made a mental note to remember that while Lieutenant Percival Martin would unquestioningly follow any order Webb gave, he was not a blind fool.

Plopping himself down at the desk, he poured himself a tall scotch. It had been a long day. Bending down, he removed a small wooden box from the bottom drawer. He lifted the lid and removed the blood-stained handkerchief from inside, laying it out in front of him. Staring at it long and hard, he proceeded to finish his drink. Lifting it from the desk, the memories started to flood back. The horrors, the panic, the cries for help, the screams.

As I swore that day in France many years ago, that man Vahlen will know the pain of torture, the pain of watching all he holds dear slowly slip away. For you Anne, I do this—for you.

CHAPTER TWO

THE SUN WAS SETTING on the horizon, and an orange glow stretched out over the rolling hills. A haze had obscured the tall mountain in the distance. The shape of it was silhouetted against the lush green fields and gnarled root trees that were tightly packed as far as the eye could see. It was an artist's dream, with picturesque vistas everywhere you looked. It would have been lovely to spend hours, taking in the countryside, the rich vegetation, and rustic stone houses. At least that's what Sergeant Peter Donalds thought for a brief second, before the sound of artillery and the slight smell of rotting flesh quickly brought him back to reality.

Donalds liked to do this, take a moment to be away from everyone while looking out at the horizon. He found it helped refocus his mind, which was something that he had less and less time for these days.

Since the landing at Anzio, Donalds and his men of the First Special Service Force had had little rest. A rugged man of thirty years, with soft eyes, an angular nose and chin, dark blonde hair, and the unkempt beard to match, he had volunteered to join the unit at the start of the war and had been with it during all its important campaigns. But even all his life experience couldn't have prepared him for what he would experience in Italy.

They had been advancing from the beachhead out towards Rome, and while they were making progress, the Germans were not giving up territory easily. Every mile they took, it seemed to cost double the amount in blood. It seemed like half the men in the unit had just arrived, replacements for those that had died. It had fallen to the non-commissioned officers like Donalds to whip these new arrivals into shape. His squad had been filled out with no less than three new soldiers, and it was these soldiers that Donalds went to check on.

In the ever-approaching dusk light, the men of Sergeant Donalds's squad were off in the ditch, some resting, some trading jokes, and others just staring blankly, deep in thought. Making his way gently down an embankment, he knelt right in front of them, commanding their attention. "Gentlemen, how are we this evening?"

The men were silent just for a few moments, and then each acknowledged Donalds in turn.

"Sarge?" asked Private Thomas, pulling at his rifle clip.

"Yes, Private?"

"When are we moving out?"

Donalds looked to the horizon, then back towards where the officers were located. "Soon, Private. We're waiting for the cover of darkness. Just a little while longer." The men looked away, two of them shifting uneasily. Donalds recognized the signs and after taking a beat, he knew what needed to be said. "This is the worst part you know, the waiting. This is the part they don't tell you about in training. Just remember what you learned in basic, and you'll be fine."

"Yes, Sergeant," they said, in unison.

"Relax for now. You'll need it before we head up the road."

"Sergeant, before you go, we were speaking earlier and I had a question..." Asked another one of the men. Donalds couldn't quite remember his last name, but it might have been Maxwell.

"Go ahead, Private." Donalds was by now standing, looking down on them.

"I... we were wondering about the boot polish on the face... I mean, does it help?"

Donalds took a quick look around. He spotted Private James Appleyard having a cigarette with a few other men and called out to him to join their group. After he cantered over, Donalds asked, making sure the recruits were within earshot. "Appleyard, these fine young men here want to know if the boot polish helps. Now, what did we recently find out the Germans call us?"

"The Black... Devils." Appleyard put extra emphasis on the *Devils*, for added dramatic effect

"And why do they call us the Black Devils?" prompted Donalds.

"Because the Jerries never see us coming, they think we actually are the devil."

"That is correct, Private Appleyard. Carry on, Private." Donalds turned back to Private Maxwell and placed a hand on his shoulder. "You—all of you—are soldiers in an elite fighting unit. The Germans are more scared of you than you are of them, I guarantee it." Donalds got up to leave, and as he walked away, he passed Private Appleyard.

"Do you really believe all that, Sergeant?" asked Appleyard.

"Private, even if I didn't, I wouldn't tell you. They taught us at Fort Harrison that you never let your men know your fears and inner thoughts, or something like that," replied Donalds, winking as he continued on his way. Appleyard saluted and then chuckled, turning back to the conversation he was having. Truth be told, Sergeant Donalds had been thinking a lot lately about the war in general and what his purpose here was. He had heard one of his soldiers describe this war as a 'bloody meat grinder' and he couldn't think of a better description. He had volunteered to join the Canadian Army when Canada declared war along with the rest of the British Commonwealth countries in September of '39. Back then, he was a fresh-faced twenty-five-year-old, helping his family raise cattle on their farm. He went through the basic training and was about to deploy to England when the call came through, not for deployment, but something else entirely. It was the Americans, and they were putting together a special unit, composed of soldiers from both America and Canada. His commanding officer asked him if he wanted to join. It was a crack unit, meant to fight a guerrilla war against the Axis forces. Without hesitation, he had agreed and was sent to Montana to join up with the other future members of his unit. The unit was called First Special Service Force, and the grueling training had already taken the ragtag group of recruits and turned them into men without fear—or at least, trained them not to show it. The training had also turned them into a unit that the Germans had a healthy fear of, as he had mentioned to Private Maxwell earlier. They had cut their teeth in a few different missions and had advanced the Allies' cause in the liberation of Italy. It was that cause that had run the First Special Service Force down. They were exhausted, and it seemed that every town they won, the Germans just dug in harder at the next one. He had seen men fall asleep standing up, unable to get out of their beds from shell shock, and even had caught one of his men ready to eat a pistol.

It had taken its toll, one way or another.

Leaving his men behind, Donalds had started to make his way down the road to where the officers were located. Finding his immediate superior, Lieutenant Walters, huddled around the table with the rest of the commanders, Donalds hung back. Once the meeting was done, he sidled up to the young Lieutenant.

"Evening, Lieutenant, I came to find out what the plan is for tonight," Donalds said, pulling out a cigarette and lighting it.

"Good evening, Sergeant. Well, I was just going over our attack plan. Here, I'll show you."

Donalds liked Walters, even though he was American. Two years Donalds's junior, Walters was perpetually clean-shaven and looked as if he was eighteen still, rather than his late twenties. Born in North Dakota, his accent gave him away immediately. He was stockier in build and a bit shorter than Donalds. But Donalds had learned early on that the smaller the man, the larger the fight in him. Walters was exactly that.

The Lieutenant pointed at the map that lay on the makeshift table, as the rest of the officers shifted off to see to other duties. A flashlight illuminated it so both men could see it in the dwindling light. "Looks like the Germans are entrenched a little farther up the road, and then we think they have some reserves in the town of Cori. If we press swiftly, we should be able to overwhelm them quite easily."

"That's what they said about the town of Cisterna, and the Germans just wouldn't give it up."

Walters looked up from the table and right at his Sergeant. "Are you okay, Peter?"

The Lieutenant's use of his first name struck Donalds, like they weren't talking about military matters anymore. "I'm fine Lieutenant, just... a little tired," Donalds spoke plainly, as was his habit with his superior officer.

Walters's eyes narrowed, and he shook his head side to side. "We're all tired, Sergeant. That's not it. C'mon, what's on your mind, Peter?"

"Permission to speak freely, sir?"

Walters waved his hand, instructing Donalds to continue.

"I know this offensive is important and all, Lieutenant. But the inch-by-inch grind for every tiny town—I just think..."

Donalds trailed off, realizing his thoughts were getting the better of him.

"Please, continue Sergeant. You just think..." prompted Walters.

Donalds shifted nervously. Even though he spoke plainly to his superior, he was entering uncharted territory. He never let anyone know what he was thinking.

"I was just thinking, what's the goddamn point? The Germans, they just kill a bunch of us, then pull back to the next position. This unit of ours, the First Special Service, we're a collection of some of the hardest bastards I've ever met. One of the reasons I joined up was because I knew that myself, all of us, would help win this war, and do something that really matters."

Acutely aware now that he had perhaps done something he shouldn't have, Donalds stopped talking and leaned against the wooden table.

Walters, his head down in quiet reflection as well, took a moment before speaking again.

"I appreciate your honesty, Sergeant. Knowing you, it probably took a lot of effort to share those thoughts."

He paused for a moment, and Donalds saw that he was trying to choose his words.

"Hell Pete, I agree with ya. The Germans don't seem up for a fair fight, and for all the time it took us to get in this war...well, it could've been a lot earlier, but you know that. I can tell you this though, we're here, and even though you may not see it, we are making a difference."

Donalds said nothing. He wanted to believe Walters, but he knew deep in his heart, that he still felt like they were spinning their wheels, like this all was just window dressing.

"If you say so, Lieutenant."

Walters patted him on the shoulder, and stuck out his other hand, pointing at Donalds.

"I need you, especially on this one, Pete. You are great at making sure your men are always in the right place. We are so close to pressing this breakout and pushing to take Rome. Rest for all of us, I promise you, will be coming soon."

Donalds sighed but nodded his head. "Understood Lieutenant. You know you can count on us, sir." The men saluted each other and Donalds started to walk back to where his squad was located. He was now facing their objective, the mountain Arrestino, or *Monte Arrestino*. Small in comparison to the Rocky Mountains, it was no doubt a defender's dream. Tonight, however, they would be moving up the road to displace those Germans at its base and clear a path for the troops to follow. Donalds didn't need to remind himself that they had trained for missions like this, and he reckoned that they were better equipped than most to handle the situation. Still, even after all they had achieved, sitting in the shadow of this new, daunting challenge, Donalds couldn't help but feel slightly nervous. Those jitters that he felt, he needed them, and wanted them; it meant that he still felt things, that he was still human. He finished his cigarette and settled into the embankment, hoping to catch a little shuteye. They would be moving out in a few hours, and he wanted to get as much rest as he could. He promised himself it would only be for five minutes, and as he did, he felt his eyes close.

———◆———

AFTER WHAT SEEMED LIKE thirty seconds, but was just under two hours, a hand on his shoulder shook Sergeant Peter Donalds awake. He opened his eyes with a start to see the fresh-faced Lieutenant Walters standing over him, helmet on and holding his carbine. "Wake up Pete. It's time to go." The Lieutenant helped Donalds to his feet, brushing some loose grass from his jacket as well.

"Yes, sir," replied Donalds, picking up his helmet and weapon. Donalds got his bearings about himself, then started to look for his men. He quickly found them milling around and starting to form into their units. Making his way over to them, he found the person he was looking for, already doing his job. Corporal Carl Mills had gotten the men moving, checking their weapons and grabbing extra clips. A baby compared to Donalds, Mills was just shy of his twenty-first birthday. He had also been Donald's first recommendation for promotion. Competent in all kinds of situations, Mills was a stickler for the rules. That made him a good candidate to be a leader, but it also limited his ability to think outside the box sometimes. Every time Donalds suggested a course of action outside regulations, Mills's face would scrunch up, and he would scratch his coffee-colored hair as if his body was rejecting a bad piece of food. Considering his facial features were already close together, it was not a pretty sight.

Donalds acknowledged him first with a nod and spoke quickly. "Thank you, Corporal, I only meant to shut my eyes for a few minutes."

Corporal Mills snapped to attention, giving a quick salute. "The men need to be prepared Sergeant. Wanted to make sure they had all the gear and were ready for your arrival."

Donalds grabbed a small tin from one of the men and began to smear some boot polish on his face, making sure no skin was left showing. Once done, he got down on one knee and beckoned for his men to do the same, "Alright boys, we've been here before. You know what you have to do. The Krauts aren't going to give up territory easily. Stay with me and we'll come out of this just fine."

"Yes sir!" the men shouted in unison, putting on their helmets. Sergeant Donalds stood up and took a quick look around his men's faces. There was fear there, but also something else.

Resilience.

Lieutenant Walters came up behind them, and began to issue orders, pointing toward the town. "We're moving up. Three prongs, the left, the center, and the right. Donalds, you and your men will be on the left flank." Donalds followed where Walters was pointing. The main road to the town of Cori lay before them, with copious amounts of tree cover on either side of the thoroughfare. Donalds and his men would be headed for just off the left side of the road, towards the west side of the town.

"I'll be with the second squad, heading up the center. Good luck gentlemen."

Donalds stood up and motioned for his men to follow. As he looked back, he saw Private Maxwell clutching his rifle. Catching his eye, he nodded and saw Maxwell's expression change; he seemed to be a little more assured.

After a few moments, Lieutenant Walters waved them all forward and the many platoons of the First Special Service Force moved out. Donalds, with his men following close behind, moved along the ditch to the left of the road, the town in the foreground, and the mountain looming in the background. Brush and a line of trees helped cover their approach up the mountain. After a few miles, they could see the outskirts of the town of Cori in the distance.

There had still been no sign of the Germans.

To his right, he saw Lieutenant Walters hold up his hand, and the whole of second squad stopped. Donalds did the same. Walters made his way over to Donalds and said, "Think we got lucky tonight, Sergeant. Do you think the Krauts pulled back?"

"I'd like to hope so, Lieutenant, but I've learned never to underestimate the Krauts."

"I agree. I want you to push your men up the left there." He pointed to the gentle incline, covered in some low-lying bushes, with a few buildings visible just beyond it. "Once you've reached the edge of the town there, I'll take the second and third squad up the road and we'll push into the town."

Donalds signaled his agreement with a brief nod. Then, with hand signals, he instructed his men they were to stealthily approach the town. From here on in, they would keep their communication completely non-verbal. Moving in behind Mills, Donalds checked behind himself to make sure the men were spread out, but still in single file. He tapped Mills on the shoulder, falling in step at the right interval, just behind his Corporal.

They started to enter the wooded area just to the left of the main road. The underbrush had thickened significantly as they crouched along until they reached a bank of trees. Donalds knew that beyond this collection of trees lay the edge of the town of Cori. Mills pushed through, doing as a scout should, keeping his eyes and his ears trained for anything. Maneuvering their way gently through the trees, Donalds could see the end of the tree-line approaching quickly. Beyond that was a grassy hill with a soft incline, on top of which sat a couple of stone houses. They had reached their objective.

Donalds tapped Mills on his shoulder and held up his right hand in a balled fist, the signal for everyone to hold their position. He watched as each man sank to their knees, their eyes trained on him. *Good, we're all in position.* He turned back towards the hill and scanned the few visible houses.

Nothing.

Their darkened windows offered no clues if they were occupied, Germans or otherwise. It was also eerily quiet, so it seemed their center and right columns had yet to engage the Germans either. Donalds wiped the sweat from his head onto his jacket sleeve. The success of the attack hinged on the three columns advancing at roughly the same time. Sooner or later, they would have to push on. Donalds took one last look at the house before he tapped Mills on the shoulder again.

Mills nodded, and emerged from the tree line, moving slowly in a low crouch with Donalds following suit. Soon, roughly half the eight-man squad was now in the open, approaching the hill, when a familiar sound pierced the air.

"MACHINE GUN!" yelled Donalds.

All eight men hit the ground immediately, as bullets enveloped them. White-hot tracers lit up the twilight sky as the gunner shifted the barrel back and forth. Donalds figured it was probably a German MG42, just by the awful amount of noise it was making. Trying to get his bearings, Donalds looked around, but it was pure chaos. Half the men had managed to retreat to the treeline, but the other three plus himself were trapped against the hill. Thankfully the incline gave them just enough defilade. He tried to lift his head slightly and see where the shots were coming from, but tracers whizzed by the instant he did.

They were trapped.

His men, in good cover in the trees, could probably see the machine gun position, and he waved at them to start firing. They started to open fire toward the houses, their rounds slamming into the stone buildings.

Donalds grabbed Mills, who was laying further up the hill, and pulled him closer so he could hear Donalds's words.

"Mills, we're going to crawl back down the hill, once that machine gun opens up on the treeline, nice and slow. Pass the word to Maxwell and Thomas."

The Corporal silently agreed and then slid slightly to his right, relaying the instructions to the other two men.

Sure enough, the shots from the rest of Donalds's men had attracted the German machine gunner, and the tracers and bullets started to rustle the treeline close to where the men were. Now was their chance.

"OKAY, MOVE OUT!"

Donalds had to shout to be heard over the deafening sounds of the gun. Then, something no one anticipated happened, catching everyone by surprise.

Private Maxwell got up and ran in a dead sprint towards the tree line.

"Dammit Maxwell, wait!" Donalds cried, reaching out with his hand as if he could stop Maxwell from his stomach.

Suddenly, a burst of shots rang out.

Maxwell collapsed to his knees on the grass, a few short meters from the safety of the trees. He cried out in pain, and as Donalds looked at his injured man, a second salvo rang out. Those ripped up his body even further, and he collapsed face down on the ground. There was no doubt he was dead.

Donalds cursed under his breath and looked down at the ground, then at his other men. Both Private Thomas and Corporal Mills looked rattled and were staring back at him wide-eyed. The machine gun started firing again, this time from a window on the other side of the building, and the tracers were back to hitting up the area where the men were in cover. Donalds turned back towards his men on the hill. "You need to listen to me, or we'll all be like Maxwell. Slide up a little bit and put whatever fire you can towards that other window. If there is another shooter in the window, any shots around there will keep his head down."

"What then, Sarge?" asked Private Thomas.

"Leave that to me. Just make sure you keep those goddamn Krauts' heads down."

Both men nodded and lined up their rifles. Donalds laid his gun across his arms and began to crawl diagonally, to the right but also towards the house. The two men behind him opened up, and he could now see their shots pockmarking the side of the house. Slowly, he inched his way forward, his eyes fixated on the building. He tried to control his breath, but his heart was beating a mile a minute.

Suddenly, a single muzzle flash came out a different window than the tracers, and the dirt kicked up a few millimeters in front of Donald's face. He froze. There must be more than just the machine gun crew in that house.

Great. Just great.

But, at least now from this new vantage point, he was away from the fire of that damn machine gun and could clearly see the house where the shots were coming from. In that chaotic instant, Donalds was proud of his men, fighting hard, surviving against all odds. Losing them was not an option, so Sergeant Donalds made a solemn decision. He waited until his men began firing at the house again, and then slowly inched his way forward. Closer to the top of the hill, the next part of his plan would require some balls and a little luck.

Taking a long, deep breath, he propped himself up and ran full speed towards the house. With the blood rushing to his head, he could barely hear a sound. Trying to run in a zig-zag pattern, he was sure that at any moment a bullet would rip through his chest. If his men stopped firing, he would be dead. Closer, closer the house came into view, and just as it seemed he would see a rifle barrel poke out of the window, a muzzle flash, and his death, he crashed into the side of the building. He looked up to the window but saw no sign of life. Barely able to catch his breath, he removed a grenade from his belt and pulled the pin with his teeth. Tossing it overhanded through the open window, Donalds ducked down, covering himself against the side of the building.

The explosion was thunderous, shaking the wall behind him. Abject silence filled the air.

Slightly disoriented, Sergeant Donalds picked himself up, grabbed his Thompson, and swung around the right side of the house. A small wooden door stood there until Donalds's right boot kicked it in. The air inside the house was filled with acrid smoke, and someone coughing could be heard in the backroom. With his gun at the ready, Donalds slowly moved towards that room. His body was pulsing with pure adrenaline and he carefully stepped to the corner, immediately seeing the effects of his grenade. One German was slumped against the window facing the road, his arm and most of his torso missing. To the right, the machine gun crew of two were also slumped down, with the German on the right coughing up blood and clutching his leg. As the German saw Donalds enter the room, he reached with his free hand for a pistol that was laying a few feet away. Watching this unfold, Donalds quickly raised his gun, firing a burst into the German's chest. The man's body twitched until it slumped down, lifeless. *That one was for Maxwell,* Donalds thought, as he went and checked the other two Germans, making sure they were also dead. Once satisfied, he returned outside the house and whistled, signaling his men to move up.

The rest of the men—Mills, Lintz, Appleyard, Thomas, Williams, and Johnson—scrambled up the small embankment, taking positions around the house. Donalds crouched down in the open doorway, surveying their position. The house was the lone dwelling on this side of the town, approximately a mile west from the main road. Ahead of them, more shadowed houses with tightly packed side streets and alleys strewn between them.

A defender's dream. Donalds swallowed hard. He waved Mills over. Once the good Corporal was kneeling next to Donalds, he spoke softly.

"We'll move towards the square, straight ahead. Two by two, cover and move. Take Johnson with you. I'll be on my own, just behind everyone."

"Yes, sir." Mills replied, signaling to Johnson with his hand to follow, and the two men were off. Next up were Thomas and Williams, followed by Lintz and Appleyard.

Donalds waited for a few seconds to give them a little space, then he exited the house.

The plan called for the three prongs to meet up in the city square and then move on to clear the rest of the town. Donalds watched as each man took corners, watching for any movement as his partner moved to the next cover, just like they'd learned in training. Like a well-orchestrated symphony, they moved seamlessly into the town, and down the narrow streets. There were no Germans to be seen.

Then, as Donalds looked up ahead, he saw Mills stop at one of the building corners, holding up his fist again.

The city square.

Donalds pushed past the men crouching in the side street, and came up beside his Corporal, now taking in the expansive view himself.

The square was a sight to behold. Ringed by red and brown stoned houses, the centerpiece was an aged stone fountain, with brass piping spewing bits of water from all four sides. A mighty brass shield sat above each spout, four in total. Aged to where the design was barely visible, Donalds thought that in the right light, they would provide some ancient scene of the past. On top, a brass spire sat upon a plateau of sculpted stone. Donalds imagined many town festivals, where the residents shared time, drank, danced, and came together. Now, it was just empty. Devoid of anything resembling joy.

Suddenly, Donalds perked up. In the distance, he could hear the unmistakable sound of boots on stone. He turned to the men and put his finger to his lips. Taking up position above Mills, who was still crouched, both men raised their weapons from behind the corner.

The steps got closer and closer. Donalds heard Mills cock the slide on his Johnson Light Machine Gun.

Then, just as they were ready to rain death upon whoever emerged, Donalds pulled back his gun and tapped Mills to do the same. Even in the twilight, Donalds had managed to recognize who was coming up the road. He stepped from out behind the corner, whistled, and waved his hands.

It was Lieutenant Walters.

Walters and his squad were at the south end of the square, and Walters quickly made his way over to Donalds.

"Good work, Sergeant Donalds. Thought we lost you for a second there. Spread out your boys on the left flank, and head down that road there." Walters pointed to a narrow, tightly packed street just to the left of them, where the main road forked into two. "I'll lead the rest and we'll clear out the right side."

Donalds waved his men forward; Walters then did the same. The two squads moved slowly up each street, single file, checking each darkened house as they moved along.

"Hey Sarge, where is everyone?" whispered Private Appleyard.

"No idea, Private. Keep your eyes open," replied Donalds.

Up ahead, they heard some wood clattering against the stone. Everyone braced themselves, crouching down, weapons ready. Donalds gave the signal to move forward slowly. The sound got louder and Private Appleyard, who was taking point, held up his hand in a fist as he approached it. Weapon at the ready, the young Private jumped from the corner and pointed his rifle down the side street. But he quickly lowered it and shook his head.

"What is it?" hissed Donalds, shifting uneasily in a crouched position.

"Just a damn window covering, blowin' in the wind."

Donalds watched on as his men gave a collective sigh of relief, but his instinct told him that the house at the edge of town was only just the beginning. He had to keep sharp; the Germans wouldn't give up the town this easily. After the false alarm, they continued down the street, the houses still dark and vacant. A widening of the road could be seen up ahead; the cobbled street continued to circle to their right and disappeared around a corner, with a smattering of houses interspersed on either side. To their left, the road led down another block and disappeared behind some more buildings. Save for the window covering, it was eerily quiet. The silence unnerved Donalds a bit, and he took off his helmet to run his hand through his hair. Placing it back on his head, he looked off to his left. There was some small movement and Donalds squinted his eyes, trying to gain a better view.

Suddenly, from the darkened street there was a flash. The sound of a bullet whizzed by their heads, and all the men instinctively ducked. "GERMANS! ON THE LEFT!" Donalds shouted, waving his men to get down. *Dammit*, he thought, they were slightly exposed, but they were in a much better position here than back in the narrow street. The Canadians quickly separated, taking whatever cover they could find on either side of the street. Donalds and Private Lintz crouched inside the doorway of a house on the right, while Appleyard and Mills had covered themselves on the left side, also in a door alcove. Deciding to take a peek, he poked his read around the corner. He spotted some shadows moving towards a house, a couple of hundred meters down from their position. It looked like the road led into a small driveway, and there was a concrete half-wall. Even though he couldn't tell how many Germans there were, he knew it had to be more than one...

SMMMMMMMACK!

A bullet slammed into the wooden frame, and Donalds pulled his head back reflexively, the splintering of wood just missing his face. That...was close. He felt a re-assuring pat on the shoulder from Private Lintz. "You okay, Sarge?"

"I'm fine, Private. Just the Germans trying to kill me."

"Oh, is that all," Lintz replied sarcastically. Donalds re-adjusted his helmet, again, and shifted himself to press against the door frame. As he was about to peer out again, a sharp whistle from the other side of the street caught his attention. It was Appleyard, desperately and frantically pointing in the direction of the Germans. Then, he took two fingers and made a motion as if it were two legs going back and forth, then finally pointed up. Donalds took a beat to understand what he was saying, and then looked down towards the German position. Looking at the concrete half-wall, his eyes trained up the side of the house, till it rested on the window that was facing them. He wasn't sure, but he thought he saw the windowpane move slightly outward. Suddenly, it dawned on him what Appleyard was trying to say.

The Germans had climbed the stairs to the house. They now had a higher position.

CRAAAAAAACK!   CRAAAAAAACK!
CRAAAAAACK!

A cacophony of shots rang out in rapid-fire, emanating from a rifle in the open window. A shriek came from Thomas across the way. Donalds watched as the man fell backward, clutching his leg. Thankfully, Appleyard reacted quickly, pulling the injured man back into the alcove before more shots struck the ground where he had just been.

Donalds knew they were trapped. The Germans were behind the wall, and now with them on the second floor of the house, they obviously had the upper hand. He needed to act, and quickly.

A plan began to form. Only one idea came to mind that would allow them to escape this trap. He also knew they would only have one shot at it. Waving his hand, he got Appleyard's attention. Using a couple of rapid hand signals, he laid out his plan for the young Private. Timing was going to be critical. He nodded and saw that Appleyard had relayed the orders to the rest of the men on the other side of the street. They were ready. Donalds dropped his left hand and held out three fingers. Slowly, he counted down from three to one. On one, he made a fist and then pointed a finger forward. That was the signal.

At the same time, all the Canadians stepped from their cover and opened fire.

The reverberation of all the weapons firing at the same time echoed off the walls of the houses. Each man emptied their clips towards both German positions and the pockmarks dotted and chipped away at the concrete. His plan had the desired effect—the Germans had taken cover and stopped firing. Seeing the moment open for them, Donalds signaled to Appleyard to attack the half-wall. If they could take it, nothing could protect the Germans on the upper level.

Donalds watched on as Appleyard handed off his rifle and grabbed a grenade from his belt. Taking a running start, Appleyard pulled the pin and underhanded the explosive, ducking into another alcove to shield himself from the explosion. It bounced a couple of times and came to rest near the base of the wall.

BOOOOOOOOOOM!

The wall exploded in a cloud of dust. Donalds could see at least one of the Germans was dead. Another was standing, coughing, covered head to toe with dust. It looked as if the explosion had disoriented him.

"FIRE AND MOVE! KEEP THE PRESSURE TO-WARDS THAT WINDOW!" shouted Donalds, grabbing Private Lintz from behind him and pulling him forward. The men on the other side of the street acknowledged and continued to fire towards the window-sill. Donalds, with Lintz closely in tow, moved towards the non-existent wall. They rapidly closed the distance down the street, and as they got closer to the wall, Donalds pointed to the disoriented German. Lintz took his rifle, aimed, and fired. A puff of dust mixed with blood came from the man's chest, he pitched forward and fell to the street. Donalds and Lintz pressed themselves on either side of the door frame. They both knew that there were more Germans inside the house—exactly how many, they were uncertain. Donalds took some deep breaths, and he saw that Lintz was doing the same.

"On three, Private. Keep your wits about you." Lintz checked his rifle and nodded. Donalds could see he was ready. He placed his hand on the doorknob and turned it slowly. The door creaked open, and both men stopped instantly. All of Donalds's muscles tensed as they waited at the door entrance.

Nothing. They couldn't hear a thing inside.

Donalds gingerly stepped inside the house, followed by Lintz. The layout was fairly basic. Straight-ahead was the sitting room, and Donalds could see the entrance to the kitchen just beyond. To his right, he saw the staircase to the second floor, followed by a hall and a series of doors. Without speaking, he pointed at himself, then the stairs, then at Lintz, and then pointed down. Lintz nodded his agreement, understanding that he would clear the bottom floor while Donalds would take the second level. After Lintz left to search the main level, Donalds carefully walked over to the staircase. Reaching the edge of the polished brown wooden stairs, he stared up ominously at the second-floor landing. A small ripple of fear made its way through his stomach. One stair at a time, he told himself. Gently, he placed his right foot on the step, then the left, and slowly began to climb the stairs. His gun, ever ready, held steady towards the landing. As he reached roughly the halfway point, he heard a sound come from somewhere on the second floor that made him stop.

A voice. And it was speaking in German.

"*Klaus, bist du da? [Klaus, are you there?]*"

Donalds did not speak one ounce of German. He looked down the stairs to see if Lintz was near; he knew he could speak German. But the young Private was nowhere in sight. Based on the inflection, Donalds could tell it was some sort of a question. He dared not move and crouched down on the step, waiting to see what happened next.

"Klaus?"

The German voice repeated its question, and this time Donalds heard it come from the left. That must be where they were hiding out. He shifted his weight and moved silently to the right banister. The darkened house made it a bit more difficult to see, and the angle from the staircase didn't help, but, he was sure he spotted a partially opened door upon the landing on the left side.

If I'm correct, Donalds thought to himself, *the German or Germans will be coming out of that room shortly, looking for their friend, Klaus.* He tightened himself up, to make a smaller target and nestled the stock of his Thompson gun into his shoulder. The door opening was clear in his sights.

After a few moments, the door slowly opened and a German soldier exited the room. *Perfect*, thought Donalds, and he depressed the trigger. The gun came to life, and the bullets arched across the wall and the door entrance. Two bullets hit the German in his chest and neck, making him collapse forward. He groaned as he tumbled down the stairs, coming to a halt not far from where Donalds sat. Wasting no time, the Sergeant got to his feet and burst up the stairs. He had to make it to the doorway. His eyes were fixated on the doorway, waiting for another German soldier to come out. Fear and adrenaline raced through his system.

But none came out.

Donalds reached the top and flattened himself against the wall on the left side of the doorway. He did a quick check into the room. The end of a small bed could be seen, as well as an old chest of drawers. The window where Donalds was sure the shots had come from was on the far wall, the lace drapes blowing in a slight breeze. Taking a deep breath, he entered the room and began to clear it. Satisfied no Germans were hiding under the bed or anywhere else in the room for that matter, Donalds made his way to the window. He waved down to his men, who by now had stopped firing on the house, and saw them both wave back in acknowledgment.

As Donalds focussed on his men below, he heard a faint noise behind him. He immediately recognized it as a metallic click.

"Keep your hands up!" a voice said, in heavily accented German. Donalds did as the voice asked, raising his arms above his head. "Turn... around." the voice said again. Donalds made sure not to make any sudden movements. Once he had turned and was now facing the room, he could see who was talking to him. A German soldier, his face darkened with soot—or boot polish—he couldn't tell. If he had to hazard a guess, he would think the man was in his early forties. His outstretched arm quivered a little, a German luger held tightly in his hand. Something else that struck Donalds was the man's pants were undone. He must have come from a bathroom somewhere on the second floor. *What unbelievably bad luck*, Donalds thought. Not wanting to give the German an excuse to shoot, Donalds placed his Thompson machine gun on the floor and kicked it towards the man.

"All clear down here, Sarge. All clear upstairs?" Lintz's voice drifted up from the first floor. The German, even more jittery now, looked towards the door and then back at Donalds. He got close to him, grabbed him around the neck, and placed the pistol barrel on Donalds's side.

"Sarge, you okay?

The German dug the barrel further into Donalds's ribs, and the Canadian Sergeant got the picture. Truth be told, Donalds wouldn't have called out to Lintz anyways. And he didn't need to. He had the situation well in hand.

"Sarge, I'm coming up." Lintz's voice preceded his footsteps, his boots heavy on the wooden planks. He reached the top of the stairs and turned to his left. Seeing the German behind Donalds, he immediately raised his rifle.

"Easy, Private. No need to be rash. He's very... jittery." Donalds spoke in a soft and even tone to Lintz. Behind him, the German soldier said something in his language.

"He wants me to lay down my weapon. I'm not doing that, Sarge." Lintz said, moving his finger inside the trigger guard, readying himself to shoot.

"I've got a plan, Private. When the time is right, you'll have your shot. Now, tell the man behind me that if he puts down his gun, he'll walk away from this.... alive." Donalds waited as Lintz translated his request for the soldier. Behind him, Donalds heard the man laugh, then say something back to Lintz. He also jammed the barrel into Donalds's ribs again... hard.

Wincing a little, Donalds asked, "What did he say?"

"He thinks we're both dumb. And, he declined our offer."

"Okay, guess we'll do this the hard way. You'll have an open shot soon, Private. Don't miss."

"Sir?"

Donalds didn't bother to answer. He arched his head and swung it backward with some force. It connected with the soldier's face, and Donalds immediately felt the soldier's grip slacken. Wrenching himself free, he dropped to his knees and grabbed the German's pants. Yanking them down, Donalds lay flat on the floor. "NOW, PRIVATE, SHOOT!"

The German stumbled around, disoriented by the blow he had taken to his face and his legs tied up in his pants. He attempted to raise his pistol, but it was already too late. Lintz fired two shots, dropping the German to the ground, on top of Donalds. Lintz came over and kicked the soldier to make sure he was dead, then laid his weapon on the floor and rolled the dead German off Donalds. "Sarge, you alright?"

Donalds sighed, loudly. "Oh yes. Never better, Private. I just have a dead German on top of me and he's got no pants on." Lintz chuckled a little as he helped Donalds to his feet. Both men dusted themselves off, then descended the stairs.

"I have to say, Sarge, I didn't think you were going to pull down his pants..." Lintz tried to hide the laughter that was creeping into his voice.

"This is war, Private. I'm pretty sure they didn't teach us to fight like gentlemen at Fort Harrison."

"No sir, they did not." Lintz slung the rifle around his back and fell in behind his superior officer. Coming back out onto the street, Donalds did a quick recon. He pointed to the end of the block. "Lintz, take Appleyard and check down that way. Then double-time it back to us." Lintz nodded, and Donalds watched on as the two men went to check the rest of the street. After a few moments, they returned, reporting that everything was clear.

"Excellent work, lads," Donalds stated, making motions with his hands for the squad to go back the way they had come to the square, "looks like we've got Jerry on the run."

They reached the square, just in time to see Lieutenant Walters and his squad emerge from the other side street. Sticking to the buildings, and trying to avoid open space as much as possible, the Canadians fanned out. Donalds crouched and made his way over to the Lieutenant.

"Sergeant Donalds, we heard you giving the Krauts a right ol' hard time on the other street. How many?"

Donalds took out his canteen, taking a brief sip of water. "A small squad, four or five men. Nothing we couldn't handle." Donalds's mind raced back to being held at gunpoint in the house—something he was not eager to repeat. He passed the canteen to Walters.

"No action down our street, just some empty houses. Very strange." Walters handed the canteen back to Donalds, beckoning to one of the men to get better coverage.

"Hey, LT, doesn't this strike you as a little odd?"

"What do you mean, Sergeant?"

"I mean, look around, this place is a ghost town. There are no villagers, and we've only seen a few Germans. Nowhere near the strength we expected, correct?"

Walters rubbed the side of his face with his hand, processing what Donalds had said. "You're not wrong, my friend, but perhaps Jerry just doesn't have the stomach for a fight anymore."

Donalds nodded politely but didn't respond. He'd learned that even if you disagreed with your superior officer, some thoughts you kept to yourself. His gaze turned back to the square, the darkened houses, and his men. *Had the Germans cleared everyone out of town? Why would they do that? Had those villagers left because they knew something we didn't?*

THHHUUNK!

Donalds felt the hand of Walters on the top of his helmet. "Sorry, LT, just got lost in my thoughts there for a moment."

Walter repeated his statement, a little unhappy he had to do it twice. "I said, Sergeant, that we've got to push on up the road and clear the rest of the town. Get your men together and we'll move out in the next couple of minutes."

"Yes sir." Donalds kept low and made his way back to his squad. He found himself a spot in an alcove, and sat down for a moment, breathing a small sigh of relief at the brief respite from the action. After relaying the orders, he removed his helmet and stared out across the square. Another town square, in another small town, in another part of Italy. This was becoming part of a bad joke. The Germans were grinding the Allies down, and Donalds felt every little bit of the one-hundred-plus days of constant fighting. He felt tired; his limbs ached even after he had slept more than a couple of hours. He found his thoughts were wandering more and more when he was alone, frustration rising to new levels at each roadblock. But, despite all of this, Donalds knew that he had no choice.

There was only one way to go. Forward.

———— ◉ ————

THE SQUAD TOOK A FEW moments to collect themselves, gently resting against the smattering of houses. A whistle came from across the square. Walters was waving and pointing with his hand, signaling to Donalds it was time to move out. The squad ambled its way out into the open square and were prepared to move up the road when Donalds heard multiple sounds that pierced the air. They immediately put fear into his heart.

Mortars.

"GET DOWN!" shouted Donalds.

A mortar round struck the square a few meters from them and exploded. He and his men dropped to the ground and tried to crawl back to the houses that rung the square for cover. A second round came down, followed quickly by a third, this time much closer than the first. Dirt and rock showered the men, and Lieutenant Walters yelled towards Donalds: "SERGEANT! THEY HAVE THE STREET PRE-SIGHTED. GET COVER NEAR THOSE BUILDINGS!"

Donalds's squad took cover back at the houses as a fourth round exploded, this one on the other side of the houses, completely overshooting their position. It was clear the German crew was changing the angle of the tube for the mortars, trying to get closer to the Allied soldiers. Donalds was about to get up and start moving towards the Lieutenant...

KA...BOOOOOOOOOOM!

The explosion knocked him to the ground hard, pinning him beneath a broken stone slab. He couldn't see, there was just a cloud of dust and acrid smoke. His chest felt heavy, and he coughed profusely.

"SARGE, YOU ALIVE?" Mills's voice seemed like it came from far away. Donalds's ears rang.

A mortar round must have hit the house; Donalds knew he was damn lucky to be alive. Putting all his strength into it, he pushed hard on the stone slab, slightly lifting it. Once his legs were free, he let the slab go and it thudded to the ground. He coughed and doubled over on the ground as his men rushed towards him.

That was too close, way too close.

Thankfully, the mortar rounds had stopped for a moment. The crews were probably re-sighting their tubes. Donalds put a hand up to signal that he was fine.

Appleyard whistled. "Sarge, I tell ya, you got some kinda death wish. Being next to you could be hazardous for my health."

"Private Appleyard... Shut up." Donalds gave a hard look to the young private, all the while examining his legs. They were a bit battered, a few cuts and scrapes, but still workable.

Lieutenant Walters raced over, and Donalds could see the look of relief on his face that the Sergeant was still amongst the living. "Sergeant Donalds, glad to see you're still alive."

"For now, LT. Jerry's trying real hard."

"No doubt, Sergeant, no doubt." Walters patted the junior officer on the shoulder. Donalds winced slightly. Turning back to the men, Walters continued speaking. "Private Appleyard, stay with the Sergeant while he catches his breath."

"Of course, sir." Appleyard came and stood next to Donalds, much to the latter's chagrin.

"Corporal Mills?"

"Yes, sir?" responded the erstwhile Corporal.

"You and the rest of your men are on me. We're taking out that mortar pit."

"Yes sir! You men, on me and the Lieutenant."

The men moved off, and soon they were slowly making their way up the street, towards the potential location of the mortar pit. They approached the turn in the road. Holding up his hand in a fist, the squad stopped and knelt. Walters must have spotted the mortar nest. Donalds watched as he disappeared behind the bend, then re-appeared and started to relay instructions.

Then the squad moved out in unison.

Gunfire echoed around the town once again, as the Second and Third squad of the Black Devils rushed the mortar pit. Donalds could hear a bit of shouting, some in English and some in German, as the firefight continued. Gently sitting up, he was at a disadvantage not being able to see further up the road.

Suddenly, the firing stopped. Donalds and Appleyard strained their ears, listening for any sign of the outcome of the battle. As they slowly got to their feet, they heard a voice call out.

"ALL CLEAR!"

It was Lieutenant Walters. Donalds, helped by Appleyard to stand momentarily, moved from their position and approached the bend in the road. Fifty meters up, a plume of grey smoke rose from a sandbagged area, and Donalds could see the Lieutenant standing around with his men.

He approached the pit, seeing the three dead Germans strewn onto the ground. A pile of mortar rounds lay not too far away, and Donalds shuddered to think what would have happened if the Germans had gotten the chance to get them all off.

"Sergeant Donalds," said Lieutenant Walters, leaning his weapon against his shoulder, "you look like hell; but, as always, some damn fine work you and your men did. Why don't you and your squad hold down this position, and we'll head up the road and clear the rest of the town. I know the rest of the boys back there on the road want to see some action."

He pointed back down the road they came, and Donalds nodded his acknowledgment.

"As you wish, sir. Corporal Mills, let's do an ammo check and set up a defensive position."

"Yes, Sergeant." Mills moved off to converse with the rest of the men.

"Colonel Fredrick will be moving up with the rest of the boys shortly, and we'll all be now moving to take the rest of the mountain tomorrow. With all the counterattacks we've been seeing, I wouldn't be surprised if they tried to come at us hard again. There was no way it should have been this easy," said Walters.

Donalds coughed a bit, then looked down at his scraped legs. It didn't feel particularly 'easy' to him.

With that, Walters and his squad started moving up the rest of the road, higher up the mountain. Donalds and his men spread out and continued to make sure the rest of the houses in the lower section of the town along the main road were empty. After searching the last house, they moved back to the intersection and took up some defensive posts.

Shortly thereafter, Donalds and his men heard a sound down the road from where they came. Turning and raising their weapons, they quickly saw that there was no need. Colonel Frederick, the Commander of the First Special Service, led the rest of the Force up the road. Extremely well-liked by his men, Colonel Frederick was the kind of soldier that Donalds aspired to. He curtly saluted as his commanding officer came over to speak with him.

"Excellent work, Sergeant, but I should know that by now. Where is Lieutenant Walters?"

"Up the road, sir. He took out a mortar pit and was clearing the rest of the houses to make sure the Germans pulled out."

"Good, tell him I would like to see him when he gets back. We won't be moving on till the morning, so post a watch and find a place to bunk in. "

"Yes sir. Thank you, sir." Donalds called over one of the men who had recently arrived with the Colonel and told him he had first watch.

Once the tasks had been sorted out, he lit a cigarette and took a stroll back down the road they had just come from. Reaching Maxwell's body, Donalds laid his weapon on the ground and stared down at the now-departed Private. *Just another young Canadian name on a tombstone in some European graveyard far away from home*, he thought, looking down at the empty eyes of the man. Yes, they had pushed the Germans back, but for how long? Those damn Krauts would re-group a few more miles up the road, or to another defensible position. Donalds didn't like to think of himself as defeatist, but perhaps the many months of war had finally worn him down. He was tired of it—the death, the brutality, the endless string of two steps forward, and three steps back.

He bent down, ripped the dog tags hanging from the man's neck and placed them in his pocket. Lost in his thoughts, Donalds failed to hear the footsteps approaching behind him until a familiar voice piped up. "How old was he?"

It was Walters.

"Twenty, just a boy really," said Donalds, sighing out loud. "I saw Colonel Frederick on his way into town. He was looking for you."

"Yeah, I ran into him on my way back down the hill. Need you to come back with me Sarge. He wants to speak with you again."

"What about Private Maxwell?" Donalds asked, pointing at the prostrate body.

"We'll make sure he gets a proper burial."

Donalds nodded his head slowly, picking up his weapon. The men started to walk back towards the town. Lieutenant Walters pointed towards one of the damaged houses and left to organize the burial detail.

Slinging his weapon over his shoulder, Donalds knocked briskly on the door.

"Come in," said the Colonel, from somewhere out of sight. Upon entering, he made his way through the house to the small parlor room and saw Colonel Robert Frederick seated at the table. He was surrounded by some other officers, going over a large map. Sergeant Donalds waited patiently at the edge of the table as their conversation continued.

"I agree, Major, let's move a squad here and here, and send another squad to the left to protect our flank there." Colonel Frederick pointed to the map as he spoke, and then quickly looked up at Sergeant Donalds.

"Alright, gentlemen, I think that will be all for now. Give us the room, please."

The officers nodded, grabbed their various effects, and started to file out of the house. Once the last officer had left, Col. Frederick beckoned Donalds to join him in the next room. In his late thirties, Frederick was beloved by all the men in the FSSF. His hair firmly combed and black as night was coupled with a clean-cut mustache that was his most prominent feature; it sat just below raised cheekbones and above a sharply defined chin. The man oozed leadership and confidence. When he was there, his presence made you feel capable of anything.

Just off where the table was located, there was a small sitting room with a couple of chairs, Colonel Frederick gestured for Donalds to sit. Lieutenant Walters had come back in by now and stood leaning against the wall. Frederick noticeably stared at Donalds's chafed legs and ripped pants.

"First of all, I have to commend the job that you did today, Sergeant. I know it wasn't an easy task we gave you boys in the first wave, but as Lieutenant Walters tells me every time, you make sure that it gets done. How're the legs?"

"Thank you, sir. And they are fine sir, just a few scrapes. Nothing I haven't had before."

Colonel Frederick fell silent, looking over Donalds while smoothing back a loose strand of hair. "How are you feeling, Sergeant?"

Donalds hesitated in answering, and Colonel Frederick continued. "Truthfully now soldier, I've seen all the signs before. Are you feeling run down?"

"A bit, sir." Donalds almost felt sheepish for voicing his agreement. Every soldier in the unit worked hard, and Donalds was not a man to talk about himself frequently.

"I appreciate your honesty, Sergeant. We all are. This campaign in Italy has been a grind, but we are making progress in pushing the Germans back. I can assure you that."

Donalds nodded but said nothing. He felt different but dared not say a thing. Colonel Frederick would not have stood for such men in his unit to say things like that.

"That being said, Sergeant, I've got something that a man of your... disposition is highly suited for. This one comes by way of London. The top, Sergeant. Even I am only privy to some of the information."

"What is it, sir?"

"It's a seek and capture mission, it seems. Some high-value German target. You are to have two to three days furlough and then report to the airfield at Castel Volturno. Once there, you will be briefed in further detail."

"And what about my men, sir?" asked Donalds.

"I'll be having Sergeant Wexler take them over, under the command of Lieutenant Walters. However, I have been requested by command to inform you that along with yourself, three other men will be required for the mission. You can make your choice as to who you would like to take with you, but you must make Private Lintz one of your selections. He speaks a little German, and my orders were to provide men with German-speaking heritage, if possible," stated Colonel Frederick.

Donalds thought for a moment and then announced his decision. "I'll take Corporal Mills, Private Appleyard and Private Lintz, as you suggested, sir."

At this, Sergeant Donalds stood as well as Colonel Frederick. Donalds saluted both him and Lieutenant Walters, shared a hearty handshake with each of them, and headed for the door.

"Good luck, Sergeant. I'll see you again very soon, I'm sure of it." said the Colonel, before heading back to the parlor room.

Donalds left them and entered the cool night time air. He lit a cigarette and stood in the doorway. A secret mission, with very little detail; a million thoughts were running through his head. Finishing his cigarette, he left to find Corporal Mills, Private Appleyard, and Private Lintz. Luckily, he didn't have to look very far—Lieutenant Walters had policed them to burial detail for Private Maxwell. He called them over and relayed the information that Colonel Frederick had provided earlier. He gave them each a choice if they wanted to join him, and each of them offered their answer individually.

"Sarge, you're telling me I get three days off and then a secret mission where I might get to kill more Krauts? Sign... me... up," said Appleyard, grabbing his shovel to go back to digging. Just like Donalds, Appleyard was a Saskatchewan boy, through and through. His gregarious personality got on some people's nerves, but every platoon had one, and Donalds appreciated that Appleyard tried to keep things light amongst the men. Some of the men teased him for his curly hair and freckles, chiding him for being 'just a boy'. Donalds knew better than that; he never underestimated the man's resourcefulness. It didn't hurt that he was also one of the best shots in the Force.

"Whatever you need me to do, Sergeant, I will be there," said Private Simon Lintz. You could only hear a hint of German in Lintz's accent, as it only revealed itself when he spoke certain words. His parents were originally from Austria but had immigrated to Canada and settled in the Prairies—Manitoba, to be specific. His family was farmers, but once the war had started, Simon Lintz hadn't hesitated, joining up immediately. No doubt he carried a chip on his shoulder with his German/Austrian heritage, but Donalds knew he was reliable.

Mills said nothing. The other two men had gone back to digging, and Mills approached the Sergeant, curtly saluting before standing at attention.

"Permission to speak, sir!"

"First of all, at ease, Corporal. Secondly, permission granted."

Mills relaxed his stance. "Sir, this mission... well, why me, sir?"

The question caught Donalds a bit off guard. He knew his reasons for picking these men, sure. Appleyard was a great shot, and his demeanor was good for morale. Lintz was mandatory, so there was no question there. Mills... well, Donalds had chosen Mills for his...fastidious nature. The Corporal had been a forest ranger from Alberta before joining up, and Donalds and Mills had ended up being bunkmates together at Fort Harrison. He was all business, but that's what Donalds would need for this mission. Donalds knew that tough decisions would always have to be made; that was the burden of leadership. A man of Mills's unwavering character would never question his orders, despite the potential outlandish nature of them. He just couldn't tell Mills that.

"Do you not want to go, Corporal?"

"If you order me, sir, then I will have to follow orders."

"No. Not on this one. I'm giving each man a choice. It will be dangerous, behind enemy lines in God knows where. I could order you, but instead I'm giving each man the freedom to make his own decision."

Mills looked at Donalds after the latter had finished this statement. Donalds could see that the man's mind was trying to process that he had the freedom to make a choice. The edges of Donalds's mouth curled into a smirk.

"In that case, sir, I decline."

The answer struck Donalds. It was not something he expected Mills to say.

"And your reason, Corporal?"

Mills looked back at the men digging but kept silent. Donalds sensed something and decided to press the issue.

"And the reason... Corporal?"

Mills hesitated again but summoned the courage. "I think you'll get us all killed."

At that statement, the men behind Mills stopped digging and stared at him. Donalds, nodding his head, removed his helmet, and stepped closer to Mills.

"I beg your pardon, Corporal?"

"Forgive me sir, but look at the facts. You're brash, you take risks, and frankly, I've been hearing you talk about wanting to make a difference in this war for some time. I'm afraid that..." He stopped, watching Donalds's face turn sour.

"Oh please continue Corporal. I find this fascinating."

"...I'm afraid, Sergeant, that your need to make a difference here—well, it will put myself unnecessarily in harm's way."

Donalds shifted his stance as he now took in everything that Mills was saying. *Was the man correct? Was he blinded by the war's grind, and desperate to make a difference in this hellish world that he would inadvertently put men at risk?* He began to question all the decisions he had made. He looked over at Appleyard and Lintz.

"How about you men, do you feel the same as Corporal Mills here? I want you to speak freely."

Both men shared a glance but quickly answered no. Then they went back to digging, now aware of the awkwardness of this conversation. Donalds turned back to Mills.

"Looks like you're alone in your opinion, Corporal. However, we'll be shipping out for the furlough tomorrow morning, so despite your apparent lack of faith in myself, I expect you to join Privates Lintz, Appleyard, and myself at 0900." Donalds started to walk over to where the two men were digging.

"Wait, sir, I don't... understand. I thought we all had a choice."

"Oh, you did. But I also get a choice. This is the First Special Service Force, Corporal, being brash and thinking on our feet are just parts of the job. I'm choosing to show you that your opinions about me are wrong. I'm ordering you to join us now." Donalds paused and walked over to Mills. He put his hand on the man's shoulder. "I need you on this Carl, is that understood?"

Mills closed his eyes. Donalds knew the answer to the question before it came.

"Yes sir!"

"Good. Now, someone hand me a shovel. Let's make sure to give Private David Maxwell here a proper burial."

CHAPTER THREE

"YES, OF COURSE, *Reichsführer*, every effort is being made, I assure you. My best man is working on a potential lead as we speak." Vahlen took a moment from his phone call and rubbed his temple. Phone calls with *Reichsführer* Henrich Himmler were always... challenging. "What's that? Oh yes, I intend to have an updated report for you by the end of next week... No, *Reichsführer*, I promise, I won't fail you."

Vahlen hung up the phone and slammed his fist on the desk. He looked around at the sparsely decorated office at the Marseille police station, hoping to find solace on its barren walls. Vahlen was an ambitious man, and he had built his career in the SS on the backs of crushing particularly difficult Resistance cells. Failure was simply not an option. He needed something to give Himmler, and fast. "Weiss? Weiss!"

The blonde *Obersturmführer* raced into the office at Vahlen shouting his name, saluted, and stood attention. "*Heil* Hitler!"

Vahlen quickly acknowledged his salute. He had more pressing matters to get to. "Have you seen *Hauptsturmführer* Teicher?"

The man thought carefully, then answered. "I believe he is still conducting his interrogation downstairs."

"Good. In the meantime, I want you to go down and assemble in the motor pool with some of the men. We'll be going on a little excursion later."

"As you wish, *Sturmbannführer*." Weiss bowed his head and clicked his heels, leaving the office. Once the junior officer had left, Vahlen went back to looking over local Resistance activity reports taken by Grassl's men. He'd been reading them for the better part of an hour before Himmler's phone call had interrupted him. After finishing reading the latest stack, he threw them off his desk and onto the ground. They were utterly useless. It was clear that the local units of the German Army had no clue how to combat the French Resistance. He put on his jacket and stood to leave the office. Hopefully, Teicher would have made some headway with the interrogation down below.

He shut the office door gently, then made his way to the marble staircase in the center of the building. Vahlen made his way across the foyer, amongst the milling officers, and then down the narrow stairwell just off the main one. Once he found the correct metal door and pounded twice. A soldier opened the door, and Vahlen instantly smelt the stale air, tinged with sweat and urine. He stepped over the threshold and found a younger man, hands bound, kneeling on the grey floor. Completely naked, the man was also blindfolded and slightly shivering. To the right of him, Teicher stood next to a table, suspenders dangling at his sides. The *Hauptsturmführer* was breathing heavily, and sipping from a cup of water. "Come to take your turn, *Sturmbannführer*?" He pointed at the various sharp implements splayed out on the table.

Vahlen shook his head. "You look like you have things well in hand. Where are we at? Time is... not on our side."

"In fact," Teicher said, putting his boot into the back of the man, "we were just getting to a list of names. Isn't that right, Pierre?"

Picking up a piece of metal piping, Vahlen watched as Teicher dragged it along the ground around the man. He tapped it twice, then poked him in the side with the end. The man winced and then whimpered a little. "Al... Al... Albert."

Teicher put the pipe squarely on his shoulder. "I think we're making excellent progress—that's the fifth name already. We can go over the list later today."

"No," said Vahlen, heading for the door, "once you have the names, let's knock on a few doors. Today." Teicher looked slightly confused at Vahlen's statement, so the large German continued. "I received a call from Berlin earlier today... the *Reichsführer* wants progress by the end of the week."

Teicher's eyes widened. He also knew that Himmler wasn't a patient man. "Of course, *Sturmbannführer*. I should be done in about half an hour." He tapped the pipe with his free hand.

"Excellent, I'll be upstairs in the motor pool with Weiss. Oh, and Eberhard..."

"Yes, *Sturmbannführer*?"

Vahlen pointed at the naked man on the floor. "No witnesses." Teicher nodded once and turned back to the man. Vahlen exited the room and as he walked down the cramped hall, he heard the metal door shut. Not long after, a loud clang and a scream of pain echoed off the walls. Vahlen could barely hold back his smile.

⸻ ⬦ ⸻

A COUPLE OF HOURS LATER, Vahlen crumpled up the sheet of paper and threw it to the floor of the car in a fit of anger. "Another name, another dead end! You're losing your touch, *Herr* Teicher, and I'm losing my patience!"

Teicher retrieved the paper and attempted to brush it smooth. "There is one more name on the list. I promise you, *Sturmbannführer*, this one will bear fruit."

"It better, Eberhard. Otherwise, it will be you that I serve up to *Reichsführer* Himmler," Vahlen said, pointing his finger directly at his subordinate. Teicher leaned forward and gave the driver the address. Both men sat in silence as the driver turned onto their path to their next destination. Vahlen looked out the window of the moving car at the passing French buildings. The beautiful vistas did nothing for him, especially compared to the Fatherland. While it may look the same to a simple tourist, he missed the mountains of Bavaria, the lakeside at Wannsee, and the many cobbled Strasse's of Berlin. As a privileged member of the *SS*, he had also been to more than a few outdoor rallies in Nuremberg, and nothing could compare to those passionate scenes.

The car made a sharp turn to the left and started down a side street. Behind them, the truck carrying his men had also made the turn. Vahlen turned towards Teicher, trying to break the tension, and gestured to the surroundings. "Do you like this country, Eberhard?"

"It is kind of hard to like a place where most people want to kill you, is it not, sir?"

"True, there are some that may wish us dead, but you and I have survived as long as we have by being one step ahead, always."

Teicher nodded and sat back as the car continued to lurch forward. As the car started to slow after its last turn, coming down the block, Vahlen looked up at the apartment building they were now in front of. He stepped from the car but turned back towards Teicher. "This is the place, correct?" Vahlen knew the information was accurate. Teicher was not a man that made mistakes often. He liked to test his men on regular occasions, to keep them sharp. He knew the question would get a subtle rise out of Teicher, which came as expected.

"Sir, my information is always accurate. Do you doubt me now, sir?" he responded, slightly annoyed.

Vahlen grimaced and waved towards the vehicle that had just turned the corner. The truck came to a stop behind the car and Vahlen's second in command, *Obersturmführer* Hans Weiss jumped down from the cab.

Weiss was every bit as ruthless and cunning as Vahlen, which is why Vahlen had put him in charge of the men. Standing slightly shorter than Vahlen's six-foot-three, Weiss stood at attention and raised his right hand in salute. "What are your orders, *Sturmbannführer*?"

Vahlen turned and pointed up to the building. "There is an apartment at the top of the building and Herr Teicher has found out the owner might have some information we need. He doesn't know we are coming, so you and I will take half the men and go up the stairs. The other half will go around back as a precaution, making sure he doesn't escape. Remember, Weiss, I want him alive."

"I understand, *Sturmbannführer*."

Weiss shouted a few commands and the men started to jump down from the truck. Vahlen and Weiss had personally selected each man in the platoon from a pool of Waffen *SS* soldiers. Each man was trained in a variety of weapons and had seen combat time on the various fronts. They worked closely together so much so that they were among the best when it came to flushing out and eliminating Resistance members. Vahlen could not have been prouder of them.

The men checked their weapons and outfitted themselves with grenades and extra ammunition. Vahlen checked his pistol and moved towards the front of the building. Once the men were finished, Weiss ordered them forward and they entered the foyer, with Vahlen leading the charge. The inside of the apartment building was pretty worn down, and the Germans started to climb the wooden stairs with purpose.

According to Teicher, the man was a former French soldier and had connections to some questionable individuals, including the man that Teicher had tortured earlier. It wasn't like they were storming a bunker, but it was still incredibly dangerous. If it wasn't so important to take him alive, Vahlen would take immense pleasure in immediately torturing and killing him. He hated the French almost as much as he hated Russians.

They reached the third floor and Vahlen spotted the door down the hall. He ordered his men forward and within seconds they had taken up positions on either side of the door. Teicher took the initiative and knocked twice on the door. When there was no answer, he shouted in French: "*Ouvre la porte, S'il vous plait*! *Police*! *[Open the door, please! Police!]*"

There was no response from inside the apartment.

Suddenly, Vahlen heard a sound and put a finger to his lips, motioning for his men to be as silent as possible. Vahlen waved the nearest soldier, Schutze Lichter, to go forward and kick down the door.

CRRRRRAAAACK! CRRRRRRAAAACK!

Lichter's body collapsed and blood spilled out onto the floor. Two rays of light came through the door now.

Vahlen and his men flattened themselves against the wall, some laying flat on the floor. It was obvious the Frenchmen had heard them, and *Schutze* Lichter had paid the price for his clumsy feet. With the element of surprise gone, Vahlen motioned with his hands for two more privates to shoot through the door with their machine guns.

"FIRE!" he shouted with vigor.

His men opened up, firing a full salvo through the door. The sound was deafening in the small hallway. When it was all said and done, the door was ragged and barely hanging onto its frame. Vahlen clutched his pistol and waved in the direction of Weiss, motioning him to kick down the door and enter the apartment.

Weiss's boot went through the damaged wood easily and the door flew off its hinges. Vahlen and his men entered the room cautiously. The apartment was sparsely furnished, dark, and depressing. It was eerily quiet, and Vahlen urged *Schutze* Kohler and *Schutze* Berger into the room to search. It didn't take long to find their target, clutching his wounded leg behind a crude barricade.

After the soldiers had made sure the room was secure, Vahlen approached the wounded man and replaced his pistol in its holster. He grabbed an overturned wooden chair, and gently set it right side up.

"Pick him up and put him in the chair. Then, Kohler, go out and find *Hauptsturmführer* Teicher and ask him to come up."

"Yes, *Sturmbannführer,*" replied *Schutze* Kohler.

Berger and Kohler put the Frenchman in the chair. He was still dazed and would have fallen if not for the men restraining him. The men made sure binds on his hands and legs were secure and then Kohler left to carry out the rest of Vahlen's orders. Vahlen grabbed a chair himself and sat in front of the Frenchman, beginning a conversation. "What is your name?"

Silence. The man avoided Vahlen's gaze as much as he could.

"Let me be clear, *mon ami*, I already know your name. Considering that we found you, that much should be clear. But I want us to start off properly, so please tell me your name," stated Vahlen. He removed his pistol from the holster and laid it on the table. The man's eyes were immediately drawn to it.

Still, the man remained silent. *He was strong*, Vahlen thought, but he had seen this type of bravery before. Many Resistance members thought they were stronger and wouldn't break, but sooner or later, everyone breaks. It was all about finding the right pressure for the right situation.

"I'm going to give you to the count of five to tell me your name."

Vahlen took off his leather glove and gripped the pistol.

"One..."

The man tried to crack a smile. Vahlen cocked the slide on the pistol and leveled it at the man.

"Two..."

Vahlen leaned forward and pressed the pistol on the man's chest.

"Three..."

"Four..."

"Albert," the man croaked out before Vahlen could say five.

"See, Albert, was that so difficult?" Vahlen asked. He gripped the man's face, focusing the man's gaze on his face. "You will tell us everything... we want to know... am I clear?" He stood up from the chair and looked down at Albert, shaking his head.

Placing the pistol on Albert's leg, he pulled the trigger.

Albert let out a scream and tried to clutch his leg, even though his hands were tied. He continued to whimper and cry as Vahlen holstered his pistol and walked out of the apartment. Outside the room, Teicher was coming up the stairwell. He saluted Vahlen and asked,

"How is our prisoner?"

Vahlen looked back towards the room and smiled. "He's ready for you. Hurry up, I want you to get all the information he has. If he names those responsible for *SS* Hauptsturmführer Kampfer's death, I might just give you the Knight's Cross myself.

"Yes, *Sturmbannführer.*"

"*Herr* Teicher, remember, the *Reichsführer* is waiting..."

Teicher noticeably swallowed and moved off towards the room, leaving Weiss and Vahlen now standing outside. Weiss spoke first. "Sir, I'm told Colonel Grassl's office is trying to get a-hold of you. He requests you contact him, immediately."

Vahlen frowned. He hated wasting time with pointless updates, especially to some useless Army officer. The conversation he was about to have would be short.

"Tell the Colonel that I am otherwise occupied at the moment."

With that, Vahlen turned heel and headed back towards the apartment.

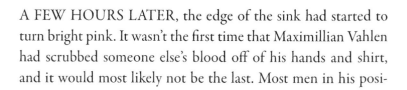

A FEW HOURS LATER, the edge of the sink had started to turn bright pink. It wasn't the first time that Maximillian Vahlen had scrubbed someone else's blood off of his hands and shirt, and it would most likely not be the last. Most men in his position would leave the interrogations and torture to their men, but every now and then Vahlen liked to take a hands-on approach. His reputation within the *SS* was built on it. All of this had led to his many promotions, and that he now carried some considerable influence with the *Reichsführer*, despite the terse phone call earlier. Satisfied finally with the state of his shirt, he grabbed a nearby towel, dried his hands, and exited the bathroom. As he did, he stopped to watch Weiss and another of his men carry the bloodied and lifeless body of Albert through the apartment and down the stairs. The man had broken rather easily, spilling his secrets. Unfortunately, those secrets were nothing regarding who killed Kampfer, or anything else of interest.

"Well, that's the last name on the list. Seems our friend back at the station lied to us, eh Eberhard?" Vahlen said, lighting his cigarette.

"Yes, sir. Accept my apologies, sir." replied *Hauptsturmführer* Eberhard Teicher.

Vahlen waved his hand dismissively, putting each of his arms through the loops in his suspenders.

"What do you want to do now?" asked Teicher, making his way toward the doorway.

One of the men moved past Teicher and caught Vahlen's attention.

"*Schutze* Kohler, get the vehicles ready." As the man left, Vahlen turned back to Teicher.

"We are getting nowhere here Eberhard, and the Army is no help either. Have the Gestapo agents you had following Colonel Grassl come back with anything?"

"No sir, they report he's acting normally."

Vahlen snorted in derision and looked away, frustrated. "Of course. The Colonel is hiding something, I can feel it. Tell the Gestapo to keep following him and find Weiss in the meantime. We'll meet back at the police station tomorrow to discuss our next move." Teicher saluted and left. It was not often that Vahlen met with failure. By now he thought he would have gleaned some sort of clue as to who committed this murder, but so far nothing had turned up. Deep in his thoughts, he contemplated this more as he got into the car. He had to admit, he was starting to become desperate. The vehicle had started to pull away from the curb. Vahlen, for the first time in his career, was uncertain as to his next step.

ON THE OPPOSITE SIDE of the street a man was pretending to look out at the beautiful blue sky, casually strolling down the sidewalk. He stopped to look in one of the many store windows, pretending to contemplate buying the fashionable garments on display. He watched the soldiers milling about in front of the apartment building through the reflection in the glass. The German soldiers were milling about below, laughing and joking.

That was it. What he was waiting for.

Stubbing out his cigarette, he lingered a little longer in front of the window, then began to walk further down the block. Once he was out of sight, he quickened his pace over another two blocks till he reached a small café. Located right near the promenade and the ocean, the establishment was thankfully sparsely populated. He strolled in, headed towards the back counter, and nodded his head towards one of the waiters. The waiter nodded back and pointed towards the phone in the corner. Ducking behind, he made his way over and picked it up. He waited until he heard the receiver and then spoke quietly. "He's there, just like you said. Him and his entire unit. They just finished raiding Albert's apartment."

"How many men did he have with him?" the voice on the other end of the line asked.

"I saw at least five on the street and probably another five go up the stairs, plus two other officers."

"Good work, I'll be in touch." The line clicked off, and the man who entered the café hung up the phone, thanked the manager of the establishment, and promptly made his exit.

———◈———

ACROSS THE CITY, FRANCK Chabert hung up his telephone. He sat back in his chair, deep in thought. Keeping tabs on Vahlen's movement was becoming more difficult, and Franck had almost the limits of his network of fellow Resistance members. He realized he was becoming more and more desperate. He had already radioed Webb to set the plan in motion, so there was no turning back now.

Franck did feel a little bad about Albert. No one deserved to be tortured at the hands of the Germans, especially a fellow countryman. But the man was sloppy; it was only a matter of time before he bungled something up and got captured anyways. So, Franck decided to use him to gain intelligence on Vahlen and his men, and keep Vahlen where Franck could watch him closely. *Cruel, perhaps*, Franck thought, *but a necessity*. His and Webb's mission now took priority.

There was another problem, however. From what Franck knew about Vahlen, the man was no fool. Eventually, he would discover that the Resistance cell here had nothing to do with the murder of their *SS* comrade. Once that happened, he would leave Marseille. Franck knew Webb would be furious if he let that happen. He couldn't let that happen. He had already exhausted giving up names to the Germans. *Poor Pierre*, thought Franck, captured by Vahlen and no doubt tortured into giving names that Franck had spoon-fed him, including the likely newly deceased Albert. This little gamble had kept the large German busy, just as Franck had planned. It had been no secret that he had also despised Pierre—there's was an alliance of convenience. Franck had tolerated the communist's affiliation with their Resistance group out of pure necessity. He had to say, this little appearance by Vahlen had allowed him to clean his ranks of perhaps the more undesirable members, which wasn't all bad.

What was he saying? These were fellow Frenchmen.

He got up and grabbed a glass of water from the kitchen. Drinking it in a single go, he watched as his hand shook, replacing the glass to the counter.

Standing there for some minutes, he started to realize the consequences of his actions.

No. Now was not the time to be weak. They died as patriots, Franck told himself.

Do you believe that? The question nagged at him. He stared out the small kitchen window and another question began to creep into his mind... *What exactly have I become?*

Franck rubbed his temples. *Vahlen. It was Vahlen's fault*, another life snuffed out by that bastard. Back to the task at hand. He had been mulling a problem that urgently needed addressing. They needed to keep Vahlen here or nearby, at least until Webb arrived. Marseille would not be ideal, due to the large garrison of German troops here.

He filled the water cup again... and put down the glass.

That was it... he couldn't believe he didn't think of it before.

There was a place that he could get Vahlen too. And the answer was so simple. Give the scarred bastard exactly what he wanted. Some of the finer details would have to be hashed out, but the plan was forming. It was time to send another message to the Major. He checked his watch, noting it was a bit early and a bit too risky to send a signal at this moment. He would wait a few hours more.

After that, he believed, a drink was in order. Something a little stronger than water.

NEAR THE PROMENADE, just outside the Old Port, The Black Rose was as lively as it had been in a while, which suited Patrice well enough. He wanted a bit of money in his pocket and a bustling bar full of patrons would definitely help. Especially with the group of German officers in the corner; their table was covered in drinks. They had been keeping him busy all night, so much so that he had barely any time to look up and see who had come into the bar. A low whistle and wave caught his attention, and Patrice's mood soured. He recognized Franck, his face grimacing as he slung the white towel over his shoulder. Making his way down the wood, the knot in his stomach got tighter. What was he doing here?

"What can I get for you, sir?" In a hushed tone, Patrice also said, "I thought I said I was done....What are you doing here?"

"Just a small glass of wine tonight, barkeep," replied Franck, loudly enough for someone else to hear. He beckoned Patrice closer and said, in a hushed tone, "Out back, ten minutes."

Patrice chewed the side of his cheek, then gritted his teeth. He went to the shelves and grabbed a corked, unmarked, dark green bottle. Removing the cork, he poured the velvet liquid into the glass. Patrice was damned if he was going to give Franck any of the good stuff. It was the house red for him tonight. Sliding the glass back to the man, Patrice reluctantly nodded. He kept a careful eye on the time, and on the state of the table of Germans. He also spent the time staring at Franck, who seemed lost inside the wine glass. When the time had passed, he saw Franck excuse himself and make a very public show of taking out his cigarettes and walking to the back of the bar. Past the off white lavatories was the door that led straight to the darkened alley. Patrice gave a couple of beats, then soon followed him down the hall. Once outside, Franck leaned against the back wall, lighting his cigarette and blowing smoke into the night air. Patrice did the same and lit his cigarette.

"Risky, with all the Germans here tonight," Patrice said.

"That's exactly why I'm here."

Patrice looked quizzically at Franck, "I'm not sure I understand..."

"I'll make it quick. I need you to tell those Germans in there that you know where the murderer of that *SS* officer, Kampfer, is. Tell them that the person they are looking for is north of here, in Serronelle."

"What? Wait a minute. I'm out of your little spy business. I said I was done with the Resistance," hissed Patrice, clearly distressed.

"Keep your voice down Patrice. Look, I need you to do this. It has to come from someone outside the normal channels. They'll believe it if it comes from you."

"Do you know what kind of a risk this is? I do not want to spend another night in the basement of that police station..." whispered Patrice, starting to pace. He looked agitated.

Franck stared ahead, the cigarette burning in his fingers. He thought of Albert—he felt a pit starting to grow in his stomach. But, time was of the essence. He flicked away his cigarette and got closer to Patrice, grabbing him by the collar, and shoving him against the back of the bar.

"I don't care if you don't like it. Just... do as I ask. Otherwise, there might be consequences. Am I making myself clear?"

Patrice said nothing, and Franck let go of his shirt, brushing it smooth of wrinkles in the process.

"Good, glad we agree. Remember, the town's name is Serronelle." Franck went back inside first, sitting down at the bar, continuing to nurse his drink.

Patrice collected himself, waiting for a few moments so as not to arouse suspicion. He then came back in and started to fill more orders. Patrice was still shaken from the confrontation outside, but without knowing what Franck would do, he had no choice but to go along with this plan. Truth be told, Franck frightened Patrice a little. He had become unstable, and there was no telling what the man was capable of.

Lost in his thoughts, Patrice didn't notice a figure approach the bar. He looked up at the last moment, realizing that it was Colonel Grassl. The man who had saved his life not but a few nights earlier was in great spirits and by the disheveled look of his uniform he was well into having a great night.

"Let's have another round for me and my men, Patrice," he said, leaning against the wood rail of the bar.

"Of course, Colonel. I just want to say how grateful...well how grateful I am for what you did for me the other night..."

Colonel Grassl held up his hand, motioning for Patrice to stop.

"Let's not speak of that again."

"As you wish, Colonel," Patrice got the glasses together on a tray, as he casually continued to speak with the officer. "Colonel, I'm glad you and your men are having a great time tonight. I, however, am not."

Colonel Grassl shifted his position, furrowing his brow. "Tell me, my friend, what troubles you?"

Patrice grabbed a glass, set it on the bar, and poured himself a little sherry. He finished it in one sip and poured another. He felt the eyes of Franck burning a hole into his back.

"I can see this issue is weighing on you Patrice, what is it?" pressed Grassl.

"Well, I overheard some men talking the other day, at one of the tables. They were talking about the death of that *SS* officer, Krieger or something..."

Colonel Grassl perked up a little at this topic. "His name was Kampfer. Tell me, who were these men?"

"They were not local; I can tell you that. I'm pretty sure I heard them say they come from a town a few miles north of here—Serronelle," lied Patrice. He placed the requested drinks on the tray and pushed them towards Colonel Grassl.

Now he waited. Grassl and his officers had been coming on and off for the last two or three years. They had learned to trust

Patrice, almost implicitly. He had to hope that the lie he told would sink in.

The Colonel, however, said nothing, grabbed the tray and walked it back to the table for his men. Patrice turned and saw Franck stare angrily. Patrice saw that he had finished his wine and had left a few *francs* on the bar. Grabbing his jacket, Franck headed towards the door. Not sure what to think, Patrice tried to forget about Franck and his Resistance. He had done his part, and he just wanted to be free from it all—the Germans and the Resistance.

As the night wound down, the Germans started to leave arm in arm, singing their wretched national anthem. Out of the corner of his eye, Patrice saw Colonel Grassl approach the bar. As the drunk German officer laid down the money for the tab, he leaned in.

"My boy... what was the name of that town... the town you told me about earlier?"

Patrice tried to steady his nerves before speaking. "Serronelle, Colonel. The town's name was Serronelle."

Grassl smiled, tapped the money on the bar, and waved goodbye to Patrice. He and the rest of the Germans bundled out of the bar, still singing.

Good, now the Germans had that info. Patrice hoped the matter was finished because, after the way Franck acted tonight, he didn't deserve Patrice's help. Something had changed in Franck ever since he had told him about the large, scarred German. He was more unstable and rasher. Patrice wondered if he had pushed the issue earlier this evening, what exactly Franck would've done.

He shivered at the thought.

———◉———

THE NEXT MORNING, HE heard the blinds open and the sun shone onto *Sturmbannführer* Vahlen's face. He rubbed his eyes and stepped out of bed. As he stretched in his room, the door opened and his adjutant, *Obersturmführer* Weiss, stood at attention. "Good morning, sir. Would you like breakfast?"

"No, I don't have the time. Is the car ready downstairs?" replied Vahlen.

"Yes sir, it's waiting for you," said Weiss, clasping his hands behind his back.

Vahlen dragged himself from the bed and went to the ornate dresser, pulling out a freshly pressed white shirt. He finished dressing in front of the mirror, buttoning his jacket and combing his hair.

Descending the stairs, which creaked mightily with each booted step, Vahlen reached the main floor. He headed straight for the kitchen. The house he was using as his billet was a large villa. Away from the ocean and the bustle of the city, the house sat on a plateau overlooking a small valley. The green-grey mortared stone gave the 18th-century farmhouse a dour look at first glance, while the bright tangerine-colored, clay-shingled roof trapped the heat in the colder months and allowed it to dissipate in the warmer ones. The twisting dirt road was obscured by overgrowth from the main road, meaning it was perfect if one wanted to disappear. He had chosen it because it was more secure and easier to protect. Every German commanding officer had read the reports of what happened to Reinhard Heydrich in the former Czechoslovakia, being assassinated on his way to his office from his house. Vahlen knew the feelings his work raised in others, and he resolved that he wouldn't die in any similar way. He always made sure his driver varied his routes. Upon entering the kitchen, he saw his driver Franz enjoying a cup of coffee at the table. He poured himself a cup, while the man stood to attention and raised his arm in a Hitler salute. "Good morning, *Sturmbannführer*."

"Good morning, Franz. Hurry up and finish your coffee, I'd like to go into town. Weiss?"

The *Obersturmführer*, who had by now descended the stairs, came up to Vahlen, standing rigid. "Yes, *Sturmbannführer*?"

"Any new reports about Colonel Grassl from our friends at the Gestapo?"

"I'm told he spent the night drinking at that horrible bar we went into the other evening. He was with some of his officers, sir."

Vahlen sipped his coffee slowly, a perverse smirk across his face. Damn that Colonel Grassl. He had the gall to lecture Vahlen on how to find Kampfer's killer, yet he drank in that establishment run by that questionable bartender. Vahlen couldn't prove it, but he was beginning to question the loyalty of the Colonel to the Fatherland. Something was not right here. He would speak with the Colonel, today.

"Let's go, Franz. Weiss, assemble the men and meet me at the police station," Vahlen ordered, heading towards the door.

Vahlen was deep in thought as the car wound around the country roads. Despite the beautiful spring day that was unfolding around them, Vahlen could think only of his failings. Every lead they had followed so far was a dead end. It was time to have a very honest conversation with the good Colonel.

The journey was uneventful, and soon enough the car once again pulled in front of the central Marseille police station. Vahlen thanked Franz and entered the building, ascending the large stairwell to the second level where Grassl kept his office. The Colonel's adjutant was at his desk outside the office, busy going over some papers.

"Good morning, Captain Sommer."

Sommer looked up, slightly shocked to see Vahlen standing before him "Ah, good morning, *Sturmbannführer*. Are you here to see the Colonel?" said the Captain, shuffling a few more sheets of paper on the desk. Captain Kaspar Sommer had been Colonel Grassl's adjutant for more than two years, or so Vahlen was told. Standing just a shade over six feet, he had carefully parted brown hair and features that were a bit sallow. Vahlen was also told he prided himself on making his superior officers happy. As an ambitious man himself, Vahlen appreciated these qualities and could see Sommer rising in the Army by getting in good graces with the Colonel. It was said that Sommer would do whatever it took to advance himself. His application to the SS was said to be in the works.

"Yes, I'd like to see him now," stated Vahlen, using his size to loom ominously over the Captain.

It did not work.

"I'm sorry sir, Colonel Grassl is very busy this morning. If you come back later..." stated Sommer, picking up a pen and filling out some reports.

Vahlen was not a man to suffer fools, and he was not a man to sit idle. He moved past Sommer's desk and entered the office of Colonel Grassl. Striding in, Vahlen was hurriedly followed by the adjutant. Grassl looked up, locked eyes with the *SS* officer, and waved away Sommer. "Thank you, Captain. You may go."

Vahlen sat down at the desk, removing his jacket and his gloves. Even sitting down, he was an imposing man, and he knew Grassl did not relish this conversation.

"Good morning, *Sturmbannführer*, so nice of you to join me."

"I wish I could say the same, Colonel. I think some things need... clearing up."

Grassl kept his head down, going through his reports, "If that's so, Herr Vahlen, then please, by all means, let's clear them up."

Vahlen brushed some imaginary lint from his uniform and looked up at Grassl.

"Ever since I arrived in Marseille, I have been stopped at every turn. Not to mention that we were told that one of our earliest suspects was vouched for... by you!" Vahlen slammed his fist down on the edge of the desk.

"Are you calling me a traitor, *Sturmbannführer*?"

Vahlen snorted and laughed, "If I could prove it, you would've already been arrested and executed, Colonel."

"And yet, here I remain. Let that be a lesson to you, *Herr* Vahlen, that your legendary powers are, in fact, fallible." Vahlen stared blankly at the Army man. Fury burned inside of him. He pushed his chair back and stood to leave when Grassl piped up again.

"Oh, don't leave yet, *Herr* Vahlen. I've got something that you will want, very dearly."

Vahlen stopped and stood impatiently. He was utterly disgusted—but his curiosity over what Grassl had to offer forced him to stay.

"What... is it, Colonel?" sneered Vahlen.

"We've heard that the person responsible for the killing is in a town fifteen miles north of here, Serronelle. An entire Resistance cell might even be there."

"Ha! A small town north of here? You can't expect me to believe this information. Where did you get it?"

Colonel Grassl opened another letter and sat back in his chair. "Then, by all means, *Herr* Vahlen, don't believe me. Keep going about your business and keep getting the results you're getting. I'm sure both Himmler and Hitler are very patient men." Grassl let a heavy sarcastic undertone hang on his words. He sat back in his chair, a small smile pulling at the corners of his mouth.

"You never answered me, Colonel. Where did you get this information?" demanded Vahlen.

"You have your sources, *Sturmbannführer*, and we have ours. I've already advised Berlin of this development, and they are eager to hear the results of your pending investigation into Serronelle."

Vahlen returned and leaned down onto the desk, his hands gripping the edge. His face was no more than a few feet from Colonel Grassl's. "I... don't like to be manipulated, Colonel. You're playing a very dangerous game here. I'll go to this town, and when we don't find anything, I'm going to make sure Berlin knows it was your information." Vahlen grabbed his gloves and jacket and got up to leave the room. As he opened the door, Grassl stood up.

"Oh, and Maximillian, one more thing. If those Gestapo goons that you had following me aren't called off, we will be having further words. Am I making myself clear?"

"We'll see about that, Colonel, we'll see about that," Vahlen said, exiting the office. While he immediately doubted the authenticity of the information, the Colonel was right in one sense—they had not made any meaningful progress on catching Kampfer's murderer. So, he would investigate and if the information turned out to be false, then he would have no reservations about killing Colonel Grassl. He needed to find Teicher and Weiss and round up the rest of his men for the trip to Serronelle. The sooner they left, the sooner he could get there and be done with this.

———◦———

FRANCK WALKED DOWN the promenade, the distant sound of gentle ocean waves lapping against the rocks of the breakwater jutting. He gripped the small pistol he had concealed in his pocket, his eyes searching the horizon for any threats. The Germans had imposed a curfew and no one was supposed to be out after dark, but there were ways around that. If stopped, he would tell them that he was on his way home from work. With the news that the Allies were making advances against the Germans on all fronts, there was genuine hope that soon France would be liberated. Franck could only hope and pray that freedom came soon to his homeland. He reached the end of the block and came to the apartment building he was looking for. He climbed the three flights of stairs till he saw the red door at the end of the hall. He knocked twice quickly, and then once more a few seconds later. The door unlocked and Yvonne's face greeted Franck. He quickly removed the pistol from his coat and put his hand to her mouth to prevent her from screaming. Using his body weight, he pushed them both into the apartment.

"Don't scream. Is he home?" queried Franck, taking a casual look around.

Franck kept his hand clamped over her mouth. Yvonne just shook her head from side to side.

Franck put the gun barrel to his lips, indicating to her to be silent. She nodded and he removed the hand from her mouth. He pointed for her to sit on the couch, while he sat in the chair opposite.

"Sorry to drop in on you like this, but you understand I must speak with your husband. And this was the only way."

She scoffed at the statement. Then she looked down at the pistol. "What will you do, shoot us in cold blood? For what? I don't know who's more dangerous, you or the Germans."

Franck bridled at the comment made by Yvonne. Nothing could be farther from the truth.

"I have never asked him to do something he didn't already want to do. Aren't you tired of the occupation?"

"At what cost, Franck? What if our daughter had to grow up without a father? For me to lose my husband? We have survived these last four years; we have too much to lose," Yvonne pleaded.

Franck thought back, to the butchery he had witnessed in the French countryside. The disregard of human life by Vahlen for the occupants of that house.

"You don't know what loss is... trust me. I have seen the devil do his work and I was powerless to stop it. You know nothing."

Before she could respond, both of them heard a key in the lock. Franck gripped his pistol again and watched as the door opened to reveal Patrice.

Patrice spoke joyously to Yvonne. "Good evening, my lovely wife." Putting down his jacket, he noticed Franck, and more importantly, the pistol in his hand.

"Franck... what's going on here?" A touch of anger crept into his voice.

Patrice came over and sat down next to Yvonne, grabbing her hand in his. Confused, he was trying to come to grips with the situation.

"I don't think you understand the importance of this. Forgive me, but I knew you would not let me in, and I must know if the Germans got the intel I gave you. This... was the only way." He turned the pistol in his hand as if showing the reason for this conversation to them.

Patrice's eyes stared at the pistol.

"But this... this is not you, Franck. There's no need for you to..."

Angry now, Franck interrupted Patrice.

"YOU DON'T KNOW ME. YOU DON'T KNOW WHAT I'M CAPABLE OF!"

Frightened now, Patrice and Yvonne recoiled from him. For a split second, Patrice thought about lunging at him and wrestling for the pistol. But at the last second, he did not. He knew he would lose against the trained Resistance man.

"Okay... okay, we don't. Ask your questions, but please, lower the pistol," Patrice spoke in a soft tone, trying to hide the fear he was feeling.

Realizing that perhaps he was taking things a bit too far, Franck sat back and placed the pistol on his leg. He took a deep breath in.

"I'm sorry... but, tell me, did the Germans tonight get the information from you? Did they question you about it?"

Patrice sighed, "I passed along the information you gave me, to Colonel Grassl no less. He even came back and asked me for the town's name at the end of the night."

Franck's expression immediately changed. His face lightened so much that it bewildered Patrice and Yvonne.

"Excellent work, Patrice, excellent work! I knew you would be the perfect man for this job."

"There was something else, Franck," the bartender said. "Earlier this evening, there were some regular German soldiers in, having a few drinks. I overheard one of them say that the SS men are packing up and leaving in the next twenty-four hours."

Franck leaned forward in excitement. "They said the SS men were leaving Marseille?"

"Seems like it. Those soldiers were quite happy, apparently that scarred German and the SS did not make many friends with the German Army stationed here. They bought two extra rounds in celebration."

Franck sat back, and a small smile crept across his face. So, Vahlen and his men had taken the bait. His plan was in motion. Now, it was time to contact Major Webb and start the second phase.

He stood up to leave and put the pistol in his pocket. "Thank you, Patrice. Your service will not be forgotten."

Patrice stood as Yvonne huddled on the couch. "Yes, yes it will be forgotten. You're a goddamn lunatic. You threaten me, you threaten my family, for what? What is this all about?"

Franck looked at Patrice, a look of anguish on his face. "You'll never understand. Nobody does."

"Get out of my house, Franck. I never want to see you again. Is that clear?"

Franck nodded and proceeded to the door. After opening it, he stopped, and turned back to them, but decided to say nothing.

Soon he was in the hall, and the gravity of what he had just done started to hit him again. *What have I done? What was I doing?*

Vengeance. Swift, righteous vengeance.

Those words echoed in Franck's head as he descended the creaky wooden steps. His purpose was clear again. Vahlen—he would pay.

He had to get a confirmation message to Major Webb tonight.

They didn't have a moment to lose.

CHAPTER FOUR

BLACKNESS. PURE, VELVETY blackness.

Major Theodore Webb looked into the distance, and there it was, looming on the horizon. He stood outside, looking up at the country house, when he heard some faint voices behind him, but saw no one when he turned around. He turned back towards the house and the door opened. A woman came out, covered in blood. She was followed by three or four soldiers. Some had limbs missing, others with holes through their chest. He tried to run, but his feet felt like cement, he couldn't move. Some of the soldiers came over to him and grabbed at his arms and legs. Then the woman approached him, her face disfigured. She spoke to him, her voice lyrical and haunting.

"Why? Why couldn't you stop them? Why couldn't you save us? Wake up, sir, wake up, wake up..."

Major Webb woke with a start, covered in sweat. Lieutenant Martin was over him, shaking him by the shoulder. "Wake up, sir, wake up."

Webb groggily sat up. He pushed away from the Lieutenant and went to the bathroom adjacent to his office. He ran the sink and splashed some cold water onto his face. The nightmares were becoming more frequent, and much more vivid. Trying to put the vision from his mind, he exited the bathroom and came back to his couch.

"Are you alright, sir?" asked Lieutenant Martin.

"Yes, yes, my boy, perfectly fine. Just had a... bad dream is all."
Wanting to shift the conversation away from his waking night-mare, he turned to Martin. "Why are you here, Lieutenant?"

Lieutenant Martin held up a small piece of paper.

Major Webb perked up, "A message from *Eager Patriot*?"

Martin nodded and handed over the slip. Webb scanned it, then poured himself a drink.

"Care for one, Lieutenant?"

"I'm good. Thank you, Major."

Major Webb clapped his hands together and yelled out a little scream of excitement. "My boy, we are in business," Webb said, picking up the piece of paper and reading it over again. "Our friend Vahlen will be in the town of Serronelle, just north of Marseille. Grab me the map, would you?"

Martin went to Webb's desk and brought back the map of France, spreading it out on the small table in front of them.

"Okay, so Marseille is here," Webb planted his finger on the map, and traced it along the road north, "and...here is...Ser-ronelle. Ah, Franck, well done."

Martin looked at the map and saw where Webb was point-ing. "Looks like there is a large set of fields not far from the town. Perfect for a drop."

"Yes... yes there is..." Major Webb said. He sat back, in slight shock that their plan had all fallen into place. In his mind, he asked himself if he wanted to go through with what they were about to do. His thoughts flashed back to the nightmare he had just had, and his decision became clear.

Martin interrupted Webb's train of thought. "So, Major, are we a go?"

"Yes, make all the arrangements, Lieutenant. Tell Jones or whatever his name was to relay the details back to *Eager Patriot*."

"Do you want me to give the Major-General an update as well on the timeline of the operation?"

The Lieutenant's question caught Webb slightly by surprise. He needed to keep this mission as secret as possible, the fewer people knew, the better.

"Uhhh... no, thank you, Lieutenant, I will brief him later about this myself."

Major Webb once again felt bad about lying to Lieutenant Martin but knew that he needed to. He had no intention of speaking with the head of SOE, Major-General Gubbins. For all intents and purposes, they would be capturing Vahlen to take him back for intelligence on the Atlantic Wall defenses. In reality, they would be capturing Vahlen so that Webb and Franck could exact revenge. For this reason, Webb had to keep everyone in the dark. The real purpose of the mission would need to be kept tight need-to-know. Nothing would be traced back to Webb, nothing that would potentially put the mission in jeopardy.

"Ahh, Lieutenant, one more thing..." Webb said

"Yes, sir?"

"I'm going to need you to join me on this one, Percival. It's positively vital to the mission's success."

Martin looked shocked. Sure, he had done his basic training, but he hadn't seen much combat if any at all.

"Are you sure, Major? I mean... I'm not exactly an experienced officer in combat..."

Webb thought carefully before he spoke next. He needed the genuine innocence and legitimacy that would come with Martin being on the mission, at least until they had Vahlen.

"We're talking about the fate of one of the biggest invasions of Europe. All hands on deck, Lieutenant. That's an order."

"As you wish, sir." Lieutenant Martin stood to leave but hesitated a few moments. Major Webb looked up from the map and sighed. "Anything else, Lieutenant?"

"Permission to speak freely, sir?"

"Go ahead."

"Are you going to be able to handle the demands of this mission? I mean, I'm not one to judge, but it has been some time since you were also in the field, sir."

Major Webb furrowed his brow. The Lieutenant was becoming suspicious, but nothing he couldn't handle. He dismissively waved away the junior officer.

"I'll be fine, Lieutenant. Your concern is noted. Now if that is all, I'd like to get some more rest," Webb said, gripping his whiskey bottle tightly. Martin nodded and proceeded to head for the exit. Before he left, Webb had already poured himself another three fingers of the brown liquid and shuffled to the couch to no doubt collapse again.

Out in the hall, Lieutenant Martin lingered for a few moments, wondering if he should pursue his concerns about battle readiness. But he knew his boss well enough and headed down the hall. He had entertained reservations about the Major leading the mission from the beginning, but the man had fought in France with the British Expeditionary Force and was evacuated with most of the Force at Dunkirk. He could handle himself, of that Lieutenant Martin had no doubt, but there was something about this mission that wasn't quite right. Nevertheless, Martin had his orders and it didn't do him any good having these idle thoughts. He went down the hall to his own office—a late-night phone call to Royal Air Force Base Tempsford was in order.

Tempsford was a secret airfield that only those in the Special Operations Executive knew of. Located deep in the Bedfordshire countryside, all the clandestine flights in and out of France originated there. Martin spoke with the commander, making sure that the C-47 Delta they had procured for the mission had arrived in good order. The commander confirmed, and Martin gave a small sigh of relief. He set about finishing up his other tasks, and then it would be home for a good night's sleep. He would need it; dropping behind enemy lines in the heart of Occupied France was no small task.

———◉———

EARLY THE NEXT MORNING, after a bit of breakfast and collecting a few personal things, Lieutenant Martin picked up Major Webb from the Baker Street office. Out of the dreariness and scarred buildings of London, the army jeep accelerated quickly down the winding roads of the English countryside. The smell of fresh rain hung thick in the air, and the roads were still slightly damp. Martin had figured the drive and fresh air would do the Major some good. As they passed the viridescent grass-covered hills, Major Webb sat there, silent, most likely nursing a slight hangover. Martin now saw his turn approaching and spun the steering wheel to the right. A seemingly unremarkable road one would think led to a small cottage or broken-down farmhouse, it was lined on either side with thick leafy trees, preventing prying eyes from doing just that. Members of the SOE knew this road well, and Martin had made this drive countless times.

Turning off the main road in a hurry, the paved concrete gave way to gravel, and the jeep briefly skidded out.

"Mind the road, Lieutenant. My head can't take much more jostling," Webb said, rubbing his temples and pulling his coat up around himself.

"Yes, sir. Sorry, sir."

After a few short minutes and some more dips and bumps that jostled the jeep, Webb coughed heartily before speaking. "You spoke to the flight crew last night?"

"Yes sir, they'll be waiting to meet us at the other edge of the field. I've only told them basic information, nothing more than that they are flying us to Italy," said Martin, attempting to keep the jeep from pitching off the road.

"Excellent."

The road wound into a wider opening, and both men could see the gate of the base now. Martin brought the jeep to a halt in front of the guard shack. The guard, a boy that looked no older than eighteen, made a thorough check of their credentials before raising the bar and waving them through. Surprisingly, the sun was out—the kind of day that you wished you could spend near the beach. The fresh air was doing wonders for Major Webb. It was also helping to cut through the last bit of a hangover from that morning. The jeep wove through the rows of planes, stacked wingtip to wingtip. It was clear the build-up for the invasion of Europe was on, and that the Allies were preparing for the inevitable crossing of the Channel. *It's ironic*, Major Webb thought, *if this build-up wasn't happening, finding a plane without drawing attention would have been quite difficult.* But, as fortune would have it, they had managed to find a one that wouldn't be missed for the next few days.

Lieutenant Martin shifted down the gears in the jeep, it pulled to a stop behind a C-47 Delta. The plane was a favorite of the airborne divisions, and its rounded nose and wide wingspan made it very distinctive. Thankfully, it had been easy to find, as it was the only one on the field. Usually, the airfield would be filled with one-seater planes, or at most, modified Halifax bombers. The Delta was the only plane that had the range that Webb and Martin needed, so they had called in a few favors and managed to procure one with the promise of a nice bottle of whiskey in return.

Under the plane, what looked to be one of the pilots was speaking in a rather animated tone with a mechanic, while another man, presumably the other pilot, dozed in the grass. Martin stepped out of the jeep and went to grab the gear as Webb wandered over to where the flight officer was finishing up his conversation with the mechanic.

"Go easy on her, she's not likely to take to your rough treatment of her undercarriage," said the flight officer. He was young-looking, with pockmarks from acne dotting across his face and a bit of unkempt blonde hair protruding from his flight cap. Webb was sure the man had trouble commanding respect from those below him, but it was also clear he took his job seriously.

"Oh, don't mind my tinkering then, just trying to keep ya in the air is all," replied the mechanic, his thick Scottish accent laden with sarcasm. He wiped his hands, picked up his tools, and seemed to storm off. Webb passed him by and waved his hand to get the attention of the flight officer. "Good morning Flight Sergeant, everything alright?"

"Good morning, sir, you must be Major Webb?" the pock-marked officer asked.

Webb nodded. The man stood to attention and saluted.

"Flight Sergeant Wiscomb at your service. Don't mind him, sir, the mechanics around here are very particular when it comes to maintenance. Sometimes they take it a bit too far, you know, sir," explained Wiscomb, gesturing profusely with his hands.

"Understood, Flight Sergeant. Now, I have a small favor to ask of you. With all the planning for the second front, there are a lot of extra ears around. We'd prefer if, essential to mission success, you kept the flight plan and mission details secret, even from some of our people here at Tempsford."

Wiscomb chuckled and tapped his nose a couple of times. "Loose lips sink ships, or something to that effect, eh Major? Fear not sir, you are in good hands. Now, let's go wake the Captain and we can be on our way."

Webb looked over at Lieutenant Martin, who was busy unloading their equipment from the jeep. He quickly made his way over.

"We should be off soon, do we have everything?"

"Yes sir," replied Martin, tossing a few more bags on the ground.

"Good. Now Lieutenant, you know I'm going to be relying heavily on you out there. The man we are after is dangerous, and his capture will go a long way to helping us land successfully in France."

"I know, sir. I'll try and be ready for whatever comes."

Webb patted his shoulder patronizingly. "Trust me, you're never ready."

While the Lieutenant finished up, Major Webb went and found Wiscomb, who by now was out from under the plane and over to the grass where the Captain was sleeping. The man was a bit portly compared to the Flight Sergeant and was aged some ten years older. Wiscomb shook him hard on the shoulders, and the man coughed and sputtered, removing the flight cap from his face.

"Rise and shine, Captain, our guests have arrived," stated Wiscomb, helping his senior officer to his feet.

The man grunted and adjusted his uniform. "Thank you, Sergeant. A pleasure to make your acquaintance, Major. I am Captain Lewis Harker."

Harker's voice boomed out in conversation, with a twinge of a Yorkshire accent. It looked like he hadn't shaved in a few days, but the one thing Webb noticed was his eyes. They had an intensity about them, something Webb suspected was quite useful in his line of work. The three men discussed what Webb had mentioned earlier about mission silence, and Harker understood completely. Both Wiscomb and Harker left to prepare for the flight, leaving Webb to his own devices. It had started to slightly alarm him how easy it was to pass off the lies, but there was the bigger picture to think about. The Scarred German had haunted his dreams and hung over everything he did since they had met four years ago. There was but one way to make sure this nightmare ended, and that was to cleanse the world of this man.

Martin finished loading all the gear onto the plane, and both climbed aboard. They got in the back and waited as Harker started up the plane's engines. Flight Sergeant Wiscomb came back and secured the door, giving a thumbs up and smile to the men.

Webb settled into the seat and pulled out his flask. He took a big swig and replaced the cap, feeling the smooth taste of whiskey go down his throat. Martin was busy checking their weapons, but Webb caught his eye. "I'm going to catch some shuteye, Lieutenant. Wake me before we get to Italy."

With that, Webb pulled the coat around himself and curled up for hopefully some nightmare-free sleep.

It wasn't likely.

CHAPTER FIVE

FRANCK HAD TO ADMIT, he enjoyed the intricate nature of making sure that every part of his gun was clean. It stemmed back to his days in the French Army, where they quickly drilled into him that an ill-kept weapon had the potential to jam. And if your weapon jammed, then you were dead. He grabbed the rag and made sure to wipe down the slide, and then slowly but surely cleaned the rest of the pieces that were laid out in front of him.

Once he was satisfied with the state of it, he put the MP40 back together. As much as he hated the Germans, he had to admit they made some pretty nice weapons. He slid the clip into the underside of the gun and cocked the slide. Placing the gun on the table, along with two other extra clips, Franck then lit a cigarette and sat back in the chair.

It was late afternoon, and the sun was starting to set, casting long shadows through the small window. Franck put his cigarette down and went to the kitchen, grabbing a piece of bread and what was left of a wheel of cheese. It wasn't much, but it had to be enough, as tonight was shaping up to be a very busy night. Now that he thought about it, the morning had been busy as well. He had spent it speaking with other members of his cell, organizing the plan for tonight.

Over the next couple of hours, Franck finished his meal and sat on his couch, thinking about what was going to happen once they had captured the Vahlen. It had focused his thoughts to think about it, and he needed it to keep him sharp, on the edge. He checked his watch; the time to leave had finally come.

He grabbed his jacket from the hook and then went to the table to stuff the clips into the pocket. He took the gun, and slung it around his back, then concealed it by putting on the jacket. Once he was satisfied that the gun wasn't visible, he exited his apartment out onto the street. The sun had set but the air was still lush and warm, thick with moisture like it was going to rain. He walked down the street with a purpose, neither dawdling nor hurrying. The vantage point, which he had chosen carefully, overlooked the entire square but was far enough away as to not draw suspicion.

Precisely ten minutes later, he turned onto the bridge near the Old Port of Marseille. The site of a recent uprising, the Germans had increased their presence here of late. Soon, he'd reached his destination, a little alcove that contained a small set of stairs. He climbed them slowly and deliberately until he came to the edge of a large precipice. From there, Franck could see the whole square laid out before him. He was in an older part of Marseille now, and the buildings reflected their age. Each was filled with apartments and lofts on the upper floors, a few cafes and shops on the bottom floor. Yellow stoned, they were reminiscent of something out of an *Alexandre Dumas* novel. They were the kind of buildings where if you brushed against them, they would leave a trail of white dust across your coat or pants.

Below the lookout, Franck took in the sights. This was the spot the Germans had chosen to keep their vehicles. This square, which stretched on almost two city blocks, contained a variety of different German vehicles, from supply trucks to half-tracks and motorcycles. All were carefully lined up in order. He slid back his jacket sleeve and checked his watch.

Twenty minutes past eight, right on time.

The show would be starting soon enough. There was no need to be cautious, the way the precipice was situated Franck was easily able to hide behind an outcrop of a nearby building. He had timed the plan to start at approximately eight-thirty, which would coincide with the Germans changing of the guard, adding to the confusion.

As he stood there, he was struck by an odd thought, that perhaps, all this preparation and time devoted to capturing and seeking revenge on Vahlen would be better used fighting the occupation. *But then*, he thought to himself, is *it so wrong and selfish to want to quiet one's demons, to right past wrongs by seeing an evil person punished?*

The four years of occupation had made the French people endure horrible atrocities; wouldn't it be just to see some of that given back to the Germans? These were questions that Franck didn't have the time nor the answers for. He had to focus on tonight, on the task at hand.

I'm doing this for her, he thought, t*he young woman that could no longer speak*. He checked his watch again, the second hand was ticking away,

Eight twenty-nine... just about time...

Franck watched as the tiny second hand ticked away—fifty-seven... fifty-eight... fifty-nine...

The second hand reached the twelve on his watch and a couple of explosions and machine-gun fire could immediately be heard in the distance. *Good*, Franck thought, *my comrades haven't delayed getting their part of the plan started.*

He emerged from behind the building and watched as the chaos below started to unfold. A few soldiers were running, loading up a motorcycle, and speeding off. Another soldier got into the cab of a transport truck and Franck looked on as five to six soldiers came and loaded into the back. A truck and another motorcycle then sped off in the direction of the explosions. Another small burst of gunfire could be heard in the distance. This was coupled with shouting in German. With the buildings so tightly packed together, the voices echoed endlessly. When most of the soldiers had cleared out, Franck saw his opening and went into action.

He unslung the MP40 from his back and took out a clip, slamming it in place and cocking the slide. He gripped the gun close to his chest as he started running across the precipice to the opposite side, where a staircase descended to the square lay. Keeping a careful watch, he bounded down the stairs, gun at the ready, and started to make his way across the square.

Spotting his target a few meters away, Franck moved quickly towards the transport truck, reaching the outer edge of the stacked vehicles. He ducked quickly behind one of the idle motorcycles. A stout German soldier came out, directing traffic. The soldier stood right next to the truck that Franck wanted, so he knew what he had to do.

Waiting until the soldier turned his back, Franck took a deep breath and moved stealthily around the bike, towards his target. Crouching, he took his gun in both hands and moved with the intent to drive it into the back of the German's neck.

Suddenly, the soldier turned around.

The butt of the gun smashed into his face, breaking his nose and spurting blood everywhere. He dropped to the ground, clutching his face and crying out in pain—and, Franck guessed, some German swear words.

Dropping to one knee, Franck placed a hand over the German's mouth and felt the warmth of the man's blood wash over his hand. He struggled to keep the soldier quiet. Leaning all his weight into the soldier's body and with his other hand, he unsheathed the man's knife. He made a quick, deliberate thrust, plunging the blade into the right side of the soldier's body, just below his rib cage. His eyes widened and stared directly back at Franck. He held firm, twisting the knife ever so slightly until the body went slack and the soldier's eyes rolled into the back of his head.

He cleaned his hands of blood on the soldier's tunic, checked around to make sure he was still alone, and then opened the door of the transport truck and climbed in.

Franck was breathing hard, so he took a moment to steady himself. Once calm, he reached under the dash and yanked down the wires. Finding the two he was looking for, he stripped them with his knife and tied the two together.

The truck roared to life.

He sat back up and pulled out the map from his coat pocket, laying it on the seat next to the gun.

TAT-TAT-TAT-TAT-TAT... SMMMMMASH!

Bullets ricocheted off the side of the truck, the door and a couple broke the driver's side window. Franck instinctively ducked down, but some of the glass hit him on the cheek, drawing blood. The noise was deafening. He peeked through the windshield and saw three Germans taking turns firing at the truck. Clearly, they were unimpressed having seen their dead comrade.

A few more bullets struck the side of the door, one piercing the metal and striking right near Franck's head. He needed to do something quickly. He had to save the truck, it was the only one left in the pool. It was time to be brave. Webb needed him. The ghost of that dead young woman needed him. Franck reached across the seat and grabbed the MP40. He sat up, braced the gun on top of the door where the glass was, aimed, and fired.

His first burst missed. One of the soldiers, who had emptied his rifle, was bracing it on his thigh, reloading rounds into it. Franck raised the MP40 slightly and fired. The burst tore across the German, striking his leg and torso. He fell backward onto the cobblestone.

TAT-TAT-TAT-TAT!

Four shots hit the roof of the truck. The Germans were shooting for his head now.

Franck had ducked down after the first one, but it was starting to make him nervous. He brought his gun up again and this time kept the trigger depressed. He sprayed the area where the soldiers were located, finishing the clip. Luckily, the only gunfire that continued was in the distance. Franck's gun barrel was smoking, but through the smoke, he saw the other two soldiers were dead.

Breathing a small sigh of relief, he set the gun down, shifted the gears, and moved the truck out of the motor pool. Thankfully, the vehicle was still drivable. Step one was done, and he settled in as the truck moved along through the streets of Marseille. Checking his watch, he was surprisingly on time for the rendezvous with Major Webb. He lit a cigarette, dangled his arm out the mangled window, and tried to relax.

A single thought flashed across his mind.

We're coming for you, Herr Vahlen. We're coming for you.

———————⊛———————

MEANWHILE, ACROSS THE Mediterranean Sea, a certain C-47 Dakota was making its approach to a small airfield in the south of Italy. Huddled on the bench, a dozing Major Webb was mumbling to himself.

"Never again... never again... never again..."

The plane touched down, rattling the manifold and waking Major Webb from his slumber. He held on to a metal handle to prevent himself from falling out of his seat. He looked over as Flight Sergeant Wiscomb and Lieutenant Martin shared a chuckle. As the plane ground to a halt, the engine still whirring, Flight Captain Harker called back: "You chaps alright back there? Low wind shears—that was a lot rougher than I would have liked."

"I think the Major was a little worried, Captain, but we are all just fine," replied Wiscomb, pulling himself upright and opening the plane door.

"Never doubted your skills, Captain. We will be here for a bit, why don't you and Flight Sergeant Wiscomb relax and we will come back once we're ready to go. Meanwhile, the Lieutenant and I will see if our guests have arrived as planned," replied the Major, adjusting his helmet and climbing down onto the metal runway planks.

The airfield was sparse this time of evening, all the planes were neatly parked, wingtip to wingtip, row upon row. Beyond the runway, Webb spotted the tops of green tents. Being late evening, the length of the shadow cast by them was getting long. As the men walked towards the tents, Webb noticed some slight gaps in between the metal planks. No wonder it was such a bumpy landing, he thought.

Webb and Martin had chosen this airfield, Castel Volturno because it was a bit off the beaten path, and it was due to be shut down shortly. They didn't need the extra eyes on them, Webb had thought, especially when everything was off the books.

They reached the tents, and Webb spotted what looked to be a crude mess and cantina. Just off to the right of that was a grouping of smaller tents, no doubt bunks for the pilots stationed here. Even farther beyond the smaller tents were stacks upon stacks of dark blue fuel drums and crates of ammunition. Just off to their left sat a small gray concrete building, which no doubt housed the airfield's operational personnel.

"Lieutenant, why don't you go in and speak with the commander. Let him know about our visit being a strictly need-to-know basis." Webb said, waving his hand vaguely in the concrete building's direction.

"Right away, sir, and you?"

Webb looked toward the cantina. "I'm going to check and see if the men have arrived yet." He left Martin and made his way to the tent, ducking his head below the low-hanging tarp. The place was very lively, mostly with Americans, from what Webb could tell. There were bursts of loud laughter and the occasional sound of broken glass. A group just off to the right of Webb was engaged in a very rousing rendition of *Oklahoma,* albeit with some of the words getting missing. Definitely Americans. Webb ordered a whiskey, which was what Americans called it, and found a ramshackle table to sit at. He downed it quickly—as it had the taste of good scotch mixed with lighter fluid—then ordered another. Normally, he would enjoy the bit of revelry that was unfolding around him but there was something concerning on his mind.

The men he had requisitioned were not here.

Webb's temper began to rise, and that mixed with the whiskey started to populate angry thoughts in his mind. *Did they not understand the magnitude of this mission? The insolence of these men!*

He fumed but started to remind himself that he had to temper his words. Both he and Martin had personally handpicked these men, and he knew that he couldn't capture Vahlen without them. Although he wouldn't admit it to Martin, Webb knew he was not the man he was four years ago. The war had taken its toll on him, in many ways. He knew that Vahlen was most likely just as crafty and sly as he was back then, so he would need the vigor of youth to stop him. Still, Webb again checked his watch, shaking his head impatiently.

Across the cantina, he spotted Martin coming in and waved at him.

"The men are not here, I take it?"

Webb's face soured. "No... where the bloody hell are they?"

Martin shrugged.

"They still have a few minutes Major. Remember, they were coming off almost one hundred days on the front... they earned some R and R."

"Thank you for the reminder, Lieutenant, I am aware of the time," replied Webb, taking a big gulp from his drink. He sighed angrily and began to drum his fingers on the table.

"Well, since it seems we will be here for a bit, I'm going to see if there is anything to eat," replied Martin, making his way to the canteen bar. He returned with a can of peaches and sat down at the table greedily shoveling them into his mouth. Webb, who had by now finished his whiskey, nudged the junior officer as four men appeared at the edge of the tent. He had seen the red patches on their shoulders, designating them as belonging to the First Special Service Force.

"Our boys, no doubt," said Martin, in between bites.

"Indeed." Webb got up from the table and marched over to the men. They had plunked down their bags and were sharing some sort of joke.

"ATTENTION!" bellowed Webb, his arms clasped behind his back. They quickly snapped to attention and saluted. Behind him, the cantina went quiet. All eyes were now on the British Major. Webb made the public show of walking past and inspecting each soldier. He stopped when he reached the older man on the end.

"Sergeant Donalds, isn't it? Tell me, Sergeant, do they make it a habit of being late in the Canadian Army?"

"No sir! Apologies, sir! We were just enjoying the time away from the front. Begging the Major's pardon, but we were only a minute or two late, and the airfield was a bit hard to fi—"

"This mission has the potential to change the outcome of this war, Sergeant," Webb said, interrupting the man, "I would've thought you'd make it a priority."

Donalds looked up at his commanding officer. The man was sweating profusely and the faint smell of liquor came from his breath. It was war, and those two factors put together could describe thousands of men fighting in Europe, but those thousands of other men did not currently make Donalds feel uneasy.

"Again, our deepest apologies, sir. My men and I are honored to be chosen for this mission, and will not let you down." Donalds held his hand high in a salute, and the rest of the squad followed suit. Webb, now seemingly losing steam from his tirade, waved his hand in acknowledgment and ambled over to the table. The bar had since returned to its regular chatter of noise.

"I will try to forget this transgression, Sergeant Donalds. Come... we have little time to spare. Would you and your men take a seat?"

Webb pointed toward the cantina, walking briskly in its direction.

The Canadians dropped their hands and all parties made their way to the furthest table, away from the other patrons. After each had found themselves a seat, Webb stood, hovering over them, and began to speak. "My name is Major Theodore Webb. That gentleman over there," Webb pointed to where Martin was standing, "is my adjutant, Lieutenant Percival Martin." Further introductions were made around the table, between the Canadians and the British. Once everyone was well acquainted, Webb took up a position opposite to them, and started to layout the contents of his briefcase on the table before them. Lieutenant Martin kept off to the side, as he had heard the rough details of the plan beforehand. Webb had rehearsed this very speech a couple of times, to make sure he inserted the right amount of gravitas into the parts that needed it.

"Gentlemen, welcome to Castel Volturno, Italy. I'll get right to the point, the mission we are about to undertake this evening has the importance to shape the outcome of the war." He let that statement hang in the air for effect, continuing once he felt he had hit home with it. "I'll run through the background, then the plan, and if possible, we can leave any questions you might have till the end. Understood?"

The faces nodded yes back at Major Webb.

"Good. Now, I want everyone to take a good look at this photo. He is our target on this mission. It's absolutely vital that we capture him... alive." Webb laid the black and white photo out onto the table, so all the men could see. He sneered a bit, seeing Vahlen's face. It had not been easy to get this photo, taken of the man at a Nazi Party rally in 1938.

The sun had set and the crude set of string lights that dotted the edge of the tent sprung to life. Each of the men picked up the photo to get a good look at Vahlen.

"Ugly bastard, isn't he, sir?" said Private Appleyard.

"Indeed, Private," Webb said, continuing his speech. "It's important to commit those features to all your memories, though it will be hard to miss the man. His name is Major Maximillian Vahlen. As you can see, he is *SS*. We have reports that he has played a large part in preparing the Channel defenses along the French coastline, and British Intelligence believes that his capture would give us an obvious advantage for our opening of a second front." Webb took a beat to catch his breath. In the pause, Sergeant Donalds piped up. "So, we're dropping into the northern of France? Isn't it going to be packed with Krauts?"

"I said to keep all questions till the end, Sergeant. Now, some of our local assets on the ground have risked their lives to bring us this information and considering he's currently tasked with hunting down French Resistance members, his capture will tick a few boxes." He looked around the table, the Canadians nodding and agreeing with everything he said, unaware of the duplicitous nature of his words. Every time he spoke, he thought they would stand up, shout that he was a liar, and storm from the building, but they didn't.

"We have reports that he travels with a bit of an entourage. His unit consists of ten to twelve men, but nothing that highly trained men such as yourselves should have to worry about." Webb pulled a map from his leather briefcase and laid it on the table. He began to outlay the locations and drop points.

"We'll be dropping into the south of France, just north of Marseille..." Webb looked over at Sergeant Donalds, making sure he knew his mistake, "...targeting this field over here. Once there, I arranged for some transportation for us to this village here. We believe he's holed up with his unit in this town, Serronelle. The idea is to get in, capture Vahlen, and then hold him captive until the next night when the plane will pick us up back in the field and fly us back to London. Simple, don't you think?"

Webb looked at the faces arrayed around the table. Each of them stared right back at him, waiting on his next word.

"Now, any questions gentlemen?" Webb asked.

"I have to ask, sir," Corporal Mills stated, rubbing his hand through his sandy blonde hair. "Why us? I mean, begging the Major's pardon and all, but surely there must have been some chaps in London for this kind of work."

I have to be careful, he thought to himself. He didn't want to rouse any unnecessary suspicion.

"A valid question, Corporal. Are you not the famed Black Devils? Do Germans not tremble at the mere mention of that name?"

The Canadians looked at each other and shared a wry smile. Webb's statement had hit the mark, so he continued, this time pacing back in forth in front of them. "The man we are chasing, he's known as a cunning master interrogator and ruthless individual. It is said he received that scar in a very unsavory manner, of which I can only imagine. Trust me when I say this, gentlemen, you must not underestimate him. He is relentless."

Corporal Mills whistled loudly and sat back in his chair. "Well, I guarantee that Kraut hasn't met anybody like us."

Sergeant Donalds sat forward, grabbing the picture of Vahlen and giving it a long look, then doing the same with the map. "What about troop strength in the area? I mean, we know the squad will be a fair size, but we are dropping into the middle of goddamn occupied France. What about the rest of the German Army units stationed around there?"

Webb pointed back at the map. "There is a sizable garrison located in Marseille, but we have calculated that by the time they realize something has happened, we will be long gone."

The Canadians sat silently in their chairs. It seemed all parties were thinking about the gravity of the situation, even Major Webb. He was about to lead these men into battle, for a purpose wholly his own. This wasn't a time to flinch.

Major Webb was the first to break the silence. "Well then, it's all settled. Lieutenant, why don't you let the commander know we'll be leaving, and Sergeant, let's get your men to the plane to load up the weapons and the rest of your gear."

Lieutenant Martin saluted and headed for the operations building. Sergeant Donalds and his men went back to their jeep, grabbing their weapons and the rest of their gear. As they left the cantina, Corporal Mills looked back, watching as Major Webb pulled a flask from his breast pocket and took a couple of long pulls from it.

At the jeep, while everyone else was grabbing their gear, Mills came upon Sergeant Donalds. "Sergeant, permission to speak freely?"

"Go ahead, Corporal."

"Does anything about this mission strike you as a bit... strange? I mean, the mission briefing at this tiny little airfield, how rushed this all seems. And there is something about the Major... I can't put my finger on it. I just saw him take a few swigs from a flask and I could smell the liquor on him from a mile away. What should we do, sir?"

"Corporal, we are not permitted to question why. Our orders are our orders, and at present, Major Webb is giving those orders. So, grab your gear, we've got a jump to make."

"But sir... this doesn't seem by the book... I'm worried..."

"You're worried, Corporal? I'm worried too. About what will happen if we don't find this German. A lot of good men will die on those beaches when we make the push to invade continental Europe. Don't you want to help those boys if we can?"

"Well... yes... but this just doesn't seem right. I mean, what exactly are we getting ourselves into here?"

Donalds bridled at the comment. "You forget yourself, Corporal. Grab your gear, and fall in. Am I understood?"

Mills shifted his stance, but once the hard stare of Donalds was on him, he brought his legs together and stood rigid.

"Yes... sir" replied Mills, grabbing his bag and joining Lintz and Appleyard walking toward the plane. As Sergeant Donalds finished grabbing his gear, he thought a little bit more about what Corporal Mills was saying. While it was true what he told Mills, that orders were orders and they were not to be questioned, he begrudgingly admitted the man had brought up a good point. There was something that struck Donalds the wrong way about the Major too. However, that could just be the man's personality.

He grabbed his bag and started walking to the runway when he saw Lieutenant Martin exiting the building, also headed in the same direction. Slinging his sack over his shoulder, Sergeant Donalds jogged and caught up with him, striking up a conversation. "Mind if I ask you a question, Lieutenant?"

"Of course, Sergeant. What do you need?"

"The Major, he's... a tough man. Anything I should know before we head out?"

The Lieutenant chuckled, slapping Sergeant Donalds on the back. "You don't miss much, do you, Sergeant. It's true, he may not be the easiest man to deal with, but I can assure you his heart is in the right place. This mission—what we are going to do in France—it's going to save a lot of Allied lives."

"I know, Lieutenant. To be honest, I've been waiting for a mission like this to come along, to really do some good and help end this war."

"Glad to hear it, Sergeant. Truth be told, I'm glad to have you lads along. Never really seen a lot of combat myself, if I'm being honest."

Sergeant Donalds smiled and chuckled a little, but inside he was shocked. *A Lieutenant with no combat experience? Very strange indeed.*

The men continued to walk toward the plane, and Donalds had to admit, he didn't dislike the Brit. Much better than Webb, of that Donalds, was sure. It had been some time since Donalds and his men had done their jump training, so this was going to be an adventure. Once they had loaded up all the supplies and said their greetings to Flight Captain Harker and Flight Sergeant Wiscomb, they piled into the back of the C-47 and waited patiently for the plane to take off.

Private Appleyard sat tapping both his hands on his thighs, a clear outlet for the man's nervous energy. Private Lintz, seated next to him, looked down and noticed the tapping. "Appleyard, let me guess, you are a tiny bit nervous about jumping out of this airplane?"

"Nahhh that's the easy part. It's the Germans down below, with all the guns. THAT'S the part I'm concerned about."

"But just think about it, you get to see the lovely French countryside. You know, I saw it as a young boy, before emigrating to Canada." Lintz had opined his thoughts in the hopes that sharing them would take Appleyard's mind off the mission.

"Is that so?" said Appleyard, stopping his hands from tapping and turning to Lintz. "Before this god awful mess, I had never left Saskatchewan. I've seen Alaska, Italy, and France now. Who would've thought that of Mama Appleyard's little boy?"

"Who indeed," said Private Lintz, laughing a bit to himself.

Across the plane, Sergeant Donalds sat alongside Lieutenant Martin and Corporal Mills. The men were deep in a discussion about their place of birth, and the possibility that their families might have known each other at some point. Sergeant Donalds gripped the dog tag he'd taken from Private Maxwell back at Cori. He was finding it hard to get the boy's face out of his mind.

"Who was he?"

Donalds looked up. Major Webb was standing over him, pointing to the dog tag.

"His name was Maxwell. He was young... too young."

"First time losing a man, Sergeant?" Webb said, sitting down next to Donalds.

"No. I've lost men before, at Anzio. But this one... I dunno, it just stuck with me."

"I know what you mean, Sergeant. Perhaps... more than you will ever know. All I can say is whatever you feel right now, use it."

Donalds looked away from the tags, and right at Webb, "Use it? I don't understand, sir."

"Don't let his death be in vain, Sergeant. Take that anger and use it to avenge him." Webb patted him on the shoulder, got up from the seat, wandering toward the cockpit. He had taken out the handkerchief from his pocket and gripped it tightly. *Very soon*, he thought, *very soon justice would be done*. Taking a sip from his flask, he went over some details in his mind that he wanted to confer with the pilots. Quietly.

"Evening, chaps, how are we looking?" queried the Major, resting against the frame of the cockpit.

"Ah Major, I wondered when you might wander up here. Same as before, right on schedule," stated Flight Captain Harker.

"Excellent news gentlemen, excellent news. Now, everything is still off the books with HQ back home as well? Secrecy is paramount to this mission's success."

The Flight Captain shot a quick look at his co-pilot, a look that said a thousand words in about twenty seconds.

"Yes, Major, we've made sure that London knows nothing of this soiree. As far as they are concerned, we are out for a training run. We'll land back in England and come back for you the second night, at the location we have predetermined," said the Captain, slightly annoyed. He had been over the details many times with the Major, and he understood the necessity to keep things secret in time of war, but this was a little extreme. The Flight Captain's answers seemed to have placated the Major, as he thanked them profusely and returned to the back of the cabin.

It was going to be a long night, the Captain thought, *a long night indeed.*

CHAPTER SIX

STURMBANNFÜHRER Maximilian Vahlen once again sat patiently in the back of the car, waiting for the interminable journey to be over. The time had done nothing to dampen his skepticism about this town he was going to; this lead that Colonel Grassl had given them was something he had been forced into investigating, much to his chagrin. He checked behind the car to make sure the other vehicles hadn't gotten lost. Never could tell in this godforsaken countryside.

The car made a sharp turn to the left and started down a single-lane dirt road. Behind them, the truck carrying his men had also made the turn, albeit more carefully due to its size. As the road twisted and turned, Vahlen turned towards his intelligence officer, Eberhard Teicher, who was busy taking in the surroundings. "What're your thoughts, Eberhard? Think we will find anything here?"

"Hard to say, sir. Look where the information came from." Teicher was sweating profusely in the heat and was busy dabbing his forehead and face with his handkerchief

"*Ja*, Eberhard, I agree. If this is another wild goose chase, I will make Grassl pay dearly."

Teicher nodded his agreement and wiped his forehead of beaded sweat. Returning the handkerchief to his pocket, he watched as the car continued to lurch forward. With the winding road, their driver had to constantly shift gears, making the men slightly queasy. In the distance, the rooves of buildings began to appear over the hill.

Nestled in the rich sage-colored rolling hills of the French countryside sat the tiny village of Serronelle. The road into the town was lined on either side by stumpy trees, their curved trunks reaching desperately towards the sky. As they passed peach-colored houses and stonewalled hedges with ivy snaking down the front, they approached what looked to be the center of town.

Vahlen leaned forward and spoke to the driver, giving him instructions; shortly after, the car pulled to a stop near the large, marble fountain. Vahlen stepped from the car just as the truck pulled in behind. *Obersturmführer* Weiss jumped down from the tailgate and shouted at his men to do the same. The men filed into the square, weapons at the ready. Vahlen approached Weiss and the men.

"*Obersturmführer* Weiss, somewhere in this town is a Resistance fighter with *SS* blood on his hands. I want you to search every inch of this town and bring its residents to the square. Be very thorough in your search, am I clear?"

"Yes, sir," shouted Weiss, standing to attention. He shouted out to his men to move, and then watched on as they began kicking in doors and dragging people out to the square.

Vahlen walked over and examined the fountain in the center square while this was going on. All around him, there were screams and gunshots as Weiss carried out his orders. It was music to Vahlen's ears. He had to admit, the artistry of the fountain was unparalleled, and for the first time since being in France, Vahlen had some appreciation for French culture. It was a very fleeting moment, however, as Teicher came up alongside him.

"Beautiful, isn't it, Teicher?" offered Vahlen, running his hand along the carved stone slabs.

"Yes, who would think to find something of such beauty in this disgusting little town," replied Teicher, waiting patiently with his arms behind his back.

"Once we have Kampfer's killer, we will need a place to have our interrogation. Can you take care of that, Eberhard? I'm sure once Weiss is done rounding up the town's residents, you won't be short of choices."

"As you wish, *Sturmbannführer*."

"Care for a cigarette?" said Vahlen, offering one from his pack to Teicher. He accepted it graciously, and the men stood there smoking for some time, each telling stories of their time in Germany. In the background, the cacophony of screams, shouting and occasionally gunshots continued. That told Vahlen all he needed to know—that Weiss and his men were almost done rounding up the townspeople. Then, he would find these traitors to the Reich.

Finishing their cigarettes, Teicher and Vahlen turned around to face the townsfolk. Vahlen un-holstered his Luger pistol and held it by his side. The townsfolk of Serronelle were all huddled in a tight-knit group, pairing off into family units and looking around nervously. *Excellent*, thought Vahlen, *they should be scared*. They were sheep and he was the wolf.

He jumped up to the edge of the fountain, putting himself slightly above everyone else and instantly drawing their gaze towards himself. He began to speak in French, which seemed to surprise a few of the people before him.

"*Mesdames and Messieurs*, I will make this brief for you. Two weeks ago, an *SS* officer by the name of Kampfer was murdered in Marseille. I have it on good authority that the person who committed such a disgusting crime against the Reich resides in this very town. Now, there are a few things that you must know about me and my men. Number one, we won't hesitate to use any means at our disposal." Vahlen let that statement hang in the air, to let its effect linger over the crowd. "Secondly, I and my men are very good shots." As Vahlen finished saying this, all of his men cocked their weapons. A few of the men and women in the crowd visibly shivered, and they murmured back and forth between themselves.

Vahlen jumped back down and started towards the huddled people. His men, strategically positioned around the huddle, had their rifles at the ready. He came upon a young couple, clutching each other, the look of fear clearly in their eyes. Vahlen reached out to touch their faces, then continued to meander through the crowd.

"Now, I would prefer we do this the easy way. Some of you know this man, this criminal, and I will make it easier on the rest of you if either this person comes forward, or someone simply tells me who he is." Vahlen stopped at a mother and her young son, waiting for something to happen. When no-one presented themself, he sighed and tightened his grip on the pistol. "So be it. I guess we will have to do this the hard way."

Vahlen grabbed the young boy away from his mother, placed the Luger barrel on the side of his head, squeezing the trigger.

Blood spattered on the surrounding people, as the young boy's lifeless body dropped to the ground. The wide-eyed mother that was clutching him let out a guttural scream, falling to her knees and sobbing as she clutched his body.

"WHO IS IT? TELL ME WHAT I WANT TO KNOW, OR I WILL KILL SOMEONE ELSE!" shouted Vahlen, gesturing with his pistol as he spoke. Once again, there was silence over the crowd. Incredulous, Vahlen walked over to a family of three. A father, a mother, and a small little girl.

"I'm going to count to three. If no one comes forward, I'm going to put a bullet in the head of this little girl." At this statement, the woman shouted an obscenity in French and screamed, while the father tried to position himself between Vahlen and the girl. Two soldiers came and restrained the man while Vahlen leveled his Luger directly at her.

"One..."

"Two..."

Before he got to three, a woman, not much older than twenty-five, came forward. Vahlen noticed her when she approached and turned to her, the pistol still pointed at the little girl. She was petite, darker-skinned, non-Aryan if Vahlen had to hazard a guess. In a crowd, she would just be another face, but there was something that struck the giant *SS* man about her.

"Something to say, *mademoiselle*?" he asked.

"Yes, I know who you are looking for. There is no need for further violence."

"Then, by all means, please, point out this man for us, and I will spare this little girl's life."

"No need," she replied, stepping a bit closer to Vahlen, "the person you are looking for is... me."

Vahlen took a moment to process what she had said. Could she, this little girl in front of him, really be the person he was searching for? His instincts told him that she might be telling the truth. Still, it couldn't be. He'd press her for the man's name.

"My dear, whoever this man is, he should thank you for your bravery, and the protection you afford him. Now, if you would be so kind as to give me his name?"

She took another step closer, showing no visible signs of fear. Her voice remained steady as she said, "You are searching for the person who killed that German officer in Marseille, are you not? I killed that *SS* man and if given the chance, I would do the same to you."

Vahlen was shocked. *Such insolence.* For that alone, he should kill her. But he needed to make sure she was the one they were searching for. Her last statement, directed at himself, turned his incredulous attitude to one of rising fury. He gripped the whole of her hair and yanked it down. She cried out sharply in pain.

"Is that so, my dear? It is unfortunate that you will not get the chance. You are also lucky that we want you alive for the time being. However, once the good *Hauptsturmführer* Teicher gets a-hold of you, I will take great pleasure in watching you suffer."

He flung her across to Teicher and two of his soldiers, who immediately grabbed each of her arms and started to haul her away. The crowd, aghast at what they had just seen, seemed to cower from Vahlen as he walked past them. He saw Weiss and made his way towards him.

"Lock the rest up in the church. If anyone resists, shoot them," Vahlen said matter-of-factly.

Weiss gestured with his arms and shouted commands to the remainder of the men. They rousted the townsfolk and started marching single file towards the church at the end of the road. Vahlen still hadn't quite decided what to do with them. While this woman had turned herself in, Vahlen was sure more Resistance members were hiding in the town and she would tell them about it, all in time. Teicher was a skilled interrogator, perhaps even better than Vahlen himself, but he was more restrained, more subtle in his technique. It would take a day or so, but they would have all their questions answered.

Vahlen left Weiss to finish up the job, holstering his pistol and removing another cigarette from his silver case. He lit it and drew a deep breath in. He headed back to where the vehicles were located, and where the radio currently was being monitored by a lowly private. Paris, and by extension, Berlin, had been requesting constant updates on his progress, which Vahlen found tedious. The alternative was to face the firing squad, so he obliged.

Once he was done, he would find some food and perhaps a drink, before joining Teicher for what would surely be a lengthy evening chat.

———————◉———————

AFTER A SHORT WALK down the main road, *Hauptsturm-führer* Eberhard Teicher pushed open the wooden door to a larger townhouse—one of the biggest in town by his estimation—just off the main road. It was separated from the other houses and seemed to be in better shape than most. Teicher waved his hand in the direction of the kitchen table and chairs, instructing his men to leave her there. They pushed her down on the chair as Teicher examined the other rooms in the house. They bound her hands and exited the room. After a few moments, Teicher came back in and sat down casually across from the girl, placing his cap and gloves onto the tabletop. He waited for a few moments, leaving the tension to hang in the air, then began to speak in the long deliberate manner he was known for.

"*Fraulein*, what is your name?"

She raised her head to look at Teicher, making sure to look at him directly in the eyes.

"Martine. Martine Cuvier."

Teicher had to give her this, she either wasn't afraid or showed no signs of it whatsoever. *A true challenge*, Teicher thought.

"A good start, Martine, a very good start indeed. Now, tell me, how long have you been with the French Resistance?"

She laughed.

"If you want to know whether I killed that pig of a soldier, Kampfer or something, then I did. I admit it, it was only me, and no one else helped. Is that what you wanted to know?"

The bluntness by which she offered her statements took Teicher aback slightly.

"I must say, *Fraulein*, you are headstrong. But it is my job to break those that think they are strong. And in this case, I find it hard to believe someone of your..." he moved his hand up and down about her, "...stature would be able to kill a man such as Kampfer."

Martine chuckled again. "It was surprisingly easy. Most of you Germans are horny, lazy, drunk, or all three."

Teicher coughed, but otherwise, he was unfazed. "You are a delight, my dear. Again, you cannot have acted alone, so we want your accomplices, one way or the other. We can do this the hard way. Or not. The choice is yours."

Martine sat in silence, her hair hanging down now in front of her face.

"As you wish, Fraulein." Teicher stood, unbuttoning his uniform jacket and placing it on the table. He then rolled up his sleeves, and shrugged out of the suspenders he was wearing, so they hung loosely around his waist. He walked over to Martine and gently grabbed her chin, turning her face up towards his.

"Such a shame to ruin such a pretty face." With that, Teicher struck her across the face with his other fist and Martine instantly cried out in pain.

He continued to strike her until her face became bruised and bloodied. After five minutes of this, Teicher stopped, rubbing his hand and doubling over, breathing heavily. He looked up at her, and although she had cried out when he struck her, she now sat in the chair, stoic as she was before. Blood dripped down on the table and the floor.

"This has only just begun, *Fraulein*." Teicher leaned in and whispered in her ear.

With that, he grabbed his jacket and promptly left the room, telling the guards outside to keep an eye on her. Once out on the street, he went to go find something to eat, and speak with Major Vahlen. He found him holed up in one of the other houses, sitting around a grey wooded kitchen table.

"We have to be patient with her, *Herr* Teicher. She will spill her secrets soon enough. I don't think it will take very long for her to give up her compatriots, despite her current demeanor. They all break, one way or the other," offered Vahlen, in between sips from a glass of wine as they sat. He pushed the bottle towards Teicher.

"Do you think if we threaten the rest of the people in the town, she'll give up her friends more easily?" Teicher said, taking his wine glass in hand.

Vahlen squinted, thinking about it.

"No, I think not. She doesn't strike me as that type. If your methods don't work, then I think we have to move directly to the scopolamine."

"Scopolamine? That's not like you, sir. Having a crisis of faith, are we?"

"Not at all, *Hauptsturmführer*. But if we beat her until she's dead, we will learn nothing. Fear not, we are making good progress here in this French shit-hole. I would like to tell Himmler that we got Kampfer's killer and shut down an entire cell."

Teicher smiled at that sentiment. It was always prosperous to be in the good graces of *Reichsführer* Himmler, and their unit had made the habit of never disappointing him. After a quick drink and some food, he would return to the house and get back to work.

They had much more to accomplish this evening.

CHAPTER SEVEN

WITH EACH SUCCESSIVE bump, Sergeant Donalds gripped his seat even harder. He hadn't jumped out of an actual aircraft in over four years. He couldn't tell if it was turbulence, but the plane seemed to shudder every thirty seconds. Each movement the bolts around them, and Donalds said a silent prayer to himself that the plane did not fall apart while they were all still in it. Flight Sergeant Wiscomb staggered back into the belly of the plane. "Coming up on the French coastline now. This turbulence should pass, but Jerry isn't gonna take too kindly to us being here. Might see some flak, hold tight, boys."

Sure enough, after a couple of minutes, loud thunderous noises could be heard outside. To those that had never heard it before, it sounded like God himself was stomping on the floor. It was a fact that German flak guns were very good and even though they were flying at night, the Germans were quite adept at finding aircraft in the dark.

Donalds glanced at his men and their faces belied their natures, stoic and unflinching. He was sure that Mills, Appleyard, and Lintz had a little fear in their hearts. It was natural to have that, but like good soldiers, they didn't let it show. Even Lieutenant Martin, with his long limbs and languid nature, seemed to have the fortitude to continue.

However, if these men were showing that they weren't afraid, then Major Webb was the exact opposite. With each tooth-rattling explosion, Major Webb gripped the nearby handle with both hands until his skin turned a visible pale white. His eyes were clenched tight, and Donalds wasn't sure, but he thought he heard a slight whimper every now then. Interesting behavior for a man that was part of the Special Operations Executive and one that trained hardened guerrilla fighters to operate behind enemy lines.

Donalds did a quick check of all his equipment and tightened the straps on his parachute. The last thing he wanted was to leap from this plane and fall to his death. He had come too far in this war to be done in by such a cruel irony. He could see that his men were doing the same, and Lieutenant Martin was getting Private Lintz to check the back of his parachute.

Standing and finding his balance, he carefully making his way over to Webb. The noise level in the cabin from the engines and the flak was quite high, so Donalds had to shout a bit.

"EVERYTHING OKAY, MAJOR?"

Webb opened his eyes and turned towards Donalds. He tried to straighten himself up, but between the flak and the plane, he still clutched the handle with both hands. Donalds leaned in closer so the Major didn't have to shout.

"Oh, Sergeant, ah, yes, just fine. Been quite some time since I've had the Germans shooting at me. Being up in the air only makes it worse, it seems."

"We'll get there, Major, don't you worry. This mission is too important for us to fail. Would you like me to check your equipment?"

"Yes, thank you, Sergeant." Donalds proceeded to check over the equipment while Webb continued speaking. "I knew when I chose you Canadians that I was getting top-notch professionals."

Donalds jiggled the parachute and tugged on a few straps, satisfied that the gear was in good shape. "Well, looks like you are all set, Major."

At that, the Flight Sergeant made his way to the back of the cabin. He grabbed a pair of gloves and made his way to the side door, signaling for the men to form up. "Coming over the drop area shortly, gentlemen, God be with you," shouted Flight Sergeant Wiscomb. He reefed on the handle and shoved open the side door, making a hook motion with his finger. This was the signal that all the men should stand up and hook their parachute lines to the cord that ran along the length of the plane. Each man did as he was told, and Donalds could instantly feel the tension rise in the plane—he had experienced it on every jump that he had been on.

Chin straps were locked into place, and each man stood ready, the wind of the door and the distant flak explosion the only sound in the cabin. Wiscomb briefly left the open door, making his way down the fuselage to where the equipment canister was being stored. He dragged it closer, just behind the last man, Appleyard, and went back to stand by the open door. The turbulence and flak had completely dissipated now, leaving each man alone with his thoughts.

Suddenly, the box directly behind Wiscomb lit up a dark green. He started waving his hand towards the open door. Lintz was the first to jump, giving a small salute as he left the plane. Martin was the next to go, practically ducking his head just to get out the side door. Webb was the next, and Donalds offered a piece of advice before he went. "Remember Major, keep your feet together and roll once you hit the ground."

Major Webb nodded, and with a little help from Wiscomb, exited the plane. Donalds was up next. He gave a quick nod to Wiscomb and leapt from the plane, feeling the cold air slam against his body like a freight train. The wind was deafening, whipping his clothes as gravity pulled him closer to France. There was little moonlight out tonight, so Donalds could only see the vague outline of the ground.

The parachutes opened upon them leaving the plane, but Donalds always felt it didn't slow them down enough. He looked up and around, but only saw a few tufts of white canvas. The wind must have scattered them

After a few disorienting moments, Donalds started to see the outline of the field below and prepared his body for impact with the ground. Just like he told Major Webb, Donalds kept his feet together and rolled once he touched the ground, cushioning the blow of landing.

He ended up on his back, his parachute fluttering away behind him, threatening to pull him like a rag doll. He unclasped the middle straps, attempting to get to his knees, which he succeeded in doing. Then, he started to reel the parachute in. He became keenly aware of his surroundings, watching the tree lines and the nearby road.

The plane had indeed dropped them into an open farmer's field, the tall grass and wheat stalks tickling his hands and face. It was a minor miracle in itself that they were anywhere close to where they wanted to be. It also made him, and his squad an easy target at the moment.

He looked up, into the darkened night sky, seeing a large stream of tracers shoot up. A German anti-aircraft gun, somewhere in the distance.

Watching on in horror, he saw a bright orange explosion.

The plane. Their plane.

One of the tracers must have found its mark. The flame burned bright against the matte black background and Donalds could see wisps of smoke trailing in the sky now as well. The light got lower and lower, until it fell behind a tree line, out of sight.

KAAABOOOOM!

A cluster of flames shot up in the distance. Donalds hung his head in sorrow, shaking his head in disbelief. More meat for the grinder, it seemed. This German officer they were after, the information he carried, it had better be worth the lives of those pilots, let alone the risk that Donalds was taking with his men.

Trying not to think about what he had just seen, Donalds gathered up his parachute and concealed it in the dirt at the edge of the field. He unslung his Thompson machine gun and kept it at the ready. Pushing through the brush, Donalds came out onto another large open wheat field and immediately saw a couple of his men on the other side. Lintz and Mills turned quickly at the sound of Donalds coming through.

"Easy boys, just me," Donalds whispered.

Lintz lowered his rifle, whistling out loud. Mills leaned his weapon against his shoulder.

"That was close, Sarge, just about shot you," said Mills.

"I knew you wanted to get promoted to Sergeant, just didn't know it was going to be at my expense," joked Donalds.

The men crouched in the field, making sure to keep their eyes on the horizon for any sign of enemy activity.

"Seen any of the others?" Donalds asked the two men.

"Not yet Sarge, but I'm sure they'll turn up," replied Lintz.

Across the field, Donalds could see some outlines moving. Taking no chances, he ordered his men to take cover in the long grass, and all three trained their weapons towards the shapes.

"Check your fire, boys, we are going to have to let them get close before we know if it's Jerry or not."

The shapes approached them and each man seemed to grip his weapon a little tighter. Fingers hovered over triggers, and eyes focused down sights as the outlines came closer. Donalds raised his gun, preparing to fire when he heard a familiar sound. One of the shapes laughed, and Donalds recognized it immediately. Private Thomas Appleyard had a very high-pitched laugh, one that got stuck in your head. Donalds would know it anywhere.

He placed his hands on the other men's weapons. "Friendlies, we are coming out. Don't fire."

Donalds and his men stood up and watched as Webb, Martin, and Appleyard approached them.

"Good to see you again, Sergeant. Tell me, how did you know it was us and not a German patrol?" asked Webb.

"And you as well, Major. To be honest, it was that laugh. Trust me, you never forget it."

Private Appleyard smiled, going over to shake hands and speak with Lintz and Mills.

"So, Major, looks like we are right on schedule. Is your local man just as reliable?" asked Donalds.

Major Webb ignored the question and waved him over, and the junior officer crouched down as Webb removed a cloth map from his backpack and laid it out on the ground. Lieutenant Martin brought out a torch and shone the light down, illuminating it for both of them. Webb pointed at an open field.

"We are here, best that I can tell." He outlined a road that ran alongside the field, now just to the east of them. "Once we get to that road, by my rough calculation, we'll be right at our rendezvous point. In terms of Germans, we chose this area as there aren't a lot of them around, but we have to be on our guard. Once we meet the truck, it's a short fifteen-minute ride to Serronelle."

All the officers nodded their agreement, and Webb packed up the map while Martin doused the light.

"Let's get moving, we don't want to keep our ride waiting," said Webb.

The group moved out from the low-lying brush and started to make their way across the large fields. After about ten minutes or so, they came to a dirt road. Private Appleyard, being the first soldier in the column, reached the edge first, kneeling at the edge. He whispered back. "What now, Major?"

"He should be here by now. Let's just wait for a few moments."

"We are very exposed here, Major. I suggest we make our way back into the field," said Donalds, shifting uneasily.

"Your concern is noted, Sergeant, but we stay here. I know this man; he would not abandon us."

The air was warm and damp, and the occasional drone of a cricket broke the silence. In the distance, the unmistakable chugging of an engine could be heard, and Major Webb ordered everyone to lay flat, their weapons pointed in that direction. The vehicle got closer and closer, and then the screech of the brakes brought it to a halt. Appleyard took a quick peek and saw a truck, its headlights shining down the road. It was roughly five hundred meters from where the men were located. Appleyard raised his rifle and aimed at the driver's side of the truck. The headlights quickly turned on and off three times and the horn honked once.

"That is the signal we arranged. That is Franck," said Major Webb. He stood up and made his way down the road and up to the truck. Martin, Donalds, and the rest of the men stood up and also made their way towards the truck. Webb and Franck were sharing an animated conversation. As the team approached, Webb gestured towards Franck.

"Gentlemen, this is Franck Chabert. He is formerly French Army and has been one of my men on the ground in France for some time now."

Introductions were made between everyone and the team started to get into the truck.

"Donalds, Mills, and Appleyard, get in the back there. Martin and I will join you shortly. Private Lintz, I would appreciate it if you would join Mr. Chabert in the cab. He's got a German uniform that should most likely fit you, and you can help in case we run into any... trouble."

Lintz went around the right side of the cab and began to put on the German uniform he found on the seat. The rest of the Canadians jumped in the back, quickly followed by Martin.

Webb remained outside of the vehicle and gestured for Franck to come over and join him.

"The time has come now, Franck. We've waited over four years for this moment. We both know what needs to be done. She has to be avenged... even if we have to die trying."

Franck's eyes widened at that statement. In his planning for this, he didn't entertain the possibility that he would have to die. He didn't know what to say.

Webb picked up on the silence. "Not having second thoughts now, are you, old friend?"

"No, *mon ami*, I am not. I think about her all the time. We'll do it, or we will die trying." stated Franck.

Webb nodded solemnly and went to the back of the truck. Franck climbed back into the cab and looked at Lintz beside him, now clad in the German uniform. Franck buttoned up his German uniform and placed a helmet on his head, pointing at Lintz to do the same. In heavily accented English, Franck gestured forwards. "How you say, get the show on the road."

He started the truck back up, and they were on their way.

CHAPTER EIGHT

VAHLEN TOOK A LONG drag from his cigarette, then placed it on the edge of the ashtray. He put his feet up on the table, watching as *Hauptsturmführer* Teicher carefully laid his cloth bag on the table. He had unclasped the latch and was rolling it out along the brown handcrafted dining table. With a bemused look, he witnessed Teicher taking the large syringe out of the bag and placing it in the small bottle of scopolamine. He drew the plunger back, filling it slowly. Through strategic planning and execution, Vahlen and Teicher had found out that the threat of force was equally effective as the force itself. The more the prisoner thought about it, the more their mind was susceptible to suggestion once the drug took hold.

"One last chance, my dear—tell us who the other members of your cell are. It will make it easier on all of us," stated Vahlen coldly, his eyes staring directly into hers.

Martine stared right back at him and spat some blood onto the table.

"Now, that is a shame. *Herr* Teicher, if you please," Vahlen said, extending his hand towards her.

Teicher came around the table and grabbed Martine's right arm, quickly tying some rubber tubing around it. He flicked the needle, depressed the plunger slightly, and squeezed out the air. He found the vein and gently pressed the needle in, inserting the clear liquid into her system. She briefly tried to fight, but Teicher held her arm in place. Her eyes rolled into the back of her head and she slumped forward.

Teicher returned the needle to its spot in the cloth bag and sat down next to Vahlen, lighting his cigarette.

"Only a matter of time now, before the effects take hold," said Vahlen, getting up to pace about the room.

As the two men waited, there was a curt knock on the door.

"Come!" shouted Vahlen, watching as the door opened and *Schutze* Kohler stepped into the room. He clicked his heels and saluted.

"Sir, the people in the church are requesting food and water, and some have to use the washrooms. What would you like us to do?"

Teicher sat silent, smoking. He noticed and then promptly removed a piece of loose tobacco stuck to his lip.

"Tell the *Obersturmführer* I will be outside in a few moments," Vahlen said, dismissing the Private with his hand.

"Yes, *Sturmbannführer.*" The Private saluted again, took a quick look at Martine, and left, closing the door behind him.

A few moments later, Vahlen exited the house and approached Weiss. Pulling the junior officer away from the pack, he spoke quietly. "Once our little friend in there gives us all her compatriots' names, we'll kill them all. Keep them happy for now."

Weiss took this information and immediately relayed orders to the other two soldiers, making sure they understood to take a small group at a time, and the two soldiers left to carry out his orders.

"Permission to speak freely, sir," said Kohler, approaching Vahlen as Weiss left.

"Speak, Kohler, speak," said Vahlen, impatiently.

"Some of the men, myself included, were wondering if we could participate in the... interrogation... of the girl."

"All in good time, *Schutze* Kohler, all in good time. Now, go about your business." Vahlen watched on as Kohler saluted and headed up towards the church.

He could see that some of his men were unlocking the doors and beginning to bring a few of the townspeople out of the church. They looked mostly frightened and worn down, exactly how Vahlen liked to see them. The first group came out without any issue, his men leading them to their respective homes and back to the church. Just as the men were taking out the second group, however, something unexpected happened.

A young boy, no older than fifteen, descended the church stairs. Vahlen watched him but turned his back for a second to look in on one of the other groups. Just as he turned, the boy shoved one of the soldiers into the other, knocking them both off balance. A third soldier raised his rifle, but the boy showed no fear as he threw his shoulder into him, tumbling the man to the side and allowing the boy to sprint across the street.

Vahlen drew his weapon and shouted at Weiss. The *Obersturmführer*, attempting to figure out what was happening, drew his pistol and aimed it at the young boy. As with most people that Vahlen had selected for his unit, Weiss was a great shot. He tracked the boy with the sight, but just as he squeezed the trigger and fired the shot, the boy ducked behind one of the buildings. Weiss cursed under his breath. *What luck this boy had!*

Vahlen started to run towards the house, at the same time gesturing to his men to get up and move in from the other side. Weiss followed not far behind until both officers reached the front part of the house. They both listened intently for any sound, any clue as to the boy's next actions. Vahlen glanced over and saw that his men had finally started to pick themselves up, and would be coming over to the side of the street shortly. He inched forward and took a quick look around the corner. The side of the building was empty.

Moving along the wall now, Vahlen was surprised when the sound of a motorcycle engine kicked up. Weiss followed close behind him and both of them came around just in time to see the boy peel out. He quickly disappeared behind another row of houses and picked up speed as he headed towards the farmers' fields and waist-high grass.

When they caught sight of him next, he had turned the motorcycle towards a dirt path and gunned the engine. Vahlen and Weiss raised their guns and fired a couple of shots, but the boy was out of range. Vahlen turned back to his men and shouted to them.

"QUICK, HE IS CLOSE. GET THE CAR!"

One of the soldiers drove the car down, and Weiss and two of his other men got in.

"Don't let him get away, *Obersturmführer*. Search as if your life depended on it," ordered Vahlen, slamming the car door behind Weiss.

Weiss swallowed hard. The car wheels spun hard as the driver pressed the gas pedal to the floor. They passed by the church as it picked up speed. The dirt path was a bit too small to get the car down, but Weiss had a feeling he knew where the boy would be going. While the sun had set, the clouds had finally cleared and the moon had now come out.

They would cut him off before he had a chance to get far.

———◉———

TWENTY MINUTES DOWN the road from Serronelle, a stolen German truck chugged along. In the back of the truck, Mills had handed out the boot polish, and the Canadians proceeded to coat their faces with it. Martin watched with slight bemusement as they covered every inch of exposed skin, with now only the whites of their eyes showing in the darkened trailer.

"I must say, I can see why the Germans have a healthy fear of you gents. I wouldn't want to run into you on a dark night," mused Major Webb, looking around at each of them.

"You know, there was a rumor going around that the Germans in Italy sent reports to their superiors. Thought there was a whole brigade of us. Little did they know it was only about twenty or so," said Mills, as he rechecked his machine gun.

"I heard they thought it was a whole division!" replied Private Appleyard, with this usual enthusiasm.

Lieutenant Martin chuckled at the last statement.

"Now, now, that's enough tall tales for the Major and the Lieutenant," Sergeant Donalds said, to which all his men went silent and looked away.

"And... it was two divisions," he said again, looking around to see the smiles on his men's faces.

"Well, I have to say, I'm glad to have you 'Black Devils' on my side tonight. The man we are—"

Lieutenant Martin's words were interrupted by a sharp knock from the cab. Private Lintz half-whispered, half-spoke through the thin wall separating them. "Something up ahead. Looks like a broken-down German Army patrol. They're waving us over. Just two of them from what I can see. What do you want to do?"

"They might be with Vahlen. We can't take that chance and it will look suspicious if we don't stop. Try and talk your way out of it, Private Lintz. If you can't... get them to come around the back," Webb ordered.

Donalds looked at Webb, who nodded slightly at the Canadian Sergeant. Donalds then made a motion with his hand, gesturing for Corporal Mills to come to the center of the truck. Mills had brought along his Johnson Light Machine Gun, a formidable weapon.

He extended the tripod, conveniently attached to the barrel, to the floor—it allowed the user to better aim the gun—and then laid flat on the bed of the truck with the barrel squarely pointed at the tailgate of the truck.

Up front, Franck eased the truck into first gear and started to slow it down. He and Lintz had both noticed the German soldier waving them down. As they got closer, they could see two soldiers now. One pushing on a motorcycle stuck in some mud, and the other waving his torch in the air. Franck buttoned up his German uniform tunic and brought the truck to a halt, keeping his lights on to make sure the soldiers didn't get a good look at either the damaged cab or themselves. As the soldier with the torch approached, Lintz eased out of the passenger side and called out to him in German.

"*Guten abend, was ist das ganze problem? [Good evening, what's all the trouble?]*"

Private Lintz's had a very thick Austrian accent; his parents had immigrated to Canada before the war started, and Lintz had to leave his native Austria behind. He missed the mountains, the cool dips in the lake during the summer, and of course, the food. He was sixteen when they left, and though he was sad to leave his birthplace, the alternative had turned out to be far worse. Nazi Germany had swallowed up Austria in 1938, making it part of the Greater German Reich. Not a night had gone by without Lintz dreaming of liberating his native land from the grip of the Nazis.

The soldier pointed back to his comrade and the motorcycle with the flashlight. "We are stuck in the mud it seems. We were headed back to Marseille from out west when we hit this ditch. Where are you headed?"

Lintz tugged at the sleeves of his uniform. It was slightly too small for him; the cuffs only came down to the end of his forearm. But it was dark. They would not be able to notice. It sounded like they were just two soldiers out for a ride. Still, Lintz had removed his Luger, casually letting it dangle at his side.

The second German soldier came up to the truck, his hands dirty with grease and his sleeves rolled up to the elbows. As they chatted, the second German pointed at the truck, and both the soldiers turned back to Lintz.

"Looks like you have seen some trouble?"

Lintz played dumb. "What?"

The first soldier pointed to the drivers' side. "There are some bullet holes here. Did you run into the Resistance?"

Lintz leaned forward, pretending to look at the damage. He saw Franck smile weakly from the drivers' side.

"Ohhhh, yes, that's from Marseille earlier tonight. We were ambushed on our way out of town. Filthy bastards."

The first soldier laughed, a high-pitched laugh. "Yes, you are right, they are so dirty. Tell me, where are you headed tonight?"

"We are headed north, towards Toulouse." Lintz pointed with his free hand, trying his best to be nonchalant. "Doing a supply run with some food for the boys up there." He watched the man intently for any sign that his lie was detected, but the man smiled at Lintz. All he needed to do was to get the men to the back of the truck, and his fellow soldiers would do the rest.

The second German's face lit up immediately, now turning to speak to Lintz straight away.

"That is excellent news! My brother is stationed in Toulouse. Tell me, what unit are you with?"

The question struck Lintz and he instantly began to sweat. He had not planned on such a specific question, and he had no idea what sort of units were stationed in Toulouse. He looked up at the two soldiers, whose smiles were quickly fading from their faces at his continued silence.

There was only one option available to Lintz, and he made up his mind that he had to do it now.

BANG!...BANG!

He fired two shots in quick succession from the Luger, both hitting the first soldier in the chest and shoulder. The man dropped out of sight behind the truck. Lintz aimed the pistol at the second soldier, the one with the rolled-up sleeves, but the German was too quick. He ducked behind the truck, starting to shout in German. Lintz looked into the cab. He couldn't see Franck. He hopefully had grabbed the machine gun that was sitting on the truck-bench. Lintz leaned against the side of the vehicle, waiting for any movement from the soldier.

But there was only silence.

In the back of the truck, the two shots that had rung out had Sergeant Donalds off his seat and moving past Corporal Mills and out the back. He crouched down, turned to the right, and looked around the edge, raising his gun to fire but stopping when he saw Lintz's outstretched arms.

Lintz pointed to the other side of the truck and Donalds shifted his position to the opposite side of the vehicle. As he poked his head around the corner, a bullet ricocheted right near his head and he pulled back quickly, letting a long, deep breath exhale.

That was close.

Suddenly, Donalds heard footsteps, and he quickly looked around the truck. The soldier had started to run back towards his motorcycle. Donalds stood up, leveling his Thompson machine gun at the soldier firing in their direction. The burst caught the soldier in the right leg, knocking him to the ground; he then tried to crawl off the road and into the ditch, but he didn't make it in time.

The added gunfire from Donald's machine gun had brought Franck up in his seat, and he opened the driver's side door, firing a volley from his gun, killing the second soldier.

"MAKE SURE THEY'RE DOWN!" shouted Donalds.

Franck called out in agreement, rushing over to the Germans. He poked each with the barrel of his gun, satisfied that they were dead.

He returned to the truck, where Donalds and Lintz were standing.

"I checked their uniforms. They are not *SS*, so probably not with Vahlen."

All three men took stock of what had just happened.

"Sorry sir, we were all good to go but ran into a problem. Figured it was better to shoot and ask questions later," stated Lintz, holstering his Luger.

Donalds, breathing heavily as the adrenaline still coursed through his body, nodded his head.

"That's fine, Private. Good shooting. I'll let the Major know this was just a random German patrol and that we still have the element of surprise."

"We should get... moving, someone might have heard those shots," said Franck, slinging the machine gun around his back and looking nervously at his surroundings.

Donalds agreed and went to the back of the truck as the rest of the men had started to exit the truck, making sure that Corporal Mills didn't accidentally shoot anyone else. Meanwhile, Franck and Lintz moved the dead bodies off the side of the road and down into the ditch.

As they climbed back into the truck and Franck started it up again, he turned to Lintz.

"I admire you, Private Lintz. You did not flinch when presented with danger. That is important."

"Important for what?"

Franck switched hands on the steering wheel and unbuttoned the top button of his tunic.

"For when you come face to face with the Scarred German. He and his men will show you no quarter."

Lintz thought about that, initially taking it as a compliment, but as the truck rolled along, something began to gnaw in the back of his mind. Something was very odd about this mission, these men. He turned away from the front of the truck and looked at the wheat fields and trees that passed by his window, trying to focus his mind on the mission ahead. Even the scenery couldn't stop the concern building in his mind. *Be extra on-guard*, Lintz reminded himself.

The next ten minutes passed without incident and the truck came around a long curve in the road. Franck, squinting his eyes ever so slightly at the terrain, brought the truck to a halt. He checked the map again, then got out of the cab. Donalds came out and joined him.

"Just over that ridge up there, is the town of Serronelle," Franck stated to Donalds, pointing up at the grassy outcropping shielding the road from view.

All the men had by now exited the truck and stood around with Franck. The Frenchman relayed the rough outlay of the village to them. Located east of the river Rhone, Seronnelle was a tiny village of about eighty people, nestled in the rolling hills of the luscious southeast French countryside. The village could be split into two sections, divided by the square that housed a large, white marble fountain. To the north were some of the larger villas and estates in the area, along with the church. The south housed more of the functionary parts of the village, containing the post office, a few scattered shops, and a tiny cafe. All in all, it would probably take a total of ten minutes to walk from one end to the other.

Donalds looked on in amazement. With the dark gray stone exteriors and clay-colored tiled roofs, it was unlike anything he had ever seen before. In a small way, it reminded him of the prairies back in Canada.

Webb, seizing the moment, started to give out his orders to everyone.

"Okay, this is it, gentlemen. Now, remember the importance of what we are here for. It's vital that this man, Major Vahlen, be taken alive. Vital. I cannot stress this enough." Webb shared a look with Franck.

Everyone else shook their heads in agreement. A brief moment of silence hung in the damp night air before Major Webb spoke again.

"Now, Mr. Chabert and Private Lintz," Webb gestured towards the two men as he spoke, "will take a stroll into town, claiming that their truck broke down not too far from here—easily confirmed by the Germans if they'd like to check. Then, once they have a rough idea of Vahlen's location, they'll report back to us and Sergeant Donalds and his men can do what they do best. Once Vahlen has been captured, we will make our way back to the truck and then back to the rendezvous with the plane. Are we clear?"

There were murmured confirmations from all the men.

It's strange, Webb thought. He had been envisioning this moment for almost four years, and now that it arrived, he didn't feel the happiness he thought he would have. Revenge was a notion that had consumed him almost relentlessly much non-stop since he had returned to England from France. But now that he was back, that the moment of completing this revenge fantasy he so desperately craved was imminent, he thought he would be feeling unbridled joy. Contrary to that, however, it felt the opposite—almost empty. He took a long swig from his flask, feeling the warm brown liquid fill his belly. There was no time for second thoughts any longer, what needed to be done had to be done.

Not just for himself, but for Franck and ultimately, for her.

"Franck, a moment of your time, if you don't mind?" Webb said, taking the Frenchman aside. Donalds watched on as the two were deep in conversation, well outside earshot of the rest of the men. They passed a flask between them and seemed to bow their heads in some sort of prayer. The Sergeant continued to watch them as Lieutenant Martin sidled up next to him, and Donalds took the chance.

"Begging your pardon Lieutenant, but what's up with the Major and Mr. Chabert? I know Franck is Major Webb's agent, but they seem... closer."

Martin took a couple of beats before speaking, as if his mind was searching for the right words to say.

"The Major and Franck know each other from the very start of this war, Sergeant. They fought side by side as the Germans invaded France. Mr. Chabert is a former French soldier, and a pretty good one at that, from what I understand. As the Germans closed around the British, they were trapped behind enemy lines for almost a week. They were reliant on each other to survive, and so their bond stretches into something I will probably never fully understand. It is the same with you and your men, is it not?"

Donalds looked over at Mills, Appleyard, and Lintz, and thought about what they meant to him. More importantly, what he meant to them. Martin was right.

"The Major is a good man, Sergeant. He may drink a little too much for people's liking, or be a bit brash in his manner, but he has good intentions."

Martin put his hand on Sergeant Donalds's shoulder and walked off towards the hill to join Webb. Donalds soon joined them, and they watched as Franck and Private Lintz made their way down the road towards the town.

———◉━———

LINTZ FELT THE KNOT in his stomach tighten a little as they walked down the hill. This was new territory to him and Sergeant Donalds had made it quite clear on the road near Cori that if he didn't want to do it, he just needed to speak up. Lintz had stayed silent, as this was a chance to do some good in this war.

At the north end, Lintz could see the spire of a church protruding over the buildings. The rustic charm of the small French town seemed to capture Lintz; he had almost forgotten that he was deep behind enemy lines.

His thoughts were interrupted as Franck tapped him on his shoulder, pointing to the edge of the village. A couple of SS-men were leaning against the side of one of the houses, sharing a conversation.

Lintz called out to them in German. "*OY! Hilfe! Wir wurden angegriffen! [OY! Help! We've been attacked!]*"

The *SS* men dropped their cigarettes and raised their weapons, shouting for Lintz and Franck to stay where they were. Both men kept their hands in the air so as not to frighten the already jittery approaching soldiers.

"Our truck was attacked by some partisans," Lintz continued in German, keeping his hands raised in front of himself, "not far from here. We managed to fight them off, but our truck was damaged. We need to speak with your commanding officer."

"Partisans, eh? We know a little about that" said the one soldier, as both of them shared in a laugh.

"Now," said the second soldier, looking Lintz and Franck up and down, "tell me this vital information and I will see it gets to the Major."

Lintz briefly looked over at Franck and let a pregnant pause develop before he said his next statement.

"My orders, Private, are to give it to the commanding officer, and the commanding officer alone."

The soldier got a petulant look on his face and stared at Lintz and Franck long and hard. Franck's facial expression was as stern as ever, and though the fear was coursing through his veins, Lintz managed to keep his composure.

The SS man finally bellowed out an angry breath of air and waved for Lintz and Franck to follow him. He led them through the town, passing the square and heading towards the church. Lintz made subtle notes to himself about how many soldiers he saw. So far, he counted eight, and they were spread out throughout the town. Strange, though, he couldn't see any of the people from the town.

They started to reach the north end of town, near the church, and the soldiers turned and pointed towards a villa just off the main road. One of the soldiers waited outside while the other opened the door and led the men into the house. From the outside, it didn't look like much, but once they entered it was surprisingly spacious. They waited in an anteroom, with what seemed to be a larger room off to the right, braced by double drawing room doors. Straight ahead, was a narrow staircase as well as a hall that stretched on, ending in what Lintz assumed was the back door. To his left, another small sitting room.

"Wait here," said the soldier tersely, as he went through the foyer and then the double doors.

As he left, Franck leaned into Lintz, starting to whisper under his breath. "This man is a master interrogator, cunning and ruthless. Watch yourself, *mon ami*." Lintz gulped a little and instantly became aware he was sweating slightly. It was one thing to fight in battle, but this being a spy business did not quite agree with him. He was going to need a drink when this was over. The door opened, and the soldier that led them into the house beckoned them into the room.

"Come, the Major will see you now."

Both men followed the soldier into the large room and were faced with a truly terrifying sight. At the end of the table was a small dark-haired woman, bound to a chair. Her face was bloody, and she hung her head slightly, a very visible bruise over her right eye. To the left was a German officer, boots on the table, jacket off, smoking a cigarette, and generally looking pleased with himself. As Lintz and Franck struggled to gain their bearings, a large officer approached them, his hands firmly clasped behind his back. He was physically imposing, standing what Lintz estimated was close to seven feet tall. As he looked them over, Lintz stared directly at the long, jagged scar running down the side of the man's cheek, where it disappeared under his shirt collar. Despite all this, it was the man's eyes that frightened Lintz the most. They were piercingly blue and seemed to have no emotion behind them.

It was Major Maximillian Vahlen, just as Major Webb had described him.

The large officer pulled out a chair for the men and stood opposite them. He looked at the soldier near the door, nodding his head in thanks, and the man left.

"Good evening, gentlemen. My men tell me you ran into a little trouble on the road not far from here, and that you urgently needed to speak with me."

Lintz's mouth was bone dry, and he tried to swallow but couldn't. He tried to speak, but nothing came out.

"Speak up, Sergeant, I couldn't hear you." Vahlen's eyes fixated on Lintz, and Franck's words about his resolve came to the forefront of Lintz's mind.

"Yes... yes, sir. Partisans ambushed our truck not far from here."

"I know something of these partisans, Sergeant, as you can see." Vahlen gestured towards the girl.

Lintz briefly looked over at Franck; his hands were clasped tightly together under the table. His eyes were affixed to the girl, never wavering.

"Now, what is this information you two so desperately need to provide me."

Lintz looked over at the man smoking on the other side of the table, then back to Vahlen. The German followed his gaze, then turned back to Lintz.

"Do not mind my good friend, *Hauptsturmführer* Teicher, what you have to say you can say to both of us."

Before Lintz could speak, Vahlen came around the back of him.

"Your accent, Sergeant—I can not quite place it. There is something... unique about it. Tell me, where are you from?"

He placed his large hands on Lintz's shoulders, and Lintz could feel the raw power as they squeezed him.

"I am from—"

"Wait, wait, on second thought, don't tell me. You see Sergeant, I am very curious. I like to solve mysteries. And you, my boy, are indeed a mystery. Now, your accent has a certain inflection at the end of some of your words. Do you know what this tells me, Sergeant?"

Lintz shook his head, staring straight ahead, trying not to flinch.

Vahlen leaned in closer to Lintz, right next to his ear.

"It tells me you are not from Germany. You see... that inflection, it's a dead giveaway."

Lintz felt the stone in his stomach sink. Panic rippled through his body like an electric current. He considered running, but he knew he wouldn't make it far. As he started to resign himself to his fate, Vahlen clapped him on the shoulders. "That must mean... you are from Austria, near Vienna, am I right?"

The question surprised Lintz, and he was still watching his life flash before his eyes when Franck kicked him under the table.

"You... you are correct sir. Very good."

Vahlen laughed, a hearty guttural laugh that unnerved Lintz even more than he already was.

"Good. Now tell me, young man, out with this information. We are very... busy" said Vahlen, returning to face Lintz and Franck head-on.

Lintz found some nerve and continued. "We were concerned, sir, that since the partisans attacked our vehicle, we thought they might be headed this way. However, that seems to not be the case."

Vahlen squinted at Lintz and Franck as if trying to ascertain whether the statement was true or not. Then he waved his hand in dismissal.

"I see. Well, as you can see, we have matters well in hand here. Thank you, gentlemen, for this valuable information, but I think we will manage just fine. You may go." Vahlen looked back at Teicher, who smiled.

Lintz stood to leave, and Franck followed suit. His gaze never left the girl at the end of the table. Unbridled anger was the only way Lintz could describe the look, and Lintz was instantly glad that Franck had kept his wits about him during the conversation. Behind them, Lintz heard Vahlen say something about music, and the deep tones of Leo Marjane's *Seule Ce Soir* echoed out into the hall. However, the sound of the music could not quite cover up the sounds of a girl screaming. Lintz turned away in disgust.

Heading straight for the outer door, they were soon outside the house. Franck grabbed Lintz by the arm. "We need to get back to the Major, NOW!"

"Okay, okay, let's not try to draw attention to ourselves..."

Lintz tried to slow down Franck, but the Frenchman was already walking quickly back towards where the rest of the team were located. Lintz scrambled to catch up as they made their way back down the road; by now Franck had no compunctions about maintaining his cover. They passed the square, and Franck was practically sprinting towards the hill. Avoiding the SS men as best he could, Lintz watched as Franck stumbled up the embankment behind some of the houses and shops. Lintz turned back to make sure that no one followed them and proceeded up the hill as well. The Frenchman approached the truck, but doubled over, attempting to get oxygen into his lungs.

"Private Lintz, since Franck here is out of breath, I take it you have confirmed our target is indeed in Serronelle?" asked Major Webb.

"Oh, he's there alright, Major. It's certainly Vahlen. He's in that house, there," Lintz pointed back at the house that they had just come from, "and there is anywhere between six to eight soldiers in the town from what I can see. Shouldn't be hard to capture him, he's quite focused on a prisoner he has in there."

Major Webb's eyes widened, and he immediately looked at Franck.

"It's a young girl, Major," Franck blurted out.

Major Webb looked away, murmuring under his breath, "Not again... not again... not again...I can't let her die."

Sergeant Donalds came over to Webb, putting his hand on the officer's shoulder.

"Are you okay, Major?"

Webb looked at Donalds briefly, then shrugged his hand off. "No time to waste gentlemen. Lock and load, let's go!"

He had started walking towards the edge of the hill when Lieutenant. Martin piped up, "Major, wait. Shouldn't we come up with a plan first?"

"No time, Lieutenant. Sergeant, get your men together, we are making a full-frontal assault. Right now."

"Major, I agree with the Lieutenant, we need to have a plan. Those are elite *SS* troops down there, not some half-strength German Army units," added Donalds.

Major Webb's face turned angry and he marched back to the men.

"Goddammit Sergeant! We don't have time to sit around and plan. I was told you Black Devils were a top-notch commando unit—real sons of bitches. Where's your stomach, man?"

Donalds narrowed his eyes. "Right here, sir!" He pointed to his belly.

Webb stepped up to Donalds, looking the Sergeant straight in the eye. "You're not getting cold feet, are you?"

Sergeant Donalds bridled at the comment from Webb. He didn't like being called out. "No, we are not getting cold feet, sir. Saddle up boys—lock and load."

He stared at Webb, long and hard, the Major matching the junior officer's gaze. This mission was getting riskier by the hour and Donalds could put it down to only one thing.

Major Webb.

Donalds felt the gaze of Mills on him. He knew what the man was thinking. Donalds would make sure they all got through this, reckless commanding officer or not.

Meanwhile, the Major had loaded his gun and was shuffling down the hill, followed by Franck struggling to catch up. Lieutenant Martin, Sergeant Donalds and the rest of the men followed suit. Donalds knew that even if Major Webb was preoccupied with capturing Vahlen, they still needed a plan of action.

By now, Webb and Franck moved towards the edge of the town. Donalds caught up to Lieutenant Martin, begging him to stop for a second.

"You're a smart man, LT. You know we need some sort of plan. This cowboy shit will only get us so far."

He took a second look at Webb going down the hill and nodded his head.

"You are right, Sergeant, what do you recommend?"

"Leave Appleyard up here. He's our best shot and can cover us easily. I'll take Lintz, if you take Mills; start on either side of the street, drawing their fire and keeping them off the Major."

"Alright, that will work."

Donalds gave out the orders to the men, and as Appleyard hiked back up the hill, Donalds and Lintz moved to one side of the street; Martin and Mills went to the other. They tried to find where Webb and Franck had gone but couldn't immediately see them. *Goddamn you, Major, what are you doing?* Donalds thought to himself. He looked at the street. A few Germans were milling about halfway up the road.

Then it all started.

BRAP-BRAP-BRAP-BRAP-BRAP!

The two soldiers immediately in front of them dropped as Webb brashly came into view, muzzle flashes from the Sten gun at his hip, lighting up the night. He and Franck ran over to check and see if they were dead, waving at Donalds and his men to move forward. They, however, did not wait and continued down the street towards the house that Lintz had pointed out earlier. Donalds split up his soldiers into two-man teams, and each moved with purpose down either side of the street, guns at the ready.

The sound of the machine gun had no doubt alerted the rest of the soldiers in the town. A group of three of them came from in between two of the houses and started firing at Major Webb and Franck. The hail of bullets from the Germans forced them to duck down, and they sought shelter in an alcove of one of the houses on the opposite side of the street. They tried the door, which was luckily unlocked, and fell into the house.

Bullets traced up the door and the front side of the house, narrowly missing them.

Donalds and the other members of the team watched on when a loud crack cut through the night. The lead German soldier dropped to his knees, his neck spraying blood.

Ah, bless his heart, Private Appleyard truly was a damn fine shot.

The two other Germans crouched immediately and moved back to the safety of the cover of the house on the opposite side of the street.

Another shot rang out, kicking up the dirt of where the Germans had just stood. They may have gained cover from Appleyard, but they were thankfully blissfully unaware of the rest of the men.

Donalds and Lintz came out from cover and unleashed a barrage from their weapons. It took the Germans by surprise, and as they tried to duck behind the house, the bullets found their mark. They lay on the ground now, writhing around in obvious pain for a few seconds, then they were both still. Donalds came upon them, checking to see if they were down, then moved down the street towards the square.

"MOVE TO THE FOUNTAIN, WE'LL COVER YOU" shouted Donalds towards Major Webb and Franck. *Bloody fools,* Donalds thought. *They're going to get themselves killed.* He watched Webb and Franck exit from the building and ran to the fountain. Soon Lieutenant Martin and Corporal Mills did the same. Mills placed his Johnson Light Machine Gun on the edge and propped it up on its tripod legs.

Webb took a long swig from his flask and patted Donalds on the leg, "Thank you for that, Sergeant. Those Jerries took us by surprise, but by George, we need to keep bloody moving up this street."

"Begging your pardon, sir, but we need to move slowly. We don't know where the rest of the Germans are in this town. And I haven't seen any of the townsfolk—where are they?"

Webb loaded a fresh clip into his machine gun, his chest heaving up and down as he took a couple of deep breaths.

"We don't have the time, Sergeant. That girl in there doesn't have long... we can't..."

His voice trailed off, and he took another drink from the flask. A few quick checks over the top of the fountain, and he was off again. Donalds could barely believe his eyes.

"Sergeant, look!" Lieutenant Martin exclaimed, pointing ahead down the road. As Donalds was busy watching Webb slink off, he could see some shapes moving in the distance. They came into the moonlight only briefly, but Donalds could see four of them, and then they were suddenly out of sight. So much for only eight Germans with this Major Vahlen. What exactly had Donalds gotten himself and his men into?

"Hold your ammo boys, keep your shots for something you know you can hit," Donalds ordered, as the Lieutenant nodded on in agreement.

Donalds was trained to think on his feet, but this was a little much. He would be damned if he didn't do everything in his power to make sure the mission was a success. The lives of millions of Allied soldiers depended on it. Even the lives of his men depended on the decisions he made. The pressure—he needed it for himself, to keep going. This was front and center in his mind as he caught a glimpse of the Major and Franck, who had by now disappeared behind the back of the houses.

CHAPTER NINE

THE BLOOD FELT AS IF it was rushing to the top of his head. His heart was beating faster and faster, threatening it seemed to burst from his chest. It had been some time since he had seen combat, and he instantly felt his age and all those scotches. Major Webb pressed himself against the side of the house, his eyes constantly scanning the horizon. Franck soon joined him, hunching over to catch his breath as well.

"Just a few more houses, *mon ami*. Up on the left, just before the church," Franck said in a hushed tone.

Breathing heavily, Webb replied, "I think we can make it around the backside of the houses there, avoid the road. How many in the inside do you think?"

Franck shrugged his shoulders and made a number two with his hand, then a number five. Webb looked around the corner, then waved for Franck to follow him. They made deliberate movements, trying to garner as little sound as possible. Webb started to feel a little deja vu, back to those days he and Webb had shared in 1940. This time, however, he knew things would be different.

They finally reached the backside of the house where Franck had met Major Vahlen a few moments earlier. Webb made a motion with his hand, directing Franck to go around back while he made his way to the front. Webb inched along the side of the house, keeping a sharp eye out for any *SS* soldiers. He turned the corner and saw the front door.

It's now or never, ol' boy, he said to himself. He gently turned the door handle and did his best to make sure the door didn't make a sound. He did a quick scan of the room, not seeing anything.

Webb immediately felt a bead of sweat running down the side of his head. A sound emanated from the closed-door room off to his right. It not only stopped him in his tracks but immediately boiled his blood.

It was the sound of a girl's voice. More precisely, a scream.

Major Webb pressed himself against the large double doors, indeed hearing voices, but he couldn't make out any words. Looking down, his memories started to fade in and out of that manor house all those years ago, the dead young girl's face... and opened the door.

He was immediately hit by not only the gruesome visual but also the smell.

The room stank of sweat, and cigarette smoke. Webb could see two German officers near the other end of the room. One was laughing and standing, smoking a cigarette, while the other was leaning over the girl, blowing cigarette smoke onto her. The girl's face was bloodied, and she looked drunk, but for a moment he thought he saw a familiar face... then it was quickly gone. The officer to his left turned nonchalantly as if expecting to see one of his men.

Webb immediately recognized him as Teicher. The large grin on Teicher's face quickly turned to one of panic when he looked at Webb. He started to lunge for the pistol placed on the table but Webb fired a burst from his machine gun, just above the man's head, stopping him dead in his tracks.

"*OY*! Nobody fucking move a bloody muscle!" shouted Webb. The second German stood up and slowly turned around, at last. Coming face to face with Webb.

It was the man that had haunted his dreams for four long, agonizing years.

Major Maximillian Vahlen.

"*Guten Abend, Herr* Vahlen," Webb said coolly in German. Vahlen looked slightly surprised to be conversing in his native language.

"And a good evening to... I'm afraid I don't have the pleasure of knowing your name?" replied Vahlen in English, leaning on the table.

"We will be keeping it that way... for now. Both of you, have a seat... slowly," ordered Webb, moving around the table as both the Germans eased into the chairs. He quickly grabbed both of their pistols, then went to check on the young woman, who was slumped over in the chair. Waving Franck to join him at the edge of the table, Webb pointed emphatically at Martine.

"What the bloody hell have you done? I thought you said they wouldn't find her..."

Franck looked down, a forlorn look flashing across his face. To Webb the guilt was evident.

"I didn't think they would—"

Webb interrupted him, "Well, they did. And they could've killed her. Then there would be two on our hands."

"I'm sorry, *mon ami*..."

"Shut up. We'll talk about this later." Webb turned away from the Frenchman, bending down to brush some hair from Martine's face.

"Don't worry my dear, you are safe now."

She groaned and tried to lift her head. Her eyes looked glassy.

"*Qui... etes... vous?* [*Who...are...you?*]" she asked with great effort.

"Someone who's here to help." Webb untied the girl's hands and picked her up from the chair. "Franck, take her to lie down. Then make sure there is no one left in the house."

"*Qui, mon ami,* [*Yes, my friend,*]" said Franck, coming over and taking the girl onto his shoulder. "What is your name?"

"M... Ma... Martine." she stammered out.

Franck patted her on the shoulder and helped her past the Germans, and out of the room. Webb's eyes bore daggers at his captives. He burned with rage... burned.

"Well, English, do you mind if I light a cigarette?" asked Vahlen.

Webb said nothing. His grip tightened on the machine gun.

"This is quite the... unexpected surprise. I have to admit, I did not expect the British to send a rescue mission for that murderer so quickly. Tell me, how long has she been working for you?" Vahlen pointed in the direction of Martine, taking a long drag from his cigarette.

Webb let out a sarcastic chuckle. "If that is what you thought, you Nazi bastard, you are gravely mistaken."

He removed the blood-stained handkerchief from his pocket and tossed it on the table in front of Teicher and Vahlen. "I'm simply here to stop the past from repeating itself. Just in time, by the state of that girl. Hope you sick bastards enjoyed yourself, as that will be the last person you'll ever torture."

Vahlen looked at the garment, then back to Webb through the curling smoke, trying to figure out what exactly was happening. "What... is all this, who are you?"

At that moment, the door opened and Franck entered the room. He walked over to Major Webb and whispered that the house was clear. He then took up a position opposite the Germans, his machine gun squarely pointed in their direction. Teicher and Vahlen had recognized him from their earlier conversation, whispering to each other in German when he walked in. Franck smiled back at them, at the same time noticing the handkerchief on the table. His anger started to bubble to the surface. Looking on at the two German's laughing faces did not help. Pulling away from the wall, he marched to the table. Using the back end of his gun, he swung it across the side of Vahlen's face. There was a loud audible crunch as the massive German doubled over, a splatter of blood hitting the floor.

"Well, now that is how you start a party, eh *Herr* Vahlen? It's time we really get down to business though," stated Webb, clasping his hands together in excitement.

Vahlen wiped the blood from his mouth with his sleeve.

"Tie their hands tight, Franck. They've got a long night ahead of them, and I don't want them leaving early."

Franck came over, binding each of their hands at the back of their chairs. Webb handed his machine gun over to Franck and walked over to Vahlen. He reached down and removed the knife from Vahlen's belt. Leaning in close to the man's ear, he dragged the knife down the left side of the German's face.

"Before this night is out, I'm going to make the left side of your face match the right... Major."

———◆———

OUTSIDE, THE SITUATION was equally as perilous. Pinned down by fire, Lieutenant Martin, Sergeant Donalds and the rest of the team were fighting just to survive. The stone fountain provided them with a scant amount of cover and both Martin and Donalds knew that they couldn't stay here for long.

"They've got us pinned down!" cried Martin, firing off a couple of bursts as bullets ricocheted right by his head. His hands trembled terribly, so much so that Donalds took notice.

"Steady yourself, Lieutenant," Donalds said, taking a few peeks over the top, "if those bastards flank us, we'll be dead."

There were a total of four Nazis on the left, about twenty yards up, keeping the squad pinned down. Donalds ducked back down and cursed under his breath. The Germans were well covered, even from Appleyard on the hill.

Donalds realized what he would have to do, and he didn't like it... not one single bit.

He slid over to Lieutenant Martin and outlined what he wanted to do, with the lanky Lieutenant reluctantly giving it his blessing. He relayed his instructions to Lintz and Mills, then crawled to the far right of the fountain.

Donalds lay there next to Martin, and managed for a brief moment to block out all the sounds, all the chaos that surrounded them. He sat there, thinking about young Maxwell, his men fighting for their lives this very evening. Donalds had recently begun to allow himself to dream of loading up on that passenger ship back home to Canada. He closed his eyes and took a deep breath. *Trust in your training*, Donalds thought, *and everything will be alright.*

The time had come once again to show the Germans what Canadians, and specifically what the Black Devils were made of!

"NOW!" shouted Donalds. Martin removed one of the grenades from his belt, pulled the pin, and quickly chucked it in the direction of the German position. At the same time, Lintz and Mills popped up and began laying down suppressing fire. As this was happening, Donalds pushed himself up and ran towards the line of houses on the right side. It struck Donalds at that moment that this was very similar to the attack they made in Italy, and if he wasn't running for his life, he would have laughed at the irony.

Bullets whizzed by him, and he could see muzzle flashes and tracers just off to his left. He called on what physical reserves he had left and pushed for the nearest house, slamming his shoulder and body weight into the window and luckily crashing straight through. The wood around the now-broken window continued to be pockmarked with bullets, and Donalds slowly slid himself away from it. Time was of the essence, and he quickly made his way to the back of the house. The firefight seemed to intensify, and Donalds moved along the back of the houses till he came to a small gap between the buildings. It looked to be a small garden, albeit un-tended to, as the growth had almost overtaken the space itself. He crouched down, slowly moving through the grass towards a hedge that covered the entrance to the street.

He peeked out through the brush, gaining a full view of the street. Thankfully, the soldiers hadn't seen him come through the garden.

It was time to get their attention, however.

Donalds popped up and squeezed the trigger on his gun and he felt it buck as he sprayed the other side of the street. The

Germans, their focus still on the fountain, now turned to fire at Donalds's position.

Mills, watching on as Sergeant Donalds put some pressure on the Germans, saw his chance. He stood up, aimed his JLM, and fired. Two of the Germans were hit, falling to the ground, dead. Mills smiled and shifted his gun to the other two when he saw a flash.

He felt the left side of his body go numb.

The gun dropped to the ground with a loud clatter. He looked down, placed his hand over his stomach, pulling it away, and saw that it was covered in blood. The pain rushed over him like a wave and his legs collapsed out from under him.

"NOOOOOOOOOOOOO!" screamed Sergeant Donalds.

The Sergeant stood up and pushed his way through the brush and out into the street. He shifted the Thompson to his left hand, grabbed a grenade from his belt, pulled the pin with his teeth, and ran straight toward the Germans. Winding up, he threw the grenade across the street, watching it bounce a couple of times and land close to the German position. Before they could react, it exploded, instantly killing one of them. The second German was dazed by the explosion and had dropped his guard. Donalds walked calmly along the street, raised his Thompson, and squeezed off a burst. It caught the German in the legs, and he fell to the ground. He approached the German and squeezed off another burst, watching as his chest ripped open from the impacts. The man gurgled something as blood dripped from his mouth before he lay still on the cobblestone.

Donalds slung his gun around his shoulder and started running back towards Mills.

The rest of the squad, Lintz and Martin, had also congregated at Mills's side. Donalds slid down onto his knees and placed both his hands on the wound, applying ample pressure.

"Stay with me, Corporal, stay with me," ordered Donalds.

Mills' eyes looked up to the Sergeant, and he opened his mouth to speak, but just gasped for air. Donalds kept his hands on the wound, but blood was quickly darkening the Corporal's shirt. Mills would need a doctor very soon.

"No, no, don't fall asleep now, Corporal Mills," said Lieutenant Martin, lightly patting the sides of Mills's face, keeping him from closing his eyes. "This man needs medical attention. I'm afraid that my skills are very limited. What about any of your men?"

Donalds shook his head, indicating they did not.

Martin thought for a moment, then looked up at one of the houses. "What about the townsfolk? I bet they have a doctor amongst them." He stood up and patted Donalds on the shoulder. He also waved his hands in the direction of Appleyard, directing him to come down and join them.

"Good thinking, LT. But where are they? I haven't seen anyone... since we arrived."

Martin looked around, and his eyes settled north. The church.

"I bet... they're in there. Germans would've kept them in a spot where they could control them."

"Worth a shot," Donalds said.

Appleyard arrived from descending down the hill, and quickly laid his rifle down next to Mills, placing his hands on the man's chest. "Aw, dammit Mills, don't do this!"

Donalds came over and relayed his instructions. "Private Lintz, stay here and keep a watch over this position. Private Appleyard, you are with me. The Germans must have locked up the townspeople somewhere here, and we need to find them. NOW."

Appleyard nodded, rising to stand next to Donalds and the two of them started down the road. Donalds had agreed with Martin, the church was the logical place to start; it was the only building that was large enough to hold all of the townsfolk. Donalds just hoped that the Germans had not taken their fury out on them. They moved with haste but also had to be careful, lest a stray *SS* soldier caught them out. The church loomed closer, and when the men approached the steps, they took a careful look around. Its small spire extended into the night sky, housing a large bell, with a smaller one sitting just atop it. Its exterior of ashen weathered stone was illuminated by two iron-wrought lamps, gently swaying in the slight evening breeze. Donalds looked to the darkened windows but found no sign of life. Both men ascended the stairs, eyes darting from side to side vigilantly, until they reached the chestnut-colored double doors.

"Look, Sarge, the doors are locked," said Appleyard, pressing himself against the stone.

Donalds looked down, and his heart sank a little. There was a large iron chain latched around the door handles. "Let's hope we find everyone breathing inside." Donalds looked down, pointing with his free hand towards the lock. Appleyard took Donalds's cue and drove his rifle down through the lock. It clanked to the ground, and Donalds pushed open the heavy oak doors, gun at the ready.

The room opened up before them, with many dark brown pews, carefully lined row upon row, and a large pulpit at its head. He couldn't immediately see anything, save for a bit of moonlight filtering through a few of the windows, but something stirred towards the back, off to the right of the pulpit. Appleyard had also now entered, and had raised his rifle in that direction.

Donalds knew it was a risk, but time was of the essence.

"We've got you covered, come out now!" he shouted.

He saw two hands raise, and then the rest of a man, no older than forty. He was of average height, with eyeglasses perched on the end of his nose. His hair, a healthy mix of brown and gray, was receding from the front of his head. Both Martin and Appleyard lowered their weapons.

"*Ne tirez pas! Anglais? [Do not shoot! English?]*" the man said, lowering his hands a little.

Donalds's French was practically non-existent. He recognized the word "*Anglais,*" and with the few words he did know, he tried to converse with the man.

"Ah... *non, Canadien...*" Donalds said, pointing to himself and Appleyard.

The man strained as he tried to listen to Donalds, but as he translated 'Canadian', his eyes lit up and a smile crossed his face.

"Ahhhh, thank you, God," the man cried out in English, clapping his hands together. Donalds and Appleyard shared a brief respite and relaxed.

The man said some words in French behind him, and both the Canadians watched as people stood up from behind the front row of pews and came out from behind the pulpit. All told, there were roughly forty people that finally appeared, half the town it seemed. They nervously stared at the two soldiers and there seemed to be a subtle murmur amongst them. Some of them pointed at the faces of Donalds and Appleyard, no doubt put off by the boot polish. A couple of them noticed that the markings on the men's uniforms weren't German and started to cheer a little bit, making their way to the door. Donalds and Appleyard stepped aside, showing that the way was clear.

"*Merci, mon ami*, I... we... all of us, we thank you for... for liberating us." the man said, gesturing to all the other people filling out of the church. Donalds and Appleyard looked sheepish in front of the man's gratitude.

As each of the townspeople came to shake their hands, Donalds grabbed the man they were originally speaking with.

"No, no liberation," Donalds pointed to his face, then back at Appleyard, "Small group, secret mission... uh, *secret...*"

Donalds hoped that by adding in the French word for 'secret', the man would understand. After a few moments, the corners of his mouth turned down, understanding the situation. However, Donalds didn't have time to further discuss it.

"Sir, we need to find a doctor... ah, *docteur*?" He tried his best to annunciate his words clearly so the man would better understand. The man removed his glasses and pointed at his chest.

"*Oui*, I...am...doctor," the man said, his broken English evident. Donalds waved for the man to follow him and Appleyard, and they pushed their way through the dispersing group of people. Once they were heading back towards Mills, Donalds reached out and shook the man's hand.

"Sergeant Peter Donalds."

"Doctor Pierre Lelievre," the man replied.

Donalds pointed towards the fountain and began to run. Appleyard did the same, and the man soon caught on and started jogging as well. They came around the marble fountain just in time to see Mills cry out in pain. Lintz had his hands on the wound. Doctor Lelievre took a long look at Mills and furrowed his brow. He turned to speak to Donalds but seemed to be searching for the right words to say in English. Instead, he pointed to himself and then at the house just on the other side of the square. He then made a lifting motion with his hands and started towards the building. Donalds helped Martin and Appleyard pick Mills up from the ground, and they moved as quickly as they could into the house. Laying Mills on the couch, the doctor left and returned a few minutes later with his bag and sat down next to Mills, feeling his forehead. It smeared the black face paint, and the doctor started to remove Mills's jacket, looking for the source of the wound. Donalds looked pensive as he hovered over the scene.

"Don't worry, Sergeant, from what I know of the Corporal, he'll pull through," Martin said, patting the Canadian on the shoulder.

"He... he has to. He just has to," replied Donalds, looking down as Doctor Lelievre peeled back the Corporal's shirt to reveal the gaping bullet wound in his chest. The doctor cursed in French and began to dab bandages on the oozing blood.

"How bad is it, Doctor?" asked Donalds.

Martin, with some working knowledge of French, translated to the Doctor.

The man pressed his glasses back up his nose and continued to dab the wound. The Doctor replied to the group quickly, then got up to go to the kitchen.

"What did he say?" asked Donalds.

Martin hesitated before he spoke.

"Lieutenant, what did the Doctor say?"

"I'm sorry, Sergeant. I really am. He said... the Corporal may not last the night."

Donalds's face turned sour. He slammed his fist down on the table. "No... no, he's not going to die. Mills is a fighter, he's tough. I can't... I can't let him die here."

Martin came up and put his hand on Donalds's shoulder. "I don't doubt it. But, the fact remains, he needs more medical attention, more than Doctor Lelievre is able to provide I'm afraid."

Donalds looked up and seconded his agreement. "Let's go get Major Webb, get what we came for, and get Mills home. Private Lintz, stay and watch over the Corporal."

The group of them left the house, moving out into the street. The townsfolk, recently liberated from the church, were milling about, making their way back to their homes. As Martin, Donalds, and Appleyard walked down the street, they were slightly overwhelmed by the scene. Every person they passed by shook their hands, in Donalds's and Appleyard's case, for the second time. Donalds almost felt guilty at the outpouring of emotion. These people thought that they were being liberated. Once the doctor told them the truth, Donalds could only imagine the hopelessness they would feel. But he had more pressing concerns to worry about. Mills was struggling to live out the night.

When they had finally extricated themselves from the grateful throngs, they reached the house that Major Webb had ran into. Donalds pushed the door open and they entered into the small waiting room. To the right, the large white drawing-room doors were shut. The house had an eerie silence to it, and all the men looked at each other as if to say "Where is everyone?"

Lieutenant Martin was the first to call out. "Major, are you there?"

The house was still silent, but then a yelp came from the drawing-room. Then rustling, and the door began to open slowly. All the men raised their weapons instinctively but were relieved when Major Webb appeared.

"Well done lads, the town is secure?" He stood in the doorway, blocking anyone from entering.

"Yes sir, the town is clear. However, Corporal Mills has been shot. He is being treated by the town doctor, but he needs to get to a hospital pretty quickly. We should get moving, sir." replied Lieutenant Martin.

A strange look came over Webb's face. "...Ah yes, well gentlemen, there has been a slight change of plans."

"What kind of change, sir?" said Donalds, subtle anger creeping into his voice.

"Well Sergeant, it seems I'm going to be staying in France a bit longer. You see, Franck and I have some things to finish up, with the Resistance."

Lieutenant Martin was visibly shocked, shaking his head trying to understand his superior's bizarre statement. Back in England, the plan was they were all supposed to fly out with Vahlen. *Why had it suddenly changed?*

"Understood, sir. We'll take Major Vahlen then, and head back to the plane," stated Donalds, starting to get a little antsy.

This time, an even darker look than the one before came over Webb's face.

"As I said, Sergeant, there has been a slight change of plans. Major Vahlen will not be leaving this place."

That statement drew bewildered and confused looks from the junior officers and amid the brief silence, a muffled scream emanated from somewhere behind Webb.

"Sir, if I could have a moment of your time. I don't understand, I thought the whole reason for the mission was the capture of Major Va—?" asked Martin. But before he could finish his question, Sergeant Donalds interrupted.

"What the hell is going on in there?"

The Canadian made a move towards the doors, but Major Webb stepped in front of him.

"Nothing in there is of concern to you, Sergeant."

Donalds's anger started to boil. *Who the hell was this Major Webb? And more importantly, what the hell is going on here?*

He stepped closer to Webb, lowering his voice to almost a hush. "We all risked our lives for this. Mills is fighting for his goddamn life. Excuse me, sir, but I believe we are entitled to know whatever the hell is in there, don't you Lieutenant?"

Caught between his superior officer, and his agreement with Sergeant Donalds's candor, Lieutenant Martin was tongue-tied. At any rate, Sergeant Donalds didn't wait for the answer and pushed his way past Webb and into the room.

He had seen much over the last year—senseless violence, man's inhumanity towards his fellow man, but he always prided himself on keeping his moral fiber. He would fight, but he would do it under his moral code, even if the Germans were vicious and cruel. Somehow, he didn't get that same feeling from Major Webb. He had to figure out what the hell was going on. But what Donalds saw in the room only confused him more.

At the other end of the room was a man tied up. Donalds could only assume it was Major Vahlen, mouth stuffed with a rag. Franck was standing next to him, holding a bloodied pair of pliers. Donalds couldn't be sure, but he thought he saw a fingernail in the clasp. The Germans's face was battered and bruised, and the man was now making indiscernible sounds of pain. To the left, another German officer was also tied up, face also slightly bloodied.

"Are you... are you torturing him?" Donalds questioned, looking at Franck and then at Webb.

"I told you, Sergeant, this doesn't concern you." The voice of Webb came from somewhere behind Donalds.

Donalds turned around, seeing both Lieutenant Martin and Private Appleyard entering the room. Behind them was Major Webb. Donalds immediately noticed his Sten machine gun pointed at all three of them, his finger on the trigger.

"Drop your weapon, Sergeant, and take a seat. We do have a great many things to discuss."

CHAPTER TEN

"WELL, IT'S NOT BLOODY scotch, but it will have to do I guess," Major Webb mused, taking a bottle of gin from the small wooden cabinet and placing it on the table. "Care for a drink, Sergeant?"

Donalds could not hide his displeasure, making a point to avert his gaze from the Major.

Webb shrugged, taking a long swig from the bottle. "Come now, Sergeant, don't you think you've earned a drink?"

Donalds gripped the table with his hands, squeezing the wood so much it hurt his hands. "You'll forgive me, sir, if I don't feel the same. Are we your prisoners now too?"

Major Webb pulled out a chair, sitting down at the table, and started to chuckle. "Of course not, Sergeant. Only these pieces of filth," he pointed at both Vahlen and Teicher, "are staying put. I just need to make sure you guys are on board with the... changes. Then you can get back to your wounded man." Webb grabbed the bottle and poured himself a tall drink.

"So generous of you, Major. But what was this all abou—"

The conversation was interrupted as Martine entered the room. Every man turned to watch her as she came right beside Webb and sat down.

"Feeling better, my dear?" Webb asked, grabbing her hand.

She nodded. "Yes, I... feel better.

"Now you see, Sergeant. This young lady here," Webb pointed at Martine, "these men were going to torture her. They would cause her enough pain to force her into giving up her Resistance comrades. Once she had done this, they surely would've killed her. Franck and I are just... returning the favor to the," Webb preached, raising his glass in a mock toast toward Teicher and Vahlen.

"You don't think I know about the cruelty of the Germans, Major? I see it first-hand every single day of this damn war. But what separates us from them, and lets me sleep a little at night, is why we are fighting this war, and ultimately, *how* we fight it."

Webb laughed out loud—a deep, coughing, stuttering laugh. He took another gulp of gin.

"I didn't peg you as so naive, Sergeant. I'm not sure whether I should admire your blind innocence or think you an ignorant fool. The Germans don't show mercy. Neither should we."

"Says you, Major. Corporal Mills might end up giving his life... for what? This... this personal vendetta? What gives you the right to be this man's personal torturer and executioner?"

At this statement, Webb slammed the bottle on the table and stood up, walked towards the seated Sergeant Donalds and leaned in. "You wanna know, Sergeant? You want to know what Franck and I have seen this piece of human garbage do to deserve th—"

"Shhhhh, listen!" said Franck, silencing the room.

All the men stopped and listened. At first, there was only silence, and Donalds started to think Franck was trying to defuse the situation. But then, the faint sound of wood creaking, not once, but twice. Every Allied man in the room froze.

"Franck, check it out." hissed Webb, taking up a position at the back of the room and keeping an eye on everyone. "My dear, help me keep an eye on all our guests if you don't mind?"

Martine nodded and picked up one of the German Lugers Webb placed back on the table, eagerly keeping it trained towards Teicher and Vahlen.

Franck exited the room as silently as he could, shutting the large double door gently. He took slow, methodical steps down the back hall, towards the location of the possible sound. He spotted a small room at the end of the hall and kept his eyes trained on it as he placed one foot in front of the other. Sweat stung his eyes, but he dared not try to wipe it away out of fear. He slid along the wall, coming next to a slightly ajar door. A monotonous tapping sound was coming from the room. He gently eased the door open with the barrel of his gun, revealing a tiny storage closet. In it sat a German *SS* soldier, furiously tapping away on a wireless set.

He looked up as Franck stood in the doorway, slowly raising his hands into the air. Franck started to lean in to grab the *SS* man, but he hadn't anticipated what the man did next. One of his boots shot up, kicking the machine gun from Franck's hand. At the same time, the soldier lunged back towards the makeshift table. Franck saw what he was lunging for.

A pistol.

Franck's eyes grew large at the impending danger. His left hand shot out, grabbing the German's arm before he could level the weapon. The men fought back and forth, grappling with each other, each man attempting to gain an advantage over the other. Franck willed his left hand to hold on. With his other hand, he pressed it into the gooey eye of the German. The man let out a sharp scream, and Franck quickly put both hands on the pistol and slowly moved it towards the head of the German. Once in place, he squeezed the trigger.

A loud *BANG* reverberated in the small room.

The German went slack, and his body lay limp on the chair. For a moment, Franck could hear nothing save for the loud ringing in his ears. As he let go of the German's arm, the body fell to the floor. Franck slumped back against the far wall, trying his best to catch his breath. Once he managed to calm himself, he went back into the storage closet and took a quick look around. Luckily, the radio was undamaged by his barrage, but he couldn't tell what the soldier was sending or to whom he was sending it. Either way, this was a big problem for his and the Major's plans. He turned to go back down the hall, where Major Webb was waiting at the door of the drawing room. "What was that? I thought you said you checked the house?" Webb said, keeping his voice low.

"I did, *mon ami*, it was clear. He must have snuck in the back," Franck replied, averting the Major's gaze.

Webb picked up on this nervousness, and his eyes narrowed. "What was he doing?"

Franck hesitated, but he had known the Major long enough to know that lying to him would do no good.

"He was using the wireless set, Major, sending a message." He waited a few moments before continuing. "Calling for help, I think."

"No shit, Franck. That certainly would have been something to prevent, now wouldn't it!" Webb grabbed the Frenchman's collar in a small fit of rage. After a few tense moments, he managed to calm down. "Unfortunate, but not completely unexpected. We knew we would only have a limited window. Let's get rid of the men and then... we can finish this." He released Franck, smoothing down the rumpled shirt.

Franck nodded, swallowing hard, and both men returned to the sitting room.

———●———

APPROXIMATELY TWO HOURS to the south of Serronelle, Colonel Grassl had just climbed into bed. It had been a long day; he had spent most of it making exhaustive defensive preparations. Just as he had tucked himself in, there was a curt knock on the door. He pretended to be asleep. Whatever it was, it could wait until morning.

A second knock, this one more forceful than the last.

"Come!" ordered Grassl, sitting up in his bed, letting his annoyance come through in his tone. It had better be a message from the *Fuhrer* himself, or an announcement that Allied troops were storming the Marseille beaches. If it wasn't, he swore he would ensure his staff were sent to the Russian front.

His adjutant entered the room, saluting and clicking his heels. "My apologies, Colonel, but this matter requires your urgent attention." Captain Sommer handed Grassl the piece of paper he had brought in.

Grassl rubbed his eyes and perused the message:

Major Vahlen's SS unit requests immediate reinforcements
Stop
Engaged with French Resistance cell in town of Serronelle
Stop
Possible All—

Grassl curtly handed the message back to his adjutant, laying back down in the bed. *It was probably still cold on the Eastern Front*, he thought, *even at this time of year*. A look of disdain crept over his face.

"And so, Captain? This looks like a routine check-in. You woke me for a routine status update?"

Captain Sommer shifted his stance. "Begging the Colonel's pardon, but the message was cut off... should we not at least investigate? We can't seem to raise the man who sent the message now."

Grassl sighed and sat back up. While he saw nothing in the message and did not like Major Vahlen, Berlin would certainly care what happened to the *Reich's* prized Resistance hunter, and more importantly, Himmler and the *SS* would raise the issue. It would be potentially hazardous, even for someone with as high a rank as Grassl.

He could see his adjutant was still waiting for an answer. "Very well, Captain, put together a squad of men. Wake me in an hour, and we'll head up there. Now... get out"

Captain Sommer saluted and left quickly. Grassl settled back into the bed and shut his eyes.

Major Vahlen of the *SS* was more than capable of taking care of himself, but a small smile crept across his face, knowing that the large Major might need the lowly Army's help. But—it could certainly wait till he had a little sleep.

———— ◉ ————

"SEEMS TO ME THAT EVENTS have conspired against us, and my timetable has been sped up. I thank you for your help getting me here, but it's best you were on your way. Well, except for you, my dear Major Vahlen," Webb stated, making his way around the table.

All sets of eyes followed Webb, but Donalds had settled on Franck. He was visibly shaken and nervously smoked a cigarette.

The blood spattered across his chest told Donalds all he needed to know about what had happened.

"What's done is done here, Major. At this point I don't care. But there is no need to hang around here. We can take Vahlen back with us. You've taken your pound of flesh. Allied High Command will want this man's information."

Webb shook his head back and forth, setting the Sten gun on the table briefly. "My good friend Vahlen here has as much intelligence on Atlantic Wall defenses as I do."

"What? Wait a minute..." stammered Donalds, an incredulous look coming over him.

Webb continued. "But he does have value to me and Franck, so he stays."

The British Major walked around behind Teicher and smacked him on the back of the head. "You can take this Nazi bastard back with you, but I think Vahlen's got a little more blood to give."

Donalds was floored. "So, your whole briefing, this whole mission, it was just to capture Major Vahlen...Just so you could torture him?"

Webb chuckled, then said angrily, "Trust me, Sergeant, he's earned it. And then some."

"DAMMIT MAJOR!" shouted Donalds, slamming his fists on the table. "We all risked our lives for this, FOR YOU! AND FOR WHAT? Why in the hell are you doing this?"

Teicher chuckled a little, an evil little cackle.

"Sadly, my dear Sergeant Donalds, we are most likely to be joined by Major Vahlen's comrades very soon. Time is something of a luxury at the moment," stated an even more agitated Webb, pacing the room frantically now.

"Major, I'm afraid I'm going to have to agree with the Sergeant here. We deserve some explanation," stated Lieutenant Martin.

"Tell us, sir." Donalds's insubordinate tone dripped from his lips.

"Yes, Major Webb, please, tell us allllll..." a deep voice slurred from the head of the table. Major Vahlen lifted his head and gave a bloody smile as he spoke. Webb gave a long hard look towards Vahlen, cursing under his breath. He looked back at Franck, nodding his head slightly.

"Well, that piece of Nazi scum was going to find out soon enough anyway, so it's your choice if you want to stay."

Donalds shifted uneasily in his seat. "Private Appleyard."

The freckle-faced Private perked up. "Yes sir?"

Donalds maintained eye contact with Major Webb as he spoke. "Go check on Corporal Mills, and double-time it back."

Appleyard got up and moved towards the drawing-room doors. "At once, sir."

After he left, an eerie silence came over the room. It seemed that everyone in the room was attempting to size up the other. Even the Germans seemed to wonder what was going on. The only one that appeared relaxed was Martine. Donalds could tell by the cautious smile on her face.

Appleyard soon returned, heading straight over to Donalds, and whispered something in his ear. "Well, Major, it seems that the Doctor says we need to let Mills rest before moving him. I guess that means we can hear the insane reason for this... mess." Donalds waved his hands at the room as he spoke.

Webb moved around the table, picking up the crumpled handkerchief from the table and tossing it in front of Major

Vahlen. The handkerchief was lace white, and Donalds and Martin could see the bottom half was stained with blood.

"This thing, right here. This is why we came to France, to this town, to find this man," Webb said, pointing at Vahlen. "As you all can see, it's covered in blood. But what you don't know is that Franck's blood, and my blood, is also on this. We made a blood oath over it four years ago, to be where we are, right now, at any cost."

"Sir, we don't... I don't quite understand?" queried Lieutenant Martin.

"You will soon enough."

CHAPTER ELEVEN

THE CLIP SLAMMED INTO the bottom of the rifle, and Captain Theodore Webb pulled back the slide, chambering a round. It was his last one—guess he had to make it count. He leaned against the tree, trying to catch his breath. He had been running through the countryside for what seemed like hours, but he couldn't stop. The adrenaline was coursing through his veins; his hand shook as he tried to unscrew the top of his canteen. A few short hours ago, in the hot summer sun of July 1940, the Germans had broken through the British and French lines. Paris had fallen a few weeks earlier, and the country was in complete chaos. He had tried his best to maintain the line, but the German forces were relentless. With most of his unit pulling back with the rest of the Allied forces to the coastal city of Dunkirk, Webb had stayed behind to help evacuate one of his young soldiers who had been wounded. In turn, they had become separated from his men and sadly Webb could not save the young man, who had succumbed to his wounds shortly after their retreat. Webb was on his own now, fighting for his survival.

The sun was high in the sky now, beating down on him. He wiped his face with his shirt, the sweat beading heavily on his face. He would rest here for a bit, and then start to make his way north. He looked up at the top of the hill. Not wanting to climb it just yet, he took another swig from his canteen.

The rustling of the brush from the open space below made him freeze.

Behind him, down the valley, a little bit, came the sound of voices and laughter. He gently put down the canteen and gingerly poked his head around the corner of the tree.

Germans.

Three of them, standing down the hill, just outside the treeline. They were a good few meters from where he was sitting.

By the sound of their conversation, Webb was pretty sure they hadn't seen him, which was lucky. He grabbed his canteen and rifle and adjusted his helmet, getting into a crouch. Taking one last look back at the soldiers, Webb moved slowly up the hill, trying to keep any sort of cover he could. Just when he thought he was free and clear, the worst thing he could think of happened. By the time he had noticed anything, the canteen had slipped out of the pouch in his belt and started to fall down the hill.

Clink, claannnnk, clank.

Each tree trunk, exposed root, and rock seemed to amplify the noise of the canteen, and once it finally settled at the bottom of the ridge, it was just a few feet from the Germans.

"Oh, bloody hell," Webb uttered.

The Germans shouted "HALT!" in unison and then unleashed a barrage of bullets when they saw Webb continue to move. Bullets ricocheted around him as he weaved his way up the hill, moving from tree to tree. At the next one he passed, he crouched down, leveled his rifle, and aimed the sight at one of the Germans. They had not yet started to climb the hill and were perfect stationary targets. He lined up the barrel and squeezed off a shot. It smacked the German on the far right squarely in the shoulder, and he dropped in agony, clutching his arm. The other two, visibly shocked, stood still for a moment, before opening fire.

Webb had taken that brief respite to scramble up towards the top of the hill. The tree cover, sparse at the top, meant that Webb suddenly felt very exposed. He looked out over the countryside, trying to find a place where he could lose the likely pursuing Germans. A flat meadow stretched away from his hill, and then led into another thickly wooded area.

Time was of the essence.

He raced off down the hill, checking over his shoulder at regular intervals. He knew the Germans would be wary of climbing the hill now that he had injured one of them. It was amazing what fearing for your own life could do to your endurance and stamina.

He made it across the field in five minutes flat, entering the second wooded area. Crouching behind one of the leafy trees, his hand scraped against the rough bark. He desperately tried to catch his breath and his heart felt like it would explode from his chest. *Remember your training*, he kept saying to himself, *and you will survive*. He needed to make it to the Channel if he had any shot of escaping France.

Peering back through the trees, Webb expected to see the whole German Army advancing against him.

But there was nothing. Just the sunlight filtering through the leaves onto the forest floor.

Taking a deep breath, he started to evaluate his options. He wouldn't survive out in the open for long, even in these woods. The Germans would catch up to him eventually. He needed a place to lay low, and quickly.

Webb stood up and began to make his way through the north. He weaved his way in between the trees, trying not to think about the pursuers that were no doubt on his trail.

After about fifteen or twenty minutes, he came to a small break in the trees. The grouping was less dense, and he spotted something to his left that intrigued him.

The beginnings of a worn footpath.

The trees were falling away now, but as he continued around the next turn, they started to thin out even further. From there, the path widened considerably, and Webb was amazed at the beauty that lay before him. The grass, which was rough along the beginning of the path, was now clean-cut and well-manicured. The thick brush of the trees beforehand gave way to sparsely placed pine trees. The light shone through much brighter in this patch, and it seemed to relax Webb, if only for a moment. Looking ahead of himself, he could see where the path led.

A large, country house.

Webb could see it now in all its opulence. Tucked away in this small clearing, a few short feet down the path, the building dominated the landscape. The outside was cream-colored carved stone, unblemished. Standing two floors tall, the upper windows were encased in black wrought iron guards, while the lower windows were larger, allowing them to be opened in the warmer months. Webb estimated the house had at least seven or eight bedrooms.

A hidden palace, lording over a secret kingdom.

He hesitated to move from his spot. Just as this might be a haven, it could also be filled with Germans. Then again, his options were limited. He crouched low and moved along the grass towards the entrance. The pine trees only provided minimal cover, so Webb was taking a huge risk. As he came up to the large entrance, he spotted a figure coming from around the far side of the house. Unsure, he dropped immediately to the ground near one of the large pine trees and kept his rifle trained towards the figure. Once he looked down the sights at his target, he realized that his panic was misguided.

It was not a German soldier coming around the house, but a young woman carrying a small basket.

She was in her late twenties, if Webb hazarded a guess, with long strawberry blonde hair tucked behind her ears. She had lush features, with rounded eyes, a button nose, and thin lips. The looks of someone unburdened by the world's troubles. She stopped on her way to the entrance, bending down to seemingly pick some flowers that were growing on the side of the country estate.

Captain Webb saw his chance.

He pushed himself up and stealthily made his way over to her. Slinging his rifle around his back, he quickly grabbed her, covering her mouth and holding her close to him so he couldn't run. She attempted to scream, but Webb clamped his hand on her mouth with force. He whispered in her ear, hoping to calm her down, "*Anglais, Je suis Anglais. [English, I am English.]*"

She nodded and turned to look at him. He put his finger to his lips and started to remove his hand from her mouth. Her eyes were wide, and she was visibly shaken. She straightened out her apron and dress and combed back a few loose hairs, seeming to steady herself.

Webb pointed at the house. "*Allemands? [Germans?]*" She shook her head. "No *monsieur*, no Germans here."

Her perfect English shocked Webb a little, and she must have noticed as she chuckled.

"You are not the first Englishman I have ever met, *monsieur*. Tell me, are you injured?" she asked.

"No, thankfully not. I am, however, on the run from the Germans. Am I able to hide here for a short time?"

She looked back at the house, and then back to Webb. She had a pensive look to her, brushing the hair out of her face nervously. "We are not supposed to accept soldiers who aren't injured. But I will see if we can make an exception for you, *monsieur*."

"I don't quite understand, *mademoiselle*, why can't I stay?" replied Webb, quickly checking behind him.

"Come *monsieur*, I will show you."

She took his hand and they started to move towards the large double doors of the entrance to the house. Webb grabbed her arm, so she turned to face him. "What is your name?"

"Anne," she replied, placing her basket on the table in the entrance.

"Pleasure to meet you, Anne. I am Captain Theodore Webb, of Her Majesty's 23rd Northumbrian Division."

She smiled and nodded politely, but Webb got the feeling she shuffled it off. Anne opened the door and led Webb into the foyer. The floor was marble and the ceilings seemed a lot higher than they looked from the outside. Ahead of them was a grand staircase, and Webb could imagine large, opulent parties being held here, with waiters shuffling around serving fancy hors d'oeuvres. Today, however, the house was packed with guests, but all of them would surely be wishing they were somewhere else.

Every inch of space was packed with wounded soldiers, each of them in various states of distress. Groans emanated from every possible avenue, and the checkered marble floor, once the picture of beauty Webb hazarded, was stained off-red with blood.

"My God... uh, *Francais*?" Webb asked, pointing at all the soldiers on the ground.

"*Oui, monsieur. Francais. [Yes, sir, French.]*" Anne replied, then in English she said, "Hurt, need help."

Webb bent down next to a French soldier, who couldn't be much older than seventeen or eighteen. There was a bandage slung around his face, covering his left eye. On his torso, he held another bandage to his lower abdomen. Caked blood surrounded his mouth, and as Webb got closer to him, the boy let out a little whimper. He grabbed the young boy's hand, thinking immediately of his men, the ones that had bravely held the line, and those that died doing so.

"Keep fighting," Webb said, making a fist with his other hand and pounding it against his chest.

While looking up at Webb, the boy squeezed his hand and nodded. Then he coughed, and blood started to ooze from his mouth. Webb backed up as Anne bent down to check on him.

There were many other soldiers like the one Webb had just seen, and it seemed that every room within view was filled with more of them.

It seemed, by all appearances, that Webb had stumbled upon a crude field hospital.

"Come *monsieur*, I will introduce you to the master of the house, *Monsieur* Faucheux." She waved for him to follow her up the staircase. Webb was overwhelmed, and while happy to escape the Germans, seeing this many wounded soldiers was not a good

sign. The fall of France was very likely in the next few weeks, if
not the next few days. He shuddered at what would happen to
these people once the Germans took over. He had to get out. As
soon as he got some rest, he'd be on his way.

Once they reached the top of the stairs, Webb could see two
large double doors to the right, which sat closed. He didn't linger
and continued to follow Anne down the hall, to the left. She
reached the door at the end of the hall and gave a curt knock
with her finger. A voice inside said something Webb couldn't
hear, and Anne turned the knob but stopped before entering the
room.

"*Attendre, monsieur, une minute. [Wait, sir, one minute.]*"

She slipped into the room and closed the door quickly behind her.

Webb wandered back down the hall to where it opened up
and a railing looked out over the foyer. He stared down at the
wounded men, quickly thinking back to when the Germans had
broken the Allied lines. They had advanced so quickly, and with
such brutality, Webb and his men had hardly had a chance to
mount a defense. The worst was the Stuka dive bombers, that
siren mounted on the undercarriage to signal imminent death.
His men had fought valiantly, but they had greatly underestimated the speed of the Germans.

Interrupting his thoughts, the door opened at the end of the
hall and Anne came out. "Come, *monsieur*."

Webb entered the room, which, after gazing at the large
bookcase, oak-framed bed, and mantled fireplace, he realized was
the master bedroom. Two large, brown leather wing-back chairs
sat facing the dormant fireplace. Behind all of that, he could see a

large, latticed window. The room smelt strongly of tobacco, and a plume of smoke emanated from one of the chairs.

A tall, thin man stood from one of the chairs, clutching a book in one hand and a black pipe in the other. His hair was jet black, slicked to his head, curling up slightly at the base of his neck. He had a sharp, well-defined beard and was dressed in a pinstripe tailored suit, shined wingtip shoes, and a gold pocket watch. He stood there, puffing on his pipe and giving Webb the once over. When he spoke, his voice had a soothing, almost lyrical quality to it.

"*Bonjour*, Captain Webb. Welcome to my home."

His English was near perfect, and his smile made Webb feel instantly at ease.

He extended his hand to Webb. "I am *Monsieur* Bernard Faucheux, and it seems you have already met my daughter, Anne."

Anne smiled at that statement.

"A pleasure to meet you, *Monsieur* Faucheux. You have a lovely home here and taking care of all those soldiers down there—I salute you, sir," said Webb.

"Thank you, Captain." Faucheux gestured for Webb to sit in the empty wingback chair. "I'm not going to lie, it wasn't by choice that we turned our home into a hospital, but when some of the soldiers started to trickle back from the front, we knew we couldn't turn them away. I have done what I can for those men, but we are hoping that some sort of relief comes soon."

Webb furrowed his brow; the news he had likely wouldn't be anything Monsieur Faucheux wanted to hear. The master of the house continued.

"I am a banker by trade, you see, but I have long since retired. I thought Anne and I might find some peace and solace in our country estate, but as you can see below, it was short-lived." Bernard took a polished wood box and opened the top, offering Webb a cigar. The British Captain politely declined. "Those men down there, they need to see real doctors. My daughter and I are poor substitutes, I'm afraid."

"Well, sir, I am afraid to be the bearer of bad news, but the front has completely collapsed. Both the British and French armies are in full retreat, headed for the coast. The Germans have the advantage now, and they are pressing. I don't believe any relief is coming."

Webb could not bear to look at Bernard and Anne.

He hated to have to tell them, but it was better they knew the truth. The looks on their faces were of deep sadness, and Anne went to hug her father, tears rolling down her face. The emotion of this finally hit Webb, as he could perhaps escape and fight another day, but these people would have to stay in their homes, to become prisoners in their own country. However, back to the task at hand.

"*Monsieur*, I beg of you, let me stay and hide here, if only for one night. There were German soldiers not far from this house. I managed to escape them, but I'm sure they are out looking for me. Please, sir..." pleaded Webb.

Bernard Faucheux took a long drag from his pipe, the smoke pluming up into the air. He looked down at Anne, then scratched his beard.

"We are civilians, you see Captain, and if the Germans are as close as you say they are, it could compromise the men here, as well as ourselves. I cannot allow it."

Webb was about to plead further when Anne interrupted him. The father and daughter had a heated conversation in French, and Anne repeatedly gestured towards Webb. Feeling slightly uncomfortable at the position he put them in, Webb stood to leave when suddenly Bernard Faucheux said, in English:

"Captain, wait. It seems my daughter has opened my eyes to your plight. You may stay, provided you keep out of sight. The lives of the men... our lives, we depend on it."

Webb nodded his agreement. "Thank you, *Monsieur* Faucheux, you won't have any trouble from me. I'll make sure to move on by morning."

The Frenchman waved his hand as if dismissing Webb.

"Anne will find you some accommodation. Tell me, Captain, before you go..." Webb shifted his rifle to his other shoulder and turned to look squarely at Bernard. The man's face showed concern. Almost fear. "What do you think will happen to France? To England? To... us?"

"Frankly, I don't know," Webb responded, hanging his head as Anne moved past him and out of the room. Bernard said nothing, sitting back down in his chair. He lit his pipe again and puffed away. Webb felt sorry for him. He didn't hide anything, he had told Bernard the brutal truth, like a proper military man was supposed to. He felt it did the man no good to be lied to. By the way Bernard slumped into his chair, Webb thought perhaps he may have been too honest.

Webb and Anne left Bernard smoking and walked down the hall, stopping at a door on the right, revealing another bedroom. Much smaller than the master, it was still one of the biggest bedrooms Webb had ever seen.

"You can stay here, *monsieur*," Anne stated, waving her arm at the surroundings. The walls were covered with smooth, eggshell wallpaper, the bright violet and rose flower pattern snaking down in regular intervals. The bed—polished chestnut tinted wood, ornamented in design—sat against the back wall, near the window that overlooked the meadow Webb had just come through. He took his rifle and gently stood it against the wall near the bed.

"This will more than do, my dear. I don't remember the last time I slept."

Anne nodded, going over to the bed, fluffing a few of the pillows and pulling back the blanket. After that, she pointed to the other side of the room, where a large chest of drawers sat.

"*Monsieur, secret pur toi, [Sir, a secret for you,]*" she said, walking over to the large armoire on the north wall. It was the same wall that was shared with the master, Webb surmised. With two hands and a great deal of effort, she pulled the armoire away from the wall, revealing a small passageway entrance.

"Bloody hell, a secret door." Webb was visibly shocked. Anne smiled and returned the armoire to its rightful position. "To hide, okay?"

"Hopefully, I won't need it," Webb said.

"You... sleep?" she asked.

"Yes, just a few hours."

She nodded and left the room, gently closing the door on her way out.

Webb removed his boots and his tunic, collapsing on the plush bed. It was not more than thirty seconds before he fell asleep, dreaming of being anywhere other than where he was.

———◆———

WEBB WOKE WITH A START. Reflexively reaching for his rifle, he sat up, getting his bearings. The late-day sun was drifting through the window, coating the room in an orange hue. Checking his watch, he rubbed his eyes, stood up, and stretched. Putting on his boots, he made his way into the hall. The double doors at the other end were open now, and Webb could see Anne milling about. As Webb entered the room, he could see that it was originally meant as a large sitting room, but instead was filled, like the downstairs foyer, with wounded soldiers. *Monsieur* Faucheux was also there, dressed down now compared to when Webb saw him earlier. He was busy changing a soldiers' bandages when he stood and waved Webb over. "You are awake, I see, Captain. I trust the room was to your liking?"

"Yes, thank you. That's the first rest I've gotten in... well, quite some time," Webb replied, walking over to help him tie up the loose bandages.

The men in this room were in much better shape it seemed, compared to the men downstairs in the foyer. Faucheux seemed to pick up on Webb's thoughts as he looked around and said, "Those that can walk up the stairs, we put here. Those that can't, we leave downstairs. Seems more and more are being left downstairs."

Webb took a second look around. There had to be over twenty men in this room alone.

"Bernard, do you by chance have a cigarette?"

He nodded, took one from his pocket, and handed it to Webb. "Outside, Captain, if you don't mind. For the men's sake."

Webb took the cigarette and stuck it behind his ear. He was headed back to his room when his stomach let out a loud grumble. He chuckled silently. With all that had gone on, food had been the last thing on his mind. His stomach had other ideas. Anne was on the other side of the room, tending to a soldier. Webb sidled up next to her.

"*Mademoiselle*, I beg of you, I'm famished. Would there be something to eat?"

Anne smiled back at Webb. She handed the man she was treating a crudely made bandage. Webb assumed it was made from bedsheets.

"Of course. Let me finish up here, and I will take you to the kitchen."

She left Webb to tend to some other soldiers, and he moved towards the door and then lingered near the stairwell. After a few moments, Anne came out, waving at Webb to follow her down the stairs. Soon they were in a hall off the foyer, walking towards the kitchen. The room was beautiful. Two large windows allowed for lots of natural light, and one was slightly ajar. A summery breeze brought the smell of fresh flowers into the room. In the center was a small wooden table and a couple of chairs.

Anne made her way over to the thick bright red cupboards, first removing a couple of plates and then opening a drawer and getting a knife and fork. She then set about making up the table. She pointed at the seat, gesturing for Webb to sit down. Webb obliged and watched as Anne went over to the icebox, grabbed two brown packages, together with a loaf of bread from the counter, and made her way back to the table.

Webb eagerly reached for the loaf, ripping off a large hunk no sooner than she set it on the table. Unwrapping the brown paper packages, Anne revealed a sizeable chunk of *Pont l'Eveque* cheese and a large piece of cured sausage. In between bites of the bread, Webb greedily reached for both and was soon shoveling it all into his mouth ravenously. The cheese was supple and creamy, and the sausage was salty and fatty. Webb couldn't get enough.

"You... very hungry, Captain. When... you eat last?" Anne asked the question as she waited by the stove, a gray kettle on the burner. In between rapid bites, Webb managed to say, "A couple of days," then ripped off another hunk of bread.

Once the low whistle of the kettle rang out, Anne poured herself a cup of tea and sat down across from Webb, smiling as she watched him eat.

"Tell me," Webb said, dabbing the corners of his mouth with the napkin, "and I mean no disrespect to you or your father, but how does a banker and his daughter end up caring for wounded soldiers?"

Anne looked confused for a moment, and Webb hazarded he might have used too many big words. But after a few reflective moments, she responded. "My mother. She was a... nurse."

"Ahh, I see. Well, she taught you lot well. I would love to meet her."

Anne stayed silent; her eyes focused on the mug of tea in front of her. It struck Webb at that moment that in all the time he had been at the house he had not seen a *Madame* Faucheux. He looked back at Anne, and the single tear coming down from her right eye told him what his statement had caused. "Oh, I'm sorry, my dear. I didn't mean to cause you any... what happened?"

"Unfortunately," a voice said behind Webb, "she passed away a few years ago. At least she will not have to see this pain inflicted upon France." Webb turned and saw Bernard enter the kitchen.

He went to the stove and poured himself a cup of tea. "But we try to honor her memory with the work we are doing here."

Bernard came over and put his hand on Anne's shoulder. She, in turn, placed hers on his and wiped away the tears with her other hand. "Your mother was strong, my dear Anne, and I hope that you have that same strength. We will need it, for the troubled times ahead."

She nodded and took a sip of her tea. "I know, Papa. I know."

Bernard took the third seat, laying his glasses on the table and rubbing the bridge of his nose. "My wife, she was a lovely woman, caring. I'm not afraid to say that in my earlier life, I was not. She was the best part of our family. And, I'm very proud to say that my daughter has all the best qualities from her. I truly believe that we are honoring her memory in the right way, with this house." He smiled and raised his cup towards Anne. She smiled back; the tears now gone from her eyes.

Webb finished his most recent bite and dusted his hands of bread crumbs. "I'm sure she was a shining light, *Monsieur* Faucheux." The Frenchman gave a curt nod in thanks. He then said something to Anne in French, and the young girl grabbed her mug and stood from the table. "*Au revoir*, Captain."

Captain Webb stood up from the table, as a proper gentleman should, when she left the kitchen. Passing by Webb, Anne gently touched his arm—a sign of affection—then continued on her way. Webb couldn't help but still feel guilty. "Monsieur Faucheux, if I offended you or your daughter, I apologize deeply…"

Bernard put down the teacup and held up his hands. "Do not worry, Captain. My daughter is made from much stronger material. But thinking of her mother still touches Anne very deeply."

"And you?" responded Webb.

"I made my peace with it, all those years ago. My daughter, this house, is all I have left. Well, and now the wounded men." Bernard sipped his tea. "Tell me, Captain, do you think you'll make it back to the front lines?"

"Honestly, I don't know. By my rough calculations, we're pretty deep behind German lines by now. I guess I'll head north, towards the Channel. Hope to make my way back to England."

"Perhaps there is still time for you and the British. France may be close to defeat, but I have to believe that there will be others that will fight on."

Webb grabbed his plate, taking it to the sink. "I hope you're right, *Monsieur*. I can tell you this, I'm not planning on letting the Germans take me prisoner anytime soon."

The two men sat in relative silence for a while, Bernard finishing his tea while Webb ate up the rest of the food in front of him. Webb went to leave when Bernard tried to get his attention.

"Oh Captain, before you go, I might put you to use tomorrow morning. Some soldiers need moving, and we could use the extra hands."

"Of course. I doubt I'll be able to sleep more than a few hours. Come get me when you're ready."

Bernard nodded his agreement. "Goodnight, Captain. Sleep well."

"And you, *Monsieur* Faucheux." With that, Webb headed out of the kitchen and back up the stairs. The soft, comforting coziness of a warm bed was calling to him.

The next morning, Webb woke with a start. *What time was it?*

He reached for his watch on the nightstand table.

7:18 am.

Damn, he had only planned on sleeping for a few hours. He swung his feet down off the bed and rubbed his face. Grabbing his tunic from the floor, he began to button it up when he heard a sound just outside the door.

The floorboard creaked. A moment later, it did it again.

Webb was frozen. His heart began to race. As silently as he could, he grabbed his rifle, checking to make sure a round was still chambered. He quickly looked over at the hiding spot Anne had shown him but realized in short order it was too far to go.

The knob on the door had started to turn.

Webb leveled the rifle at the entrance. If they were coming to take him, he wasn't going to go down without a fight. Seconds ticked by and tension filled every crevice of Webb's body. The door creaked open, and Webb moved his finger to the trigger. He'd make sure the ugly face of whatever German soldier came through would get a bullet squarely in it.

The wooden door opened... Webb steadied himself to shoot. Just a few more seconds and he'd have a clear shot...

A shrill yell pierced the air; at the same time there was a loud crash of glass hitting the floor. Webb quickly pointed his gun barrel to the sky, letting out a sigh of relief.

He recognized the person coming through the door. It was Anne.

"Anne!" he exclaimed, both relieved and still a bit jittery from the jolt of adrenaline. "I'm so sorry, my dear. I thought you were the bloody Germans!"

He put down the rifle and rushed over to her. She had collapsed against the door frame, no doubt scared at seeing a rifle pointed directly at her. Webb came over and saw what she had been carrying. A tray filled with delicious croissants, jam, coffee, and white china lay shattered on the ground. The coffee was starting to leave a dark stain on the claret-colored floor runner.

"You... scare me... Captain," Anne said, breathing heavily and wiping her head with a napkin. Realizing the mess she had caused, she bent down and began to clean.

"Please, my dear, allow me." Webb crouched down and started to pick up the shattered pieces of the cup. Once most of the mess had been cleaned up, Anne grabbed the tray and smiled at Captain Webb. "*Merci*... Captain," she said, heading out of the room and towards the stairs.

At the end of the hall, the large double doors to the drawing-room flew open. Bernard appeared, a concerned look on his face. "Oh... Captain, good morning. I heard a noise... Is everything okay?"

Webb looked at Anne and smiled. "Just a little accident, *Monsieur*. My apologies, I may have surprised your daughter with my rifle. In my defense, I thought the Germans may have taken the house."

Bernard furrowed his brow, then threw his hands up. "Well, I'm relieved they haven't!" He pointed to the floor below. "But, since you're here now, there are a few more soldiers that I will need your help in bringing upstairs." They would spend the better part of an hour moving the two men to their new station. Muscles strained, Webb took a moment after helping the second soldier to catch his breath.

"*Monsieur*, I need a cigarette."

Bernard bent down, helping one of the soldiers put his arm into a crudely-made swing. "Remember, outside Captain."

"Yes, I haven't forgotten." Webb went back down the hall and grabbed his rifle.

Rifle slung around his back, Webb descended the grand staircase and out the front doors. To his surprise, there was already a soldier outside smoking.

"Spare a light? Uh, sorry, lum... luuumi...?" Webb stumbled with his French, deciding on pointing at his cigarette to help. The soldier chuckled. He was a bit shorter than Webb, with dark brown hair and stout legs, and arms. It seemed he had a perpetual five o'clock shadow on his face, despite looking like he was in his early twenties. He walked over to Webb, visibly limping, his right ankle completely bandaged up.

"Your French is terrible, *monsieur*." He brought the lighter out of his pocket and pointed to it. "*Lumiere*." He held the lighter still so Webb could light his cigarette.

"Ah, *Lumiere, Merci,* sir," replied Webb, holding out his hand. "Captain Theodore Webb."

The man placed the lighter back in his pocket and grabbed Webb's hand. "Sergeant Franck Chabert. Pleasure to meet you, Captain."

"What happened to the ankle, Sergeant?"

Chabert patted his leg with his free hand. "I twisted it in a ditch, retreating from the front. Luckily, some of my squad brought me here. The Faucheuxes took us in, and soon others began to show up," he said, taking a drag from his cigarette, and giving Captain Webb a long look. "Are you staying with us long, *mon ami*?"

"Not if I can help it. Just resting up for a bit, and then gonna try to make it back to the Allied lines." Webb looked off towards the horizon, towards the trees he had run through yesterday. He had been lucky to lose those Germans soldiers, but it was only a matter of time before they closed in on him. The sun was starting to crest over the treetops and the warmth of early spring would be enveloping them shortly. Webb took a long drag, letting the smoke stream from his nose.

Suddenly, in the distance, he heard some rustling.

"Sergeant, do you hear that?" Webb asked, straining his eyes to look along the tree line.

"No, *mon ami*, I cannot hear a sound."

"Perhaps we best go inside." Webb stubbed out his cigarette and made for the door. Franck shrugged his shoulders and followed suit. As Webb walked through the door, he felt a hand on his shoulder. He turned to see a panicked Franck, gesturing towards the trees. Webb instantly recognized what was coming through them.

A line of German soldiers.

"What should we do, Captain?" breathed a visibly scared Sergeant Chabert, limping into the foyer.

Webb shut the door. "We will stand a better chance of holding them off in the house. Do we have any weapons?"

Sergeant Chabert shook his head. "We might have a few rifles around, but no ammunition."

Webb swore, and then rubbed his hand over his face. They only had a few short minutes before the soldiers reached the house. He had maybe three more bullets left in his clip. It was impossible, they would never be able to fight off the Germans. At that moment, Anne came down the stairs hurriedly.

"Germans! You... hide." she pointed back up the stairs towards the rooms. Webb was slightly confused for a moment or two until he realized what she was talking about.

The hidden passage behind the armoire.

"What about you and your father?" Webb asked concernedly. Anne waved her hand to dismiss his comment. She grabbed his arm to pull him up the stairs.

"Wait," Webb said. "The Sergeant can walk, he's coming with me." Webb stepped back down and put his arm under Chabert's.

Anne took a long look at Webb, as did Franck.

"My friend, I will be fine. Besides, you will move much faster without me."

Webb shook his head vigorously.

"If I'm going to survive, I need someone that knows the terrain and speaks the language. And you're the most able-bodied chap I've seen since I got here. I need your help, Sergeant."

Franck opened his mouth to speak but ended up saying little. He nodded his head slightly, resigning himself to Webb's logic. Webb took that cue to put Franck's arm on top of his while gesturing for Anne to take the other one.

She did the same on the other side, and together they helped him up the stairs. They moved as quickly as possible down the hall to Webb's room. While Anne held Franck, Webb dropped his rifle and pulled open the armoire. It creaked open, and Webb could see into the dark passage. It was more spacious than he imagined and large enough for at least three or four people to move around comfortably. He came back and helped Anne put Franck in the passageway, and as she turned to leave, Webb grabbed her wrist.

"Please, *mademoiselle*, do not go."

She smiled up at Webb, and even though she was younger than him, it was a reassuring smile that a mother would give a child. She rested her other hand on his, tapped it twice, pulled it away, and shut the door. It clicked shut, and Webb could hear her footsteps back along the floor and out of the room. All they could do now was hope, and pray, that the Germans didn't find them. Rules of war dictated that injured soldiers would be given help, but if *Monsieur* Faucheux or his daughter were found to be harboring enemy able-bodied soldiers, the consequences might be dire.

Webb felt guilty; he had begged them to stay, and now he had put everyone in danger. He sat back, leaning against his rifle, wondering what this day would bring next.

The passage was filled with acrid air and musty odor but it seemed to be well insulated, as they could only hear muffled voices and faint sounds. Webb kept his rifle at the ready, his ears pressed to the wall. There was a flurry of steps up the stairs, and Webb could make out some shouting in German. The soldiers had made it into the house and they were no doubt searching for him. He looked over at Sergeant Chabert, trying to make himself comfortable in the tight space.

The two men sat there in silence for what seemed forever until that silence was broken by the sharp tonal notes of the German language. The words were barely audible, but they were echoing from somewhere further down the passage. Webb got up, slowly making his way down the tiny corridor. By his estimation, the passage stretched behind the wall of the master bedroom.

Sure enough, at the other end, there was an air duct near the floor. Webb bent down and was able to see four German soldiers.

They were wearing different uniforms than the men he had encountered in the woods earlier. One was quite large, and Webb could see he was an officer, as the other men routinely saluted him when they entered the room. He leaned against the fireplace, watching, but saying nothing. Webb waved for Sergeant Chabert to come closer. He would need his help to translate.

The lead German stepped forward, gesturing wildly while he spoke. Faucheux did not respond. Angrily, the German started switching to French. Chabert whispered to Webb. "They are asking him if he has seen a British soldier."

Webb gulped.

So, his worst fear was confirmed. Had they tracked him directly here?

It had been quite some time since he escaped from the patrol. Did those soldiers go back and get more help? That would explain these men and their uniforms.

His attention was drawn back to the room as the German began talking loudly again, with Bernard responding to him in an even tone. Webb turned to Chabert, who once again translated. "The Germans insist you are here. They want to search the house... room by room."

"What did *Monsieur* Faucheux say?" said Webb, trying to shift his weight as quietly as possible.

"He agreed to let them search the house, but not to disturb the wounded soldiers."

Three of the Germans left the room, leaving one behind to watch Bernard. Around the house, there was a cacophony of footsteps, as the soldiers moved from room to room, no doubt conducting their search. Both Webb and Chabert sat there, trying not to make a sound. At some points when the footsteps came closer, they tried not to breathe even. Being cramped in this tiny space began to aggravate Chabert's ankle a bit, but he managed to keep his movement to a minimum. Their very freedom depended on it.

After what seemed like an eternity, the Germans returned to the master bedroom. This time, the large German began to speak. Webb couldn't quite see through the grate, but the man truly was an imposing figure. He towered over his fellow soldiers and dwarfed Bernard. While the previous soldier had shouted angrily and waved his arms, this giant German instead spoke in a direct, but almost soft manner. Chabert once again leaned in close. "He is asking *Monsieur* Faucheux one last time to give you up. Or else..."

Or else? Webb immediately felt the pit in his stomach grow larger. His presence here had put the target on not only Bernard but Anne as well. He had to do something to stop the situation from getting worse. He moved away from the vent to stand up when Chabert put his hand on Webb.

"Don't, *mon ami*, you will spend the war in a prison camp... or worse, they will just kill you."

Before Webb could respond, they watched as the large German waved his arm at two soldiers. They came over and pushed Bernard down by the shoulders into one of his leather-back chairs. They kept a hand on each of his shoulders so Bernard couldn't move. Off to their left, they heard the door open, and another soldier entered the room, carrying Anne, who had been kicking and fighting until the soldier released her. Webb tried to move again, but Chabert kept the hand on his shoulder. The larger German removed his Luger from the holster and laid it on the side table. He said something to Bernard, and the translation was just as quick.

"He told Bernard he's going to count to five..." The large German grabbed the pistol and calmly pointed it at Anne. She let out a scream and said something to her father, who tried to reassure her with some words of his own. Meanwhile, the German kept counting down. Finally, as he got down to the last number, Bernard held up both his hands.

Webb and Chabert both held their breath. Would this kindhearted gentleman give them up?

Time seemed to stop in the room when finally, Bernard said something that even Webb knew what it meant. "*Je t'aime*, Anne. *[I love you, Anne.]*"

She began to cry, and Webb and Chabert watched in amazement as Bernard wrenched himself free and lunged at the German. While he certainly surprised the German a bit, the large man was too quick and brought the pistol to bear. The sound was deafening in the small room as the German fired two quick shots into the gut of Bernard. He collapsed back, knocking over the leather-back chair, crying out in pain. The German got up, sauntered over to where Bernard was writhing in pain, leveled the pistol, and fired a third shot. Bernard stopped moving. Anne was sobbing uncontrollably now, while Webb and Chabert could barely contain their seething anger. The German walked back toward his men, which gave Webb a clear look at his face now. The features would be forever burned into Webb's memory, especially the large scar that stretched down the right side of the man's face. Unbridled rage coursed through Webb, and it took all his strength not to burst through the vent.

The Germans shared a laugh, and then the large one with the scar began giving orders. Some of the soldiers left the room, but two remained. The German with the scar bent down, and both Webb and Chabert instinctively moved back from the vent, even though he couldn't possibly see them. He said something to Anne, and Chabert looked up to the heavens, his eyes closed.

"What? What did he say?" whispered Webb.

Chabert shook his head as if trying to build up the courage to say the words. "He said that it was a very brave thing that her father did and that he believes him..." Chabert trailed off.

Anne sobbed louder and choked back some screams. "I don't understand..." Webb said before Chabert continued. "...For her father's insolence, they are going to execute every single man in this house. And the men will then have their way with... with... her."

Webb sat there in shock. The pit in his stomach was the size of a boulder now, and he felt physically ill. He tried to move away from the vent, guilt racking his body and rage filling his heart.

Then, the shots started to ring out throughout the house. The Germans were starting to execute the French soldiers. The only thing Webb and Chabert could do was weep in the silence of their hiding place, helpless to do anything at all. The sounds were horrific, shouting and cursing in French, coupled with men pleading for their very lives, which was quickly followed by a gunshot. It continued this way for the following half hour, each shot and voice clawing at the men in the passage.

After some time, the sounds of the massacre died down. Both men sat in silence, patiently listening for any clue as to what would happen next. Then, when it came, it was something they were both dreading.

A blood-curdling scream of pain. It was from Anne.

Webb pressed his ear against the wall; the soldiers' and Anne's voices became slightly louder, which meant they must be in the room adjacent to their hiding spot. Webb's room.

Both men froze.

Anne screamed again, and Webb and Franck could hear the soldiers laughing. Gently picking up his rifle, he started to make his way to the secret door. Franck, leaning against the wall for stability, grabbed Webb by the arm and shook his head back and forth. He then took his thumb and drew a line across his throat, pointing silently towards the screams. Webb understood what he meant—that they would surely die if he went out there. But it was his fault the Germans were here. Maybe if he could surprise them...

Franck tugged on his arm again, and with the last pull, Webb turned to face the Frenchman, but the last tug has loosened Webb's grip on his rifle, and it clattered to the floor. Both Webb and Franck pressed themselves against the walls, both trying not to make a sound.

Shit... thought Webb. *Maybe they didn't hear it.*

The laughing outside in the room had stopped, and the German voices began to speak in quieter tones. Webb couldn't be sure, but the inflection sounded like they were asking questions to each other. Then, suddenly, they heard a knock on the wall, then another.

Damn, he thought, *so the Germans had heard the rifle dropping, but they couldn't quite figure out where the sound came from.*

More knocking on the walls, and more questions in German. Webb was sweating heavily now.

The Germans were getting closer, and closer...

ON THE OTHER SIDE OF the wall, Anne could see with her own eyes what was unfolding. She was pinned to the bed by one of the German soldiers, his strong hands keeping her still. He kept staring down at her, smiling, which turned her stomach. But she also noticed that more and more he was paying attention to the rest of the soldiers searching along the wall. She too had heard the sound and knew it was only a matter of time before they found the entrance, and the two men hiding there. Anne lay there, feeling utterly helpless. She knew if she did nothing, the men in there would be doomed. She was their only hope. The image of her father being shot entered her mind, and tears began to stream down her face. It was now or never, and Anne decided right then and there that she would do more than just tend to wounded soldiers in this war. She slipped her left leg in between the Germans' legs and watched his face. When he turned back to his comrades, she took her chance.

Anne brought her leg up swiftly, catching the German soldier in his most vulnerable spot. His grip on her immediately loosened, and Anne kicked again, this time with her other foot. It connected with his chest, and he let out an audible groan, dropping his rifle and falling to the floor. She wasted no time reaching down and grabbing it.

Once the rifle was in her hands, she tried to steady herself. The gun was much larger than she anticipated, and she had trouble holding it up. She finally managed to aim and pointed it at the Germans tapping on the wall. Squeezing the trigger, the muzzle flashed and the power of the gun nearly knocked her off her feet. The bullet impacted the wall above the Germans, and all three of them immediately ducked.

Good, Anne thought, *now I've got their attention*. She tried to reload the rifle, but couldn't quite get the bolt to pull back, so she threw down the rifle and ran out the bedroom door. She could hear their rapid footsteps chasing after her. The staircase was right in front of her if she could just make it down...

As her foot touched the first step, she felt a giant hand grab her shoulder and jerk her backward. She was now face to face with the large *SS* officer. The man who had brutally murdered her father. His grip was strong, and he spoke in French to her. "Tsk, tsk, tsk, my dear, where are you going in such a hurry?"

His eyes pierced into her, and she could only stare back. There was nothing there, just cold, unflinching malice. He grabbed a handful of her hair and wrenched her head back. Anne let out a cry of pain. He dragged her by that handful along the floor, back towards her father's bedroom. She kicked and screamed, but it did little good. Once they reached the bedroom, he threw her down to the floor. He continued to talk to her as she lay on the ground. "You French, you're all the same. You think you are better than everyone else. It's the same with the Jews. But like them, the French will see how we Germans like to do things."

Webb, hearing the voices now coming from the bedroom, gently walked over to the grate and crouched down. He could see Anne now, prostrate on the floor, the German standing over her.

"*Vive... le... France.*" Anne stuttered, attempting to push herself up from the floor. The *SS* officer came over, and put his boot onto her back, letting the full brunt of his weight press her down to the floor. "This is where you belong, French. Under... my... boot."

Anne whimpered as she struggled under the leather jackboot. For a brief moment, she looked around for salvation—someone to save her...anything. Her eyes fixed on the vent along the wall, and she saw Webb. They shared a brief moment, Webb nodding his head, and Anne sharing a small smile, albeit a brief one. The large German chuckled and removed his pistol. He slowly aimed it at Anne's head and pulled the trigger.

BANG!

The sound broke Webb's heart. He looked at Franck, who just closed his eyes and shook his head. Webb leaned his head against the grate. She didn't deserve to die that way. In between his self-guilt, Webb noticed that more soldiers had entered the bedroom. One of the men was hunched over and seemed to be grabbing his groin.

"You fools," shouted the German officer, "do I have to do everything myself?"

One of them tried to speak up, but the German with the scar shut him down immediately. "I don't want to hear it! Now, help the rest of the men finish up and let's get out of here."

The Germans left the room, and Webb collapsed on the ground, broken and in a state of despair. Chabert started to cry, tears rolling down his cheek. Then he started to smile, which caught Webb off-guard.

"What could make you smile at a time like this?" asked the Captain.

Chabert wiped his face on his sleeve, "Don't you see, *mon ami*, don't you see what she did for us? She saved our lives by giving hers. That brave little girl."

Webb looked back through the grate into the bedroom, at the bloodied bodies of his hosts. *They were so innocent*, he thought to himself, *just two people trying to help as best they could. Now, look at them. Dead, sacrificed for me and Chabert.* Webb wished for a drink, badly.

After a few more hours, the screaming, the footsteps, and the shots seemed to stop. Webb and Chabert, with much consternation between them both, decided they should venture out. They pushed the secret door gently, trying to listen for any sound of the Germans. Once they were satisfied that they were gone, they set about the house, trying to gather any supplies they could. The house was a bloodbath. Webb and Franck went room by room, checking for survivors.

There were none.

As Franck entered one of the rooms, he cried out, "*Mon Dieu*! [*My God!*]" and collapsed to his knees.

So many of his wounded countrymen, executed in cold blood; it was more than the good Sergeant could bear to witness. Webb wandered back to the master bedroom. He crouched down, next to Anne, and tried to brush the hair from her face. It was matted in blood from the gunshot. Looking at her young face, Webb was overcome with emotion; he put his hand to his face as tears began to stream down. Brave little Anne. Defiant to the very end. She didn't deserve this fate. Nor the wounded men, nor *Monsieur* Faucheux.

Webb's blood boiled, and he clenched his fists till his fingers turned white. Something had to be done. Sergeant Chabert limped into the room and winced as he looked on at the corpses of the Faucheuxes.

"Well, *mon ami*, what do you want to do now?" asked Franck, leaning himself against the door frame. Webb reached down and removed the handkerchief from Anne's head. It was bloodied and burnt from the bullet.

He stood and approached Franck. "We can't stay here. The Germans could be back at any moment." He clutched the handkerchief to his chest.

"*Qui*, I agree with you, Captain. I know a place, but we can't go looking like we do," replied Chabert, pointing at his clothing. Webb looked around the room, settling on Bernard's closet. "We might be able to find something in there." The men stripped out of their uniforms and grabbed some of Bernard's clothing. Surprisingly, the suits they found fit Webb perfectly, but Franck was smaller than Bernard, so it was a little baggy on him. Nonetheless, now dressed in civilian clothes, the men started to leave. Passing by Anne once more, Webb knelt. He brushed a couple of strands of hair from her face. The guilt was beginning to rack him.

Once outside, Webb pulled Franck aside. "Sergeant, we have to swear on it."

"Swear on what?"

Webb removed the bloody handkerchief from his pocket, holding it out for the Frenchman to see. Franck was initially uncertain but then nodded his agreement solemnly. He held up his finger, then limped back into the house. He came back out holding a bayonet.

Webb took the bayonet from Franck. "Promise me something, Franck. Promise me, that if we ever see that German again, we will get revenge, for Bernard... for... for Anne."

"I..."

"PROMISE ME! You have to me promise me..." shouted Webb, grabbing Franck by the shoulders.

"I... promise. We will avenge her. On pain of... death" said Franck. He took the bayonet and felt the blade slice into the flesh on his hand. He gripped the handkerchief.

Webb echoed his statement, "On pain... of death." He also took the bayonet, cut his hand, and gripped the handkerchief. They stood there for a few moments, squeezing tightly.

Then, Webb left Franck outside while he salvaged what he could for supplies. He soon came back out, put his arm under Franck, and both soldiers headed off into the forest. Webb hoped that they would blend in with refugees and somehow get back to Allied lines. Walking through the brush, there was one thing that Captain Theodore Webb and Sergeant Franck Chabert knew beyond a shadow of a doubt.

The throbbing cuts on each of their hands and the blood-stains on the handkerchief would be their reminders.

CHAPTER TWELVE

"FRANCK AND I WERE TRAPPED behind German lines, running for our lives. We hid out on a farm for three weeks before we managed to smuggle ourselves aboard a fishing vessel. France had fallen, and the continent belonged to the Nazis. These last four years, this bastard over here was never far from our thoughts." Major Webb paused, seemingly to catch his breath. He walked around the table to Vahlen and grabbed him by the hair. "This man," said Webb, pointing at Vahlen as he spoke, "he's a taker of lives. The Grim goddamn Reaper. He sows destruction wherever he goes." Webb slapped Vahlen upside the head, drawing an angry look from the German.

"My God, sir, you never told me this," said Lieutenant Martin, visibly shocked.

"I never told anyone, Lieutenant. You see, after the Germans were done with their orgy of violence—after they were done killing an innocent young girl and her father, Franck and I had to wade through all the... dead. We... we couldn't even bury them." Webb's eyes welled up, and he looked over at Franck. Webb now looked down to the table, at the bloody handkerchief. "And we swore on that day, Franck and I, we would make him suffer as everyone in that house did."

"A pact of vengeance then?" asked Sergeant Donalds.

"Exactly, Sergeant. A pact of vengeance."

Vahlen coughed intermittently due to his injuries and said, "I... remember that house. So, you... were there after all. You are lucky we did not find you; I would've done to you what I did to them..."

"SHUT UP! You don't get to speak," Webb shouted, striking the butt of his gun across Vahlen's face.

Teicher winced at the audible crunch, briefly looking away. Vahlen doubled over, the gash in his head visibly gushing blood now. Webb was breathing heavy, bracing himself against the table. Donalds could see it now, see it on Webb's face. He was tired... very tired.

"Sergeant, I believe it's time for you to take your men and leave." Webb sighed, rubbing his eyes. "As you can see, Franck and I have much to finish."

Donalds stood, waving at Appleyard to do the same. "So, what, you've got some sort of death wish, Major? You're going to torture this man to death, and go out in a blaze of glory?"

Webb approached Sergeant Donalds, jabbing a finger into his face. "You've got some nerve, Sergeant. Speaking to a superior officer in that tone. That's exactly what we are going to do. This piece of filth deserves everything he gets, and then some. For everyone at the house, and probably countless others over the years. Franck and I, you see...we are willing to make the ultimate sacrifice ourselves to make sure that he doesn't do anything... ever again."

Donalds thought carefully before he spoke next. "I... I can't let you do this, Major. Despite your story, despite what he's done, I can't allow it. It's not right."

"You just don't understand, do you, Sergeant? You won't stop us... We... I need to do this."

Donalds stood up and removed his pistol, pointing it at Webb. The room fell silent.

To the left, Martine, who had been sitting quietly, stood up. She began to gesticulate wildly and launched into a tirade in French. Everyone's eyes were on her, and when she was finished, she stared vehemently at Major Vahlen.

"What did she say?" questioned Donalds.

Franck cleared his throat. "She said that the German Major shot a child when he arrived in town and that if we weren't all here, she would remove his body parts, one by one."

At that last statement, Martine smiled.

Donalds found that he had some burgeoning respect for the young French woman. Still, he couldn't let this happen. No man deserved to be tortured, even one as detestable as Major Vahlen.

"That may be true, but I can't let you torture that man. Any of you. It wouldn't be proper."

Webb moved closer to Donalds so that the barrel of the Canadian's gun touched his chest. "DO IT, Sergeant. Pull the trigger. I know you want to." He pointed at his head, his hand shaking. "Every night, I see those images of that house in my dreams."

"You need help, Major. That much is clear now. So, I'm willing to excuse your earlier behavior, and I know that in your heart, you don't want to do this," said Donalds sternly.

"You don't know me, Sergeant. Let's be completely honest, you're going to have to kill me to make me stop."

The tension in the room was palpable. Donalds was wrestling with the notion of shooting his superior officer, in cold blood. And over a German. If he wasn't so angry, he would have laughed at the irony.

But then he noticed something on the periphery. Franck raised his machine gun in the direction of Donalds. Appleyard, seated at the table, also noticed.

"Whoa! What do you think you're doing, my friend?" announced the young Canadian, standing up and raising his rifle squarely at Franck. Donalds's hand trembled on his gun. His finger lightly brushed the trigger. The anger he felt, at being used, letting down Mills, the danger they had all faced—it all boiled to the surface. There was a very real possibility they could die right now.

He hesitated for a moment, adjusting and re-adjusting the grip on his pistol.

"You can't do it, can you Sergeant?" taunted Webb, pressing himself against the muzzle further. It seemed like time had stopped. Donalds and Webb locked eyes, waiting for the other to flinch.

After what seemed an eternity, Donalds finally shook his head and lowered his pistol. He placed it back in its holster. The tension, while still high, dissipated slightly.

When Webb turned away, Donalds called out, "Hey! Major."

The Brit turned back, and Donalds swung his fist. It connected on his cheek, knocking the man backward.

Donalds shook his hand in pain. *Damn, that hurt, but it also felt really good,* he had to admit. If he was honest with himself, he was a few short seconds away from pulling that trigger. This had surprised even him. Teicher said something to Vahlen in German, and the two shared a laugh.

Webb stood back up, wiping the blood from his mouth on his sleeve. He chuckled a little.

"You see, Sergeant, despite your altruistic morals, you know... you know you want justice for those people too." Webb grabbed a couple of glasses, set them down on the table, and poured gin into each. He handed one to Sergeant Donalds. "Have a drink, Sergeant. We've both earned it, don't you think?"

Donalds was still rubbing his hand gingerly, and he pushed the glass away with the other hand. He got up to leave the room. Private Appleyard and Lintz also stood to leave, falling in behind their Sergeant.

"No, in fact, Major, we've done nothing... nothing at all. The only thing that was accomplished was you put us all in grave danger."

Major Webb shrugged his shoulders, finished his glass, and quickly poured another. "It's war, Sergeant. Men die. I have my reasons for what I've done, and those consequences I will live with. But after tonight, my conscience will be clear."

"To me, Major, it seems that what you're quite good at is putting lives in danger." At that statement, Donalds flashed back to what Mills had said to him outside of Cori. The man's words were, at the time, insubordinate and unfounded. But as Donalds grappled with Webb's betrayal, he realized Mills had been right. He had put them in danger, even if it was inadvertently. His zealousness to pursue this mission had blinded him to the fact that Webb had ulterior motives. He hung his head in sorrow briefly until the anger began to return. "First it was that father and daughter and now... me and my men."

Webb turned away from Donalds, swirling the gin in the glass, looking out the window.

"Him," Donalds said, pointing across to Vahlen, "him I actually understand, disgusting as he is. But you, Major, I will never understand. You're a goddamn alcoholic pretending you're a soldier. You're lucky that I haven't put you down."

Webb went to open his mouth to speak but instead said nothing.

Donalds turned to Martin. "Lieutenant, we are leaving. You can join us if you like."

Lieutenant Martin took the glass spurned by Donalds and finished it in one go. "Major, these revelations are most disturbing. You used me. You used these men. I never thought you were capable of something like this."

Webb's face twisted into a bemused grimace. He got up and stood in front of the large bay window, avoiding looking at his men. "Good evening, gentlemen."

Donalds wanted to say what was on his mind but then thought better of it. It was pointless. Major Webb was a zealot and could not be reasoned with. He grabbed his gun and pack and opened the drawing-room double doors. Lieutenant Martin and the two other Canadians followed him out. They all gave Franck a long stare as they left the room, and received an equally terse one back from him. The men started to trudge back towards the house where Corporal Mills was being treated, with no words spoken between them. The news that the mission had all been part of Major Webb's vendetta with Major Vahlen had hit them hard, especially Lieutenant Martin.

Finally, it was Martin that dared to speak first. "I want to apologize, Sergeant. I feel that I have played some unwitting part of this charade."

"Save your apology, Lieutenant. You can buy us all a drink when we're the hell out of Occupied France," barked Sergeant Donalds, quickening his pace. Once they reached the house, they saw Doctor Lelievre wiping his hands as he stood outside. "Your friend is... stable now, but he needs a better surgeon than me. I have done all I can do."

"Thank you, Doctor, we are very grateful. I suggest you lock yourself away, more Germans are coming," said Martin, patting the Doctor on the back.

Donalds said his thanks to Doctor Lelievre as well, moving over to the prone Corporal Mills. He was lying still, a large, crude bandage wrapped around his torso. Donalds cursed under his breath. *This was Webb's fault. Damn that bastard.* And, out of earshot of the other men, Donalds cursed himself as well. He grabbed a cloth and dabbed Mills's forehead. He would make sure Mills made it back to England, one way or the other. He owed the man that much.

The men set about fashioning a crude stretcher out of some old pieces of lumber they found strewn about the town. They then lifted the comatose soldier onto it. Carefully, they maneuvered him out the doorway and started making their way back towards the truck. It was a difficult climb over the hill with the stretcher, taking much longer than expected since they had to be careful jostling Mills. At the truck, after helping place Mills on the floor, Lintz went to the cab and started the engine as a test. Donalds and Appleyard sat in the back, sharing a cigarette. Donalds was particularly preoccupied in thought, thinking back to the first day he signed up for the First Special Service Force. His training officer, a rather ornery man by the name of Saunders, had told him, "Boy, there are going to be times when you will be knee-deep in shit. When that happens, trust in your chain of command, and you'll be alright." Donalds chuckled at that thought—if only Saunders could see the amount of shit Donalds had gotten himself and his men into.

"The Krauts will be here shortly, no doubt. We can get back to the field, but will they send another plane for us?" Donalds realized he was voicing his inner thoughts.

Martin, also taking in the night's events on the bed of the truck, sat up abruptly at Donalds's question. "What do you mean, another plane?"

"After we jumped, as I got my bearings on the ground, I watched our plane pass over the treetops. It was hit with AA fire, a helluva lot. It burned up, poor bastards."

Martin looked away from Donalds and slammed his fist into the side of the truck, visibly distraught.

"What is it? Wait, let me guess... Major Webb screws us again?" asked Donalds.

"Yes Sergeant, sadly you are correct. That plane was our only way back home."

"Wait, what? How can that be?" asked Lintz.

"Operational secrecy, you see, Private Lintz. Major Webb kept the entire plan out of the regular channels at SOE—I should say he and I did. We and the aircrew were the only ones aware of this plan."

"Which means, what?" piped up Appleyard, taking an interest in the conversation.

"Which means, my dear young Appleyard, if what Sergeant Donalds saw is true—that the plane was indeed shot down—then we have no way home," said Martin, slumping against the side of the truck.

The Canadians stood silent. Donalds particularly stood fuming, beaten down by the evening's events. He had suffered many close calls before, and always when he thought his time was up, he had managed to scrape through. But tonight, it just might be the very night that this war would claim him. They needed to find a way back to England. They had to.

Then, an idea struck him. A potentially life-saving idea. He couldn't believe he hadn't thought of it before. "Lieutenant, if you were able to contact London, could you get us a ride home?"

Martin thought for a moment, then nodded his head. "Yes, in theory, but we don't have a radio."

"Correct, we don't. But I'm pretty sure the Germans do. Remember when Franck came back to the room in the house. How did they know that German reinforcements were coming...? I bet there was a radio in that house."

Martin clapped his hands together and stood straight up. "I'll be damned! You're right, Sergeant."

Donalds put his hands on Appleyards's shoulders. "Private, I want you to go back and..."

"No," Lieutenant Martin said, interrupting their conversation. Both men turned and stared at the Brit.

"Sir, what do you mean... no?" asked Donalds.

"I mean... no, I can't let you, in good conscience, risk your men any further. I'm partly responsible for this... I have to fix it."

Martin turned to leave, but Donalds stopped him. "Why don't I come with you, sir, in case something happens."

The offer was genuine. Despite what Major Webb had done, Donalds could not in good conscience hold Martin responsible as well. Martin shook his head and patted the Canadian on the shoulder. "Thank you, Sergeant. I believe that your company will be well needed."

"Appleyard," Donalds called out, waving for the freckled-faced private to come join them. "I'm leaving you in charge, son. Keep an eye on the Corporal for me, will you?"

Appleyard snapped to attention, giving a curt salute.

Lintz, now leaning against the truck, came to see them off. All the men, conscious of the danger, stood in silent acknowledgment. A few moments later, Martin and Donalds grabbed their weapons and started back down towards the town.

"Oh sir, before you go, a word?" Appleyard said, walking away from the truck.

"Of course, Private."

Once they were out of earshot, Appleyard started.

"Before you go, sir, I want you to know that I know what you're thinking. It's not your fault."

Donalds looked up, shifting uneasily.

"Is that so, Private? Please, tell me, how am I not responsible for you all?"

"Begging your pardon, sir, but you shouldn't blame yourself. We all agreed to this mission, and we were all deceived, even the Lieutenant."

Appleyard finished his statement, acutely aware that perhaps he had spoken too much out of turn, and turned to look at the horizon.

Donalds smiled. "Private, do you want to make Sergeant someday?"

"Yes, sir, I suppose I do."

"Then let me give you a little advice—don't go around thinking you know what's in your superior officers' heads, they don't like that too much."

"Yes, sir." Appleyard gave Donalds a sheepish, curt nod, and then started to give his rifle a check.

"But… just 'cause I said you shouldn't do it; doesn't mean you weren't right. Thank you, Private."

Donalds patted the young soldier on the shoulder and turned back towards Lieutenant Martin. It was now Appleyard's turn to smile.

⟹ ◉ ⟸

LT. MARTIN AND SERGEANT Donalds double-timed it back down the road and up over the hill. They passed through the light brush, down the hill to the edge of the town. It looked solemn now, much more than before. None of the citizens Donalds had freed from the church had dared venture from their homes. Blinds were firmly shut, and lights non-existent. Donalds didn't blame them.

Keeping to the slightly darkened shadows of the buildings, the men moved quickly. The thought of daylight approaching, and truckloads of German soldiers appearing at any moment, spurred them along.

Donalds saw the pensive look that had come over Martin's face since they left the house the first time. He also had been shocked at the clandestine manipulation by his commanding officer, but he suspected that Martin felt worse. He considered himself a very honorable person, and to risk the lives of men they didn't know for private vendettas infuriated him. At the moment that Webb had revealed his secret to them all, Donalds had found his anger bubbling to the surface uncontrollably. With the gun pressed firmly to Webb's chest, he had been agonizingly close to pulling the trigger. Martin hadn't so much as moved to stop Donalds. He was as much a pawn as the rest of the Canadians.

The sun was now just beginning to crest on the horizon, and the town was illuminated with an eerie glow, the color of which was tangerine. They passed by the bodies of the dead SS men that they had battled earlier that morning. As he approached the center of town, they heard the faint rumble of an engine. Moving quicker, they ducked down into a small alley and peered around the corner, trying to see the direction of the vehicle the loud sound was coming from. Locating it finally, they realized it was coming from the other end of the town, near the church and house where Webb was conducting his torture chamber. Both men shared a side-eyed look as they came to the realization of what the sound was.

It was a car.

More specifically, a German *Kubelwagen*. Dammit, they were too late. The German reinforcements had arrived.

Peering around the corner, Martin looked on as the car pulled up in front of the house. He watched on as three soldiers stepped out from the vehicle. Inside the vehicle, Martin could see a young boy, not much older than fifteen. He had close cropped brown hair, along with a cream colored over-shirt stained in patches. A loose strap from his suspenders hung loosely at his side. His head hung low and from look of him his hands seemed bound behind his back. Two of the Germans, one with stocky features and ill-fitting helmet, followed behind what looked to be a junior officer. Barking to the men, the officer seemed unhappy to Donalds eyes and ears. Slightly shorter than the soldier he was speaking with, his facial features were angular and gracile. Reaching back with his gloved hand, he smoothed a loose piece of golden blonde hair back onto his head, before replacing his cap. They both took a small look around, then headed back towards the house. The third stood in the car, watching over the young boy.

"You see that there, Sergeant? We're sunk, aren't we?" asked Martin, his eyes as big as saucers.

"Well, it's not going to be easy, if that's what you mean, Lieutenant. But that's why I'm here."

Martin leaned back against the wall of the house and closed his eyes. Fear had paralyzed him. There was no way he could deal with German reinforcements and his renegade commanding officer at the same time. The task, he had to admit to himself, seemed impossible. He clenched and unclenched his hands. *Deep breaths*, he told himself, *deep breaths*.

"You okay, Lieutenant? You look a little... pale."

Martin shook his head and opened his eyes.

"I... I... think so... You'll forgive me, Sergeant. Seems my stomach is doing backflips."

Donalds smirked, then crouch-walked towards the jittery Lieutenant.

"You have men depending on you...and that means you don't have the luxury of being scared. Now, pick up your weapon, and let's come up with a plan."

Martin opened his eyes, re-focused, and stood up. Grabbing his gun, he took the corner next to Donalds, staring down the road.

It was still just a single car.

Not only that, but the German he saw in the car earlier was also now gone. *Maybe this was just more of Major Vahlen's men,*

Martin thought to himself, *and we aren't going to have to face a whole German division!*

"It's just the one car still. Might just be some more of Vahlen's men," mused Donalds, pushing up his helmet to scratch his scalp. "They'll be busy with our good friend, Major Webb. I think it's now or never, Lieutenant."

"I agree, what's your plan?"

Donalds pulled his helmet back down, and his facial expression turned hard. "Follow me and stay low."

Guns locked and loaded, Martin and Donalds moved along the line of houses towards their goal, like shadows.

"HALT!"

The voice was German, and as Donalds turned back, he realized that he had made a critical mistake. The soldier from the car had reappeared and was yelling at them, making motions for them to lay their guns on the ground. Donalds saw Martin hesitate—he wagered the man was contemplating if he could get off a few shots before the German did the same—but then acquiesced to the soldier's demands. Crestfallen, he and Martin started to lay their weapons gently on the cobblestone and raise their hands above their heads.

The two Allied soldiers stood there, staring down the barrel of a German semi-automatic rifle. The soldier, using his weapon to gesture at the commandos, pointed to the wall of the house opposite to where Webb and Vahlen were. Both men, hesitant to move at first, stood fast.

BANG!

The German had fired a round into the air. They slowly shuffled over—Martin first, followed by Donalds. The Canadian watched as Martin held his hands up, his legs knocking together.

"Steady, Lieutenant, steady. No sudden movements," Donalds said, in a calm, reassuring tone.

"I'm... I'm... dreadfully sorry, Sergeant... for... for everything..." Lieutenant Martin stammered out. Both men expected the execution to come any moment.

Just then, something rather unexpected occurred.

From behind the German, the young boy Donalds had seen earlier launched himself from the vehicle, driving his head into the back of the soldier, knocking him off balance. After hitting the German, he fell to the ground face first. In a fit of rage, the German turned around and fired a couple of rounds. In the confusion, Donalds acted quickly and retrieved his machine gun, aimed, and fired off a couple of shots.

One of the bullets hit the German, the other the car behind him.

The man's body fell to the ground and Martin quickly rushed to check on the young boy. He felt for a pulse but sadly found no heartbeat. Pressing his hand to the boy's face, he gently closed his eyes.

Donalds picked up Martin's machine gun and rushed over to him. With a free hand, he picked up the Lieutenant, urging him along.

"We need to get to cover. God knows where those other two krauts are."

The two soldiers took cover near the bullet-riddled car. Martin, adrenaline coursing through his veins, sat wide-eyed. He silently thanked the boy, who had most likely saved their lives. Donalds, checking his clip and locking it back into place, sat with his head just above the car top, his eyes scanning the horizon.

We can't risk going any further, Donalds thought, *till we figure out where the other Germans from the car are.*

———◉———

"DID YOU HEAR THAT?" Franck said out loud. He had taken a break from his duties as torturer to give Major Webb another turn. No one answered straight away; the rest of the party was busy having their fun with Major Vahlen. Even Martine had had her moments, surprising the men by taking the Major's knife and removing one of his fingers. The man had let out a subdued scream and it had been music to Franck's ears. People didn't realize that, but torturing a man was laborious work, but it was work he had been dreaming about for many years. He wanted to make sure to savor every ounce of it.

"Yes, I think it came from out front," said Webb, drinking gin straight from the bottle now.

Franck went to the window and peeled back the curtain. "*Mon Dieu*, there is a car outside! And look, two dead bodies."

Webb and Martine came over to look. All three were so transfixed by the events outside, they failed to hear the small creak of the floor just outside the room.

Suddenly, the double drawing room doors burst open.

Two Germans entered, and one of them started to spray the area near the window. Webb instinctively ducked, but the combination of the night's events and the gin had slowed his reflexes. He barely made it to the cover of the dining table. Franck had been closest to the door and took the brunt of the salvo. Martine looked like she was clipped as well; she lay face down on the floor, a small pool of blood forming near her head. Webb wanted to go to them, but he knew if he did, he'd be done for. The

Frenchman had collapsed quickly to the floor; all the while the German soldier continued to fire. The splintering of wood could be heard as the bullets impacted the wall behind Webb.

After a few moments, Webb managed to pull out his revolver and cocked the hammer, firing a shot. It impacted near the top of the door frame. The soldier instinctively ducked and stopped firing. Webb fired off a second shot, hoping to push the soldier back even further. It was now every man for himself. He groped with his hand on the top of the table, searching for his Sten machine gun. All he needed was to find it, and he'd cut down that bastard. The soldier began to fire again, this time wildly. It was so aimless, it caused Teicher and Vahlen to panic a little and try and duck their heads. The sound was deafening in the room. Webb's fingers searched until they finally felt what they'd been looking for. Pulling down the machine gun, Webb stood up, keeping it waist high. He pointed it in the direction of the soldier and pulled the trigger. It chewed up the side of the door and caught the German in the arm. He cried out in pain. Webb slowly walked towards the man and fired again, the bullets piercing the man's uniform. He dropped to the ground dead.

That was for Franck, Webb thought to himself. He had reached the edge of the door and was looking down at the dead German when he heard a loud noise.

BANG!

He didn't feel it at first. He was slightly drunk, and his body felt numb. But soon the fire spread from his belly and radiated up his chest. He looked down at the burnt hole in his midsection. To his right, he saw the source of the bullet.

A junior German *SS* officer.

Webb dropped his gun and stumbled back into the drawing room. His feet tripped over themselves and he fell to the floor, hard. Webb clutched his chest, trying to stop the bleeding, but more and more his shirt was starting to darken. He groaned in pain. Over to his left, a sound came from Franck. Webb looked on as the Frenchman struggled to breathe, his lungs desperately gasping for air. The bullets looked to have pierced his chest and throat. Webb's face grimaced, but his eyes locked with those of Franck. For a single glance, the old friends shared one last moment together. To be honest, Webb hadn't thought when they made that pact all those years ago, that it would end like this. He couldn't be prouder of the way...

BAM!

He jumped in shock as Franck's head exploded. The German officer had entered the room, the smoke rising from the barrel of his pistol. Webb closed his eyes in anguish, and felt a few tears rush down his cheeks. Franck deserved better. They all... deserved better. After a few moments, he opened his eyes to a frightening sight.

The pistol now pointed toward him...

Webb thought back to Anne, to that country house, to Franck lying there dying as he closed his eyes, waiting for the inevitable...

"*Nein, noch nicht. [No, not yet.]*" said *Hauptsturmführer* Teicher.

Webb opened his eyes and watched on as the recently arrived officer nodded and holstered his pistol. He untied his fellow officers and then helped carry the imposing *Sturmbannführer* from the chair over to where the British soldier sat. Instinctively, Webb had crawled towards the wall by the window and propped himself up into a seating position. They pulled out a chair and Vahlen eased into it. He looked down at Major Webb as Teicher and Weiss tied a handkerchief to his hand where the finger was gone, but it still dripped blood on the floor. He dabbed his face with the edge of his sleeve and coughed twice, blood now dribbling down his chin.

"I have to extend my admiration, Major. You were diligent, meticulous. It's what I would have done. But...not quite enough it seems," said Teicher, standing over the wounded Brit.

Webb nodded his head and winced in pain as he pointed at the bottle tipped over on the ground. "Mind if I have one last drink?"

Teicher thought for a moment, then picked up the bottle and held it out to Webb. With one hand Webb reached out to take it, his fingers just getting around the bottle, when Teicher let it go. It tumbled to the ground, spilling what was left onto the blood-soaked floor. Webb looked up at Vahlen, whose now slightly bloodied face struggled to force itself into a grin.

"*Auf Wideresehen*, Major. Give my regards to that stupid French girl, Amie, or whatever her name was, when you see her in the afterlife." Teicher took out his pistol. He went over the chair and put the gun into Vahlen's good hand. "The honor is yours, *Sturmbannführer*." Vahlen propped his disfigured head up and did his best to smile. He gripped the pistol, aimed it, and unleashed a single round. Webb felt like he got hit with a concrete slab in the chest.

His vision started to tunnel, and it felt as if time slowed. Blackness was about to overtake him. In his final moments, as his eyes rolled into the back of his head, he whispered, "Anne... forgive me, Anne... forgive me."

OUTSIDE, CROUCHED BEHIND the car, Donalds was trying to figure out his next move. Martin was a jittery mess. Thank goodness he hadn't let him come alone.

They had heard the cacophony of shots inside the drawing room. Webb was probably dead now.

The radio they so desperately needed was in that house, so tantalizingly close, but with more *SS* men here, the task seemed impossible.

Donalds threw his helmet to the ground, as he slumped against the side of the car, dejected.

They were, for all intents and purposes, dead in the water.

Further up the hill, Private John Appleyard was pacing back and forth outside the truck. He checked his watch. It had been almost half an hour since his officers had gone back for the radio, and Appleyard was getting worried.

Lintz joined him outside the truck and lit a cigarette. "Going to be bright in a couple of hours. Do you think the Sergeant and the Lieutenant ran into trouble?"

Appleyard stopped pacing and asked Lintz for one of his cigarettes. Lighting it up, he replied, "Hard to say. You know the Sarge, he'll get the job done. He always gets the job done."

"And if they don't come back?"

Appleyard didn't answer right away, considering his options. "Then Simon, I don't know..."

Lintz nodded solemnly. Nothing further needed to be said. Both men knew what was at stake. They stood there in the very early morning sun, as the chirps from nearby robins rang out. Appleyard looked out to the horizon, thinking about when he used to watch the sunrise over the prairie in his native Saskatchewan. There, on countless perfect mornings, he stood watching it coat the wheat fields with a warm cup of coffee in hand. He couldn't think of anything that he wanted more than that, right at this very moment.

Sadly, that memory was shattered by a familiar sound.

Gunfire.

Both men stood still, Appleyard's lit cigarette dangling from his mouth. Yes, it was coming from the direction of the town. It was quickly followed by a few more bursts and then silence again.

"Simon, start the truck, and be ready to move once I get back."

"You're not thinking of going down there—what about the reinforcements? We can't take on a division..." pleaded Lintz.

"Sarge needs me, Simon. I can feel it. He wouldn't leave us, and we can't leave him. Just keep that truck idling."

Lintz looked like he was going to put up more of a fight, but slowly nodded his head. Appleyard picked up his rifle and started back down the road.

Reaching the hill where they had been when they entered the town Appleyard stopped and looked down at it. It became clear at that moment that he was one man, deep behind enemy lines, facing a ruthless enemy. The odds were not in his favor.

The ridge.

Appleyard remembered that when they were coming back from the town, there was a ridge that skirted along the backside of it. He might be able to give some cover to Sarge if he moved to that vantage point.

He started to make his way across the dipping hills. Just ahead and slightly off to the left, the ground planed out, leaving a flat piece of land amongst the grassy knolls. The sightlines were clear—a perfect sniping position. Appleyard took off his jacket and laid it on the fertile ground. He then got himself to a prone position, adjusting his rifle and himself until he was comfortable.

Sweeping the rifle from side to side, Appleyard started looking for targets. He aimed it towards the front of the car. Something was moving, but he couldn't quite tell what it was.

Might be Sarge, might be a German... but it could be a local. Thoughts bombarded Appleyard as he stared down the sight.

He hoped that Lieutenant Martin was in there right now, calling London. His mind turned back to what he had heard earlier. Was that gunfire the sound of Webb and Franck finishing off Vahlen before fighting the rest of Vahlen's men?

A movement to his left turned his eyes back towards the house where they had left Webb and Vahlen.

Through the back door, two German soldiers carried the body of what Appleyard had to assume was Major Vahlen, just by his size. Beyond that, Appleyard recognized the other German officer, Vahlen's second in command, with the slicked-back hair. They were quickly followed by a junior *SS* officer and another soldier bringing up the rear.

Appleyard lowered his rifle and shook his head. So, the gunfire wasn't Webb going out in his blaze of glory, taking Vahlen with him. Even worse, this probably meant that Lieutenant Martin and Sergeant Donalds were also most likely dead. His heart sank. He thought of Mills, dying for a mission that wasn't even real.

Just as quickly as he had allowed himself to entertain the thought, Appleyard spotted some faint movements toward the front of the house. He popped his head up and squinted, doing his best to see what was near the car. Sure enough, he spotted the green helmet of Sergeant Donalds, and it seemed the Lieutenant was there as well, huddled behind the German car.

Well, I'll be damned, Appleyard exclaimed in his head. The men were still alive.

He now turned his attention to the group of Germans making their way towards the car. He needed to give Sergeant Donalds and Lieutenant Martin an opening.

He shifted his body slightly and closed his left eye. Taking a deep breath in, then slowly exhaling, he squeezed the trigger for shot number one.

CRAAAAAAACK!

The German on the left of Major Vahlen dropped; the bullet had ripped through his chest. Without support on the left side, Vahlen toppled to the ground dragging down the man supporting his right side.

Appleyard pivoted his hands slightly, quickly firing off a second shot.

CRAAAAAAAACK!

A helmeted *SS* Private that was bringing up the rear of the group fell as the bullet passed through the side of his head. Now crouching down, and having seen two shots, the remaining *SS* men turned towards the hill where Appleyard was located. A German soldier aimed his rifle and fired a shot towards the Canadian, kicking up a bit of dirt in front of him. The rest of the Germans did the same, and soon Appleyard was under a hail of gunfire.

"Well, guess I got their attention," said Appleyard to himself, keeping his head low.

Sergeant Donalds, who was huddled behind the car, heard the first shot and looked at Martin.

"That sounds like a Garand... Ohhhh... Appleyard, you freckled beauty!"

"What... What's happening?" Martin said, clutching his machine gun for dear life.

"Appleyard is giving us covering fire. We might just pull this off, LT."

Donalds pushed himself up, using the car as cover, and unleashed a barrage from his weapon. He managed to injure Weiss, who doubled over now. The rest of the Germans turned back towards the car and started firing, forcing Donalds to duck.

This opened up another chance for Appleyard.

He aimed the rifle, this time at the junior *SS* officer, Weiss, and squeezed the trigger.

CRAAAAAAACK!

The bullet hit him square in the back, and he fell flat to the ground.

Unsure where to turn, the remaining soldier fired a couple of shots towards the hill. He then started to make a beeline towards the house.

Donalds recognized the soldier running for the house as Teicher. He shifted his gun, aimed slightly ahead of the sprinting German and squeezed off a sustained burst. The bullets seemed to catch the German, before splattering over the side of the house.

"This is our only chance, Lieutenant," Donalds said, looking on, weapon still raised. He waved his hand towards the hill, in acknowledgment of the help.

Martin stood up from behind the car, straightening his jacket. His weapon firmly pointed in front of him, he slowly made his way towards the house.

"Call that plane, Lieutenant. I'll make sure they're all down."

Lightly stepping over the dead bodies, Martin slammed himself into the corner of the house, then did a shoulder check to look around the back.

Clear, just the swinging open door.

Martin slunk along the back, feeling the wooden stairs creak under his weight as he approached the entrance. Shrouded in shadow, the hall looked foreboding. Entering the threshold, he headed for the radio room. Just as he passed the open door, it suddenly slammed shut. Martin turned, but a grey blur crashed into him, and he saw two hands trying to wrestle the gun from him. Martin fell on the wooden floor, hard. His gun clattered a few feet down the hall, out of his reach. Looking back, he saw what had jumped him.

Teicher.

The SS Captain now groped and pulled at Martin's right leg, holding the British Lieutenant from moving forward. He tried his best to kick the German, but the man now gripped his leg with both hands. The men struggled back and forth until Teicher pulled himself up on top of Martin, face to face. His hands wrapped around Martin's neck and he started to squeeze with all his might.

"I don't know why you came back, English, but I'm going to make you regret it!" shrilled Teicher, pressing his fingers further into Martin's throat. Martin clawed wildly at the German's hands, to no avail. The pressure was building in Martin's chest, and his limbs flailed back and forth. The corners of his vision started to go dark, and Martin realized he was dying.

Then, something happened that may just have saved his life. As his foot lashed back and forth, it struck the back of Teicher's thigh. The spindly German winced in pain, and Martin felt the hands around his neck loosen just slightly. *He must have a bullet wound back there*, Martin thought.

He had only a few moments to act.

Taking his leg, he struck his foot down on the wound again with significant force. The second time the German arched back, and his hands instinctively moving to clutch the wound. Martin took that moment to bring his right forearm across the German's face, just like he'd been taught in training. He felt the nose bone crunch, and Teicher fell backward, clutching his face. Martin turned over on his side and coughed profusely. He collected himself, and crawled forward, grabbing a hold of his gun. Propping himself up against the wall, he aimed the machine gun at Teicher.

"The only regret I have is not killing you earlier." Martin pulled back the slide and squeezed the trigger. The gun rattled in his hand; Teicher lay motionless on the house floor.

Donalds appeared at the door, kicking it in, his gun raised. "Martin... Martin, you okay?"

"Yes, I'm quite fine, Sergeant. Just a little... tired... is all."

Exhausted, Lieutenant Martin picked himself up and went straight for the back room. He ducked into the storage closet and found what he was looking for. The radio. He pulled out the dead radio operator and started twisting and turning the knobs, searching for the frequency he wanted. Donalds waited at the door, looking on with slight bemusement. When Martin had reached the right combination, he took the microphone and started speaking.

"This is Lieutenant Percival Martin, calling London Station. Come in, London Station. Over."

Martin released the transmission button, hearing nothing but static. This was against protocol, but Martin had to hope that someone was listening. The radio crackled again, then a few faint sounds started to come through. He adjusted the headphones to try and hear a bit better.

"What's your mission code name, Lieutenant? Over."

"No mission codename. I repeat, no mission code-name. Requesting transport to exfil an Allied team trapped in France. Over."

"This is highly irregular, Lieutenant. Will need proof of identity before we can proceed. Over."

"Look up service records. Martin, Percival, service number 02054891. Over."

"Checking, standby Lieutenant."

Martin sat back in the chair.

"It will take them some time to confirm my identity. Pray those London boys don't take too long."

"I'm well past praying, Lieutenant. We're in miracle territory now."

Setting down the headphones, Martin got up and started down towards the drawing-room.

"I know what you're doing, Lieutenant. But, it won't do you any good." Donalds shook his head as he stared at the British officer.

"I know, Sergeant, I know. But I have to. He was my commanding officer, and in some cases... my friend."

"Alright, let's go."

The men inched their way down the hall, Donalds's eyes moving from side to side. Pushing open the door, the scene that greeted them was exactly what they had expected. Martin moved over to Franck's limp body, and seeing not much left of his head, he turned away in disgust. Donalds also looked around the room, and he immediately noticed Martine was nowhere to be seen. *Had she made it out of this hellish situation?* He picked up one of the overturned wooden chairs, and that's when he saw him.

Major Webb, propped up against the window.

A large, dark red stain had covered his tunic. Martin came over, bending down to examine the Major.

"For what's it worth, Lieutenant... I am sor—"

Behind them, the sound of shoes on a floorboard forced Donalds to swivel, gun at the ready. Someone was coming into the drawing room. Expecting some German *SS* straggler, Donalds prepared to fire.

However, they were greeted by a much more pleasant sight.

"Don't shoot, English." It was Martine. She held a crudely made bandage to her head, which was damp and bright red with blood.

"You are hurt... Do you need help?" Martin asked slowly.

"I can speak your language just fine, you don't have to speak to me like I'm an idiot. And I'm fine, the bullet just grazed me," Martine retorted, heading over to the drinks cart. Martin, a little put off by her direct comments, allowed his shock to wear off and it was replaced by a smile. Martine poured herself a drink and downed it quickly. "Came back to make sure he was dead?"

"I beg your pardon?"

She pointed at the corpse of Major Webb. "Your friend—did you both come back to make sure he was dead?"

Both men stood dumbfounded at her blunt nature.

"No... I actually... I came to pay my respects. Whatever happened here... what happened tonight... he was still a good person."

"And you?" She pointed at Donalds. "Did you come to pay your respects?"

Donalds pushed his helmet back on his head. "If I'm being honest, ma'am, I did not. I came to make sure that bastard was dead. But he was still a soldier, and so I am forced to pay my respects."

Martin bent down, tearing off one of the dog tags from Major Webb's chain. "It's possible, Sergeant, that any one of us might have done the same, you know."

Donalds pondered that statement, but his face quickly turned to a scowl.

"I wouldn't have tortured a man and cut off his finger. That, I am very sure of!"

Martine chuckled a little while pulling the damp bandage away from her head for a moment. "You should worry less about your morals and more about the Germans. They're the ones that need killing."

"And torturing, right?" retorted Donalds. He surprised himself how quickly he responded, but the emotions of the night's events were still fresh.

Martine snorted. "You British and Canadians, you have the luxury of being free of occupation. All this," she said, waving her hands at the room, "we have to live this every day. If some German officer gets his nails pulled out or his leg broken, it's been a good day."

"And I suppose, my dear, that the lives—our lives, your life—that these two men put at risk—that's worth it too?" said Martin, making his way towards the table. He went to the drinks cart, rummaged for a few moments, and then came out holding a oddly shaped bottle. Donalds noticed he had poured himself a tumbler of the liquid.

Martine looked puzzled. She put down her drink. "What are you talking about, English?"

"I'm talking about the Germans coming to this town. How do you think they found you? They didn't just magically come here, and we didn't just accidentally arrive to save the day. It was Major Webb and Franck that told them where you were. They used you as bait."

Shocked, Martine stood there in silence.

"Not so confident now, are you, ma'am. He used us, he used us all." Donalds gestured vociferously at Webb.

Martine looked away from the men, shuffling towards the large window, and subsequently, Webb.

"And—the town, what about them?" she asked, stifling back tears.

"I doubt the Major or Franck gave them a second thought. They would have been collateral damage, just like us."

Martin went over to her, putting his hand on her shoulder. He wanted to comfort her, but he knew this wasn't the time.

The distant sound of crackling and a tinny voice let Martin know he needed to return to the radio quickly, and he left Martine standing in the drawing room. He went back down the hall, where the voice became clearer. "Come in, Lieutenant Martin, come in. Over."

"I am here. Over," replied Martin, putting the headphones back on.

"Identity confirmed, Lieutenant. Please provide coordinates for extraction. Over."

Martin fumbled with his sack, taking out a leather-bound book, and turned halfway through. He had written the coordinates before they left London and thank God that he had.

"Map Grid 48. Coordinates 1000824.5. Over."

"Map coordinates confirmed, Lieutenant. Pick up will be at the usual time. Over and out."

Martin acknowledged London and signed off. He grabbed his gear and went back to the drawing room. Martine was now sitting at the table. "Perhaps I owe you gentlemen an apology, Lieutenant."

"Not at all, my dear. We were all in this together."

"So, I guess you'll be leaving then?" she asked.

"Yes, and I suggest you do the same. More Germans will be here shortly." Martin slung his bag around his body and turned to leave. Donalds did the same with his weapon.

"Lieutenant..." Martine called out.

Martin stopped. "Yes?"

"Your commander... he did save my life tonight. For that, I will always be grateful."

Martin paused at her statement. Again, a sly smile broke out across his face. "What was your name again?"

"Martine. Martine Cuvier."

"Perhaps we will meet again, Martine." With that, Lieutenant Martin and Sergeant Donalds headed out of the drawing-
room and towards the front door.

It was time to get the hell out of this place.

———◉———

APPLEYARD BREATHED heavily as he started to run back
up the hill. Pushing himself, he deftly navigated the ridge and arrived back at the truck, gasping for air greedily.

"Lintz, let's get moving! The Sarge and LT need a ride."

They both jumped in the truck, and the large piece of machinery lurched forward as Lintz put it in gear. Soon enough,
they reached the edge of town and Lintz was maneuvering it towards the square. He pulled it to a halt as Donalds and Martin
came running up, hopping into the back. Appleyard helped
them up into the bed, then dropped the canvas cover.

As the truck roared along the road, Donalds looked down at
Corporal Mills. He could feel the eyes of Martin on him.

"Something on your mind, Lieutenant?"

"I—wanted to say thank you, for saving my life back there.
And, for what it's worth, I'm truly sorry about your man, Mills.
Major Webb was wrong in what he did, I know that. Hell, he
even manipulated me to get what he wanted. But you mustn't
hang your head, Sergeant, you've done some good here today."

Donalds let out an incredulous gasp of air. "I doubt that very
much, Lieutenant. Do you want to know why I agreed to take
this mission?"

Martin said nothing but waved his hand to signal Donalds
to continue.

"I took this mission not because I thought it would get me promoted, or curry favor with the British. No, you see, I took this job in the hopes that I would be able to tell my kids, my grandkids, that someday their father and grandfather did something to help end this terrible war. I'm not looking for glory. I'm not looking for medals. I just want my sacrifice here to mean something... to someone."

"It has, Sergeant. It has..."

"Oh really, Lieutenant. And tell me, what would that be?"

Martin looked directly at Donalds. "Well, for one, you saved that town from a massacre. Those people owe their lives to you. Second, despite Major Webb's misguided approach, we have put a stop to Major Vahlen. Based on what I've seen of the man, we did the world a favor. Finally, you saved my life and the lives of your men, and of that young woman back there, fighting for liberation."

Donalds sat back in the truck, his head leaning against the rattling frame.

"Am I wrong, Sergeant?"

"No—just don't feel like congratulating myself right now."

That seemed to end their conversation and Donalds sat back, deep in thought.

He remembered back to the house in Italy, where he and Colonel Fredericks had spoken. When this mission first presented itself, Donalds had taken it on the chance that he could finally feel that he was doing some real good in the war, to help save lives. Despite not securing any usable intelligence to help the impending invasion of Europe, Martin was right, they had saved lives. Just not the lives he thought he would be saving.

However, as Corporal Mills lay prostrate on the truck floor, his wounds bandaged now and pumped full of morphine, the guilt began to wash over the Canadian Sergeant like a wave. Mills had also told him that his sometimes reckless nature put them at risk, and now here was the proof. Up until now, Donalds had blamed Webb for everything, and rightly so. But, as he mulled it over more and more, he realized, despite his obvious objections, that Mills may have been right.

The emptiness in his stomach was growing larger by the moment.

He looked out of the truck as the town of Serronelle faded behind them. He looked back over at Appleyard, exhaustion written over his face, as it probably was on his own as well. He replaced the canvas cover and sat back, feeling an overwhelming urge to sleep. *Maybe just a few minutes,* he thought. It was going to be a while before they reached the field to meet the plane. As Donalds drifted off, Lintz shifted the truck into third gear, letting it pick up a little more speed. The truck came to a fork in the road, and Lintz pulled the steering wheel to the right, directing the truck down the dirt path.

VAHLEN COUGHED, SPITTING up the mud that invaded his mouth. A mouth that hurt like hell. Rolling over to his side, he tried to push himself up but failed miserably. His hand's crudely made bandage by Teicher earlier had fallen off, and the dirt stung the wound where his middle finger had been.

Now on his back, he stared out the one eye that would open at the early morning sky. The strangeness of the evening struck him... so much so that it was hard to wrap his head around all the events that had happened.

Tiredness overtook him quickly, but before he passed out, he heard the rumble of truck engines in the background. As his eyes became heavy with sleep, he was struck by a thought.

I am still alive.

CHAPTER THIRTEEN

AS THE CAR CAME UP to the edge of Serronelle, Colonel Grassl shifted nervously in his seat. The streets were empty, and a plume of smoke billowed up in the distance. In the middle of the road sat two greyish objects; Grassl couldn't quite make out what they were.

The car got closer, and the realization dawned on him.

Dead Germans soldiers. Leaning forward as the car passed, he could see the *SS* markings on their collars. They must be Vahlen's men.

Stepping from the car, he removed his pistol and waved towards the nearest troop truck.

"*Raus! Raus! [Out! Out!]*" he shouted, waiting for his trusted second in command, Captain Sommer, to finish organizing the men. Once he was done, he returned to Grassl, saluting and eagerly awaiting orders.

"Captain, get the people of this town out into the square. Then have some of the men police up these bodies and start burying them."

"*Jawohl, Mein Her, [Yes, sir,]*" replied Captain Sommer.

"And Captain," Grassl said, leaning in close to avoid being in earshot of others, "let me know right away if Major Vahlen is alive or not."

Captain Sommer clicked his heels together and moved off. The rest of the soldiers dispersed, knocking on doors and getting the people back to the square again. Grassl stood in the square, looking over everything like a schoolmaster looking over his pupils. His men began cleaning up the bodies of the dead *SS* soldiers, and Grassl realized he had stumbled into a disaster. It was no secret that the regular German Army and the *SS* had a fractious relationship; neither one fully trusted the other. To be honest, Grassl had detested the manner they went about their business, Vahlen's accusation of Grassl as a traitor being a case in point. That said, he hated to see dead German soldiers, *SS* or otherwise. What exactly happened here would be his responsibility to find out.

The townspeople, now forced from their homes for a second time, unbeknownst by Grassl, tirelessly shuffled their way to the square. Suddenly, a group of them got pushed aside as a soldier came running from the north, his helmet almost falling off his head. He spoke in a hushed and hurried tone with Captain Sommer, who in turn walked briskly over to Grassl.

"*Mein Herr*, there is something that needs your immediate attention."

Colonel Grassl furrowed his brow. "What is it, Captain?"

"Private Kruze has found something. It's to the north, at the other end of the town."

"Lead the way." Grassl started towards the location, with Captain Sommer and two other soldiers in tow. It didn't take long for them to make the trek, but once they arrived, Grassl couldn't believe his eyes.

"*Mein Gott, [My God,]*" uttered Grassl, as the rest of the men stood beside him.

The house was riddled with bullet holes across its front, but it was the pile of German bodies that lay just outside that had drawn everyone's attention. To the right, there was a shot up

Kubelwagen, no doubt the source of the smoke that Grassl had seen earlier.

"Check the house," Grassl said to his men, as he watched some of the others sift through the bodies. As the men turned over each body, it became clear they were all dead. So, the information the bartender had given him was accurate. He knew that reports of Resistance activities in the area were up, but this was something different. He looked back at the huddled masses in Serronelle, milling about in the square. *Had the town risen up and killed the SS men?* So many questions ran through his mind.

"Colonel, over here, this man is alive!" shouted one of his men.

Grassl turned his thoughts back to the house and walked over, as did Captain Sommer. Had it not been for Major Vahlen's distinguishing large physique, they may never have identified him, thought Grassl, as the man's grotesque face came to view. It was bloodied and battered almost beyond recognition. Grassl brought his handkerchief to his mouth, partially to block out the smell, but also to prevent himself from vomiting.

"He's unconscious..." Sommer bent down, pressing two fingers to the man's neck. "...For now."

"Get the Major loaded into the truck," Grassl said, standing up. He dusted his hands and pointed towards the house. "Is there anything inside?"

"I will check, *Mein Herr*," said Sommer.

The truck pulled up, and Grassl watched on as they loaded the disfigured body into the back. It took three of his men to do it, and once he was inside, one of the men set about tending to his wounds. Grassl checked his watch when he saw Captain Sommer come to the doorway. He waved at Grassl hurriedly, and the Colonel made his way over. Once through the door, Sommer led the Colonel through the small foyer and into the large entertaining room.

"Well, what have we here?" said Grassl, thinking out loud. He bent down and looked at the two dead bodies lying before him. "A British Major—that is not something one sees very often these days. And who is this?" Grassl attempted to shift the other body—that of Franck Chabert—with his foot, to take a better look at the man's visage.

"Another British spy?" the Captain asked. "He wears an Army uniform, but he is not German."

"So, it would seem. Very interesting, would you not say, Captain?"

Grassl's second in command nodded. "What are your orders, Colonel?"

"I need a cigarette to think. Join me outside."

Both men exited the house and went over near the shot-up car. Grassl pulled a cigarette from his silver case, offering one to Sommer. As they were lighting up, a Private appeared, flanked by an older man. Grassl took a long look at the man through a couple of puffs and waited for the Private to speak. The soldier stood at attention, saluting, then said, "Colonel, this man wishes to speak with you."

Grassl nodded and waved for the man to step forward as the soldier moved aside. "Do you understand German?" Colonel Grassl asked.

The man nodded. "I do."

"Good, so speak then."

"I want to plead mercy from you, sir. You have no doubt seen what has happened here."

Grassl did not speak but slowly nodded.

"I speak for those in Serronelle, sir. I am Doctor Lelievre. We had no part to play in those men's deaths. We are innocent, and just simple townsfolk..."

Grassl held up his hand, and Doctor Lelievre stopped speaking.

"That will be all... Doctor. Thank you for your time."

"But sir..."

"That will be all...Doctor," Grassl said tersely. The soldier that had brought him to Grassl quickly ushered him away, and back down the road to the square. Once he was out of earshot, Sommer began speaking to Grassl.

"I don't believe him, Colonel. He's lying. Major Vahlen was onto something here, we should interrogate everyone. Burn this town to the ground if we have to. I'm willing and able, Colonel."

Grassl finished his cigarette and flicked it away. "Get the men back in the truck. I want us on the road back to Marseille in the next fifteen minutes."

Sommer stood in shock, then quickly ran after Grassl. "But Colonel, protocol dictates that we..."

Colonel Grassl dismissed his subordinate with a quick wave of his hand and started to make his way back to the car. Frustrated, Sommer hung back, mulling over his next move. He stewed on the evidence for a bit, but quickly came to a conclusion. This town's people knew more than they were telling. At the very least they should question a few of them. He knew what he had to do.

Discreetly gesturing to a Private, Sommer gave him instructions to follow him. They then made their way to where Doctor Lelievre was standing. The man looked up frighteningly at him, and Sommer made sure to speak with him quietly.

"Show me your house, Doctor."

The man just stared back at him. Sommer returned his glare equally conveying the seriousness of the situation. After a few seconds, the Doctor relented and pointed to a house on the other side of the square. The Private stood him up, and the people around them looked away immediately. As soon as they reached the house, the Private pushed the Doctor inside, then stood by the door as Captain Sommer entered and shut the door.

"Now it's just you and me, Doctor. And I don't like to be lied to. Do you understand?"

The Doctor swallowed heavily and nodded his head.

"Now, I highly doubt that an aging British Major and his greasy accomplice managed to take down an elite unit of *SS*. There were others, weren't there? Resistance? Other Allied soldiers? TELL ME!"

Doctor Lelievre shook his head vociferously. "I don't know what you mean, sir."

Captain Sommer didn't know how, but he knew the Doctor was lying. His patience was running thin. "Doctor, what did I say about lying..." Sommer picked up a vase from a side table. He threw it hard at the opposite wall, shattering it into a thousand pieces. Doctor Lelievre ducked instinctively and looked up at him with wide eyes.

"I swear, sir, there was no one else here. I am not lying!" Doctor Lelievre pleaded, holding up his hands in front of him. Sommer knew the signs; the man was begging for mercy. He removed his pistol and grabbed the barrel so the handle was free. It seemed that he would have to "entice" him to tell the truth. The handle of a gun across one's face tended to do that. He raised his hand when a voice shouted from behind him.

"CAPTAIN! AT ATTENTION!"

It was Colonel Grassl.

Sommer lowered his hand and stood straight. Grassl slowly walked up, inspecting first Captain Sommer, then the Doctor. His eyes also looked over at the smashed vase pieces lying on the floor. "What's going on here, Captain?"

"Sir, I thought this man had some infor—"

Grassl interrupted his junior officer. "Captain, you forget yourself. This is not the conduct of an Army officer. Now, I ordered you to get the men packed up. Perhaps you should see to that."

"Sir, if I could speak..."

Colonel Grassl pointed outside, and both men exited Doctor Lelievre's house. Grassl turned and stepped closer to his subordinate. Captain Sommer stood at attention again; he visibly sweating. Grassl tapped the side of Captain Sommer's head. "I can see you won't let this go, Captain, so listen up. Major Vahlen came to see me before he left Marseille. I had given him the information that led him to this town. He was searching for a French Resistance member responsible for killing *Hauptsturmführer* Kampfer."

Captain Sommer stood silent, caught off-guard at what he was hearing.

Grassl continued, "And it seems that Major Vahlen did indeed find this agent—the man with the black hair in the German uniform back there. You see, Captain, there was a report last night of a truck being stolen from the motor pool. A soldier was found dead, and his uniform stolen. I believe the man we found in the house with the British soldier was that same man. As for the British Major, he was most likely this agent's commanding officer and a spy. However, both are now dead, and I doubt *Herr* Vahlen will be able to speak anytime soon. So... I consider... this... matter... closed."

Captain Sommer opened his mouth to speak, but then closed it. Grassl patted him on the shoulder.

"I'll try and forget your insubordination when I make my report to Berlin. The Russian Front always needs more soldiers, Captain." Sommer swallowed heavily, saluted, and left to see to the loading of the truck.

Despite Grassl's explanation, Sommer knew something wasn't right. There was something here that just didn't add up. He couldn't investigate while Grassl was around, but Sommer knew where to get answers. And he would get them.

Grassl watched on as Sommer and the soldiers began to pack up. He then looked back at Doctor Lelievre. Grassl wouldn't waste a minute more in this little town. He had bigger concerns, and what Vahlen was up to here was not high on the list. The Allies would be coming, that Grassl was sure of, and he had defensive preparations to see to. He would tell Berlin and the *SS* what they wanted to hear, and that would be that. To be honest, Grassl still felt bitter about the way that Vahlen had treated him. While he would never admit it out loud, Colonel Grassl believed the *Sturmbannführer* Vahlen got exactly what was coming to him. Besides, the condition that Major Vahlen was in, Grassl's report would be the only one that mattered.

This little adventure would be filed away soon enough.

⸺◦⦿◦⸺

THE SCREECH OF THE brakes and the sudden stop of the truck jolted Sergeant Donalds from a brief nap. He stood, stretching his cramped limbs, and stepped out from the trailer of the truck. The midday sun was beating down now, and Donalds removed his jacket.

Looking out, he recognized the field where they had arrived the night before. Black dirt rows were neatly organized, with large, thick trunked tree lines spaced in between them. In the distance, a small stone building sat adjacent to one of the vast fields, dark grey stone topped with tangerine colored clay tile. It looked marooned, like a stranded vehicle on the side of a highway. The trees—their thin leaves and long spindly branches—rustled with every tiny breeze. Lintz had left the truck parked under an outcrop of them on the edge of the field. From the air or the road, the truck would be mostly hidden from view, and this is where they would wait for their ride home. Martin and Appleyard were off by a stump, sharing a cigarette, so Donalds wandered up to the cab and spoke with Lintz.

"Fine spot you've got us here, Private."

"I thought you might like it, sir. You know, this place would be a nice place for a holiday, I guess. You know... if it wasn't for all the war-type stuff, the Germans...you know."

Donalds chuckled and agreed. "Yeah, they kind of dampen the mood."

Lintz took a sip from the canteen, offering it to Donalds. "How is the Corporal?"

"He's in rough shape. I gave him a bit more morphine, but he's in a lot of pain."

Lintz gave a solemn nod. Both men had lost people they knew. They had seen the brutality that the Germans were capable of. And, after tonight, the brutality that their side was capable of as well. Donalds walked over to where Martin and Appleyard sat by the large tree. "How long till the plane gets here again, sir?"

"After sundown. I've got a couple of flares so we can mark the field. Till then, we just have to wait," said Martin.

"Five or so hours until we are home free. Great," said Appleyard, shifting his weight so he could lean against the tree.

"Five or so hours till we can get Corporal Mills some real help," Donalds said, reminding his man of the predicament of their comrade. Donalds decided to get a little exercise and took a short walk up and down the road and then back to the tailgate. Between the wind and the sunbeams filtering through the leaves, he barely noticed as two hours drifted by. Behind him, he heard a large cough and a groan from Mills. Climbing up, he looked over at the man, who reached up and grabbed Donalds's coat and started to speak. "Morph... Mmmorph... Mmmmorphine."

"Alright buddy, I got you covered." Donalds filled the syringe from the vial of morphine and flicked it twice with his fingers. During his time as a forest ranger, he was given rudimentary medical training; being trapped in the wilderness for weeks on end, he had to be prepared to treat himself for any injuries.

He found the vein on the Corporal's arm and gently inserted the syringe. After a few seconds, the man's groans started to subside. His face, grimaced in pain moments earlier, had returned to a more serene state. He pressed two fingers against Mills's neck; his pulse was steady now, but weak. As he replaced the syringe, he heard a distant sound and couldn't quite place it. Curious, he poked his head out of the truck. After a few more moments, he heard the sound a second time. His heart began to race.

It was motor engines. Lots of them.

Quickly, he frantically waved for Martin and Appleyard's attention. They looked over at him quizzically, then heard the sound as well. They raced over to the tailgate, along with Private Lintz.

"Where are they coming from?" Appleyard said, slamming a clip into his rifle and chambering a round.

"The main road, to the north. What do you want to do, Lieutenant?" asked Donalds.

"Appleyard, can you get up into that tree?" Martin pointed towards the giant oak tree they were currently parked under. "That should give you a perfect vantage point to see what we have coming."

"Shouldn't be a problem, LT," said Appleyard, slinging his rifle around his shoulder. He began to climb the tree, concealing himself beneath the foliage.

"The rest of you, back into the truck. If they come down the side road, Private Lintz, just make it look like you're taking a break from a long journey."

"You got it, sir." He climbed back into the cab of the truck, grabbed his MP40, and came to the back.

Donalds looked on approvingly at Lieutenant Martin. "Someone might think you've done this before, sir."

Martin smiled. "It seems to get easier every time you do it."

Donalds and Martin climbed in the back, and Lintz shut the tailgate and pulled down the canvas. Donalds slid down to the end of the bench so Lintz could relay the information from Appleyard as soon as he saw it.

The engine sounds droned on in the distance, and Lintz stood near the back, smoking a cigarette. Up in the tree, Appleyard had a good view of the main road, south, and north. As the vehicles came around a bend, Appleyard could make out their color as grey, which probably meant they were German. Then, Appleyard saw something in the distance that took precedence. He frantically relayed the information to Lintz on the ground. Running back to the truck, Lintz informed the others.

"He saw five vehicles in the column. Command car in the front, two motorcycles, what appears to be a troop truck, and... a tank.

"A tank? *A tank*?" said Donalds incredulously.

"Yes, sir, said it was lagging a bit behind the rest of the column."

"Hopefully they'll pass us and be none the wiser," said Martin, nervously rubbing his hands together.

Up in the tree, Appleyard watched on as the column continued, passing the turnoff they had taken. He let out a large sigh, unaware that he had been holding his breath. The tank, which Appleyard could see much clearer now, was a Panzer Type III, and it was losing ground rapidly on the rest of the column. The large armored vehicle chugged uneasily along the road, belching plumes of black smoke. It was now roughly five-hundred meters or so from their position when the back end spewed an even larger amount of smoke and the engine pitch went higher. He then watched as it stopped in the middle of the road and turned right slowly down a side road just north of their position. It stopped halfway down the throughway, and Appleyard saw a man pop open the hatch with smoke emanating from the top.

"Lintz, Lintz, are you there?" said Appleyard in a hushed tone. No response—*he must be back at the truck*, thought Appleyard.

The command car and one of the motorcycles had now also turned around and come back down the side road, stopping near the tank. Taking a chance, Appleyard climbed down the tree, doing his best to stay out of sight. Confident that they had not been seen, he and Lintz snuck to the back of the truck and climbed up.

"What is it, Private?" queried Donalds.

"We've got a big problem. That tank, which was lagging behind the rest of the column, appears to have some sort of engine trouble. It turned off the main road and is currently sitting on the other side of the field."

"Dammit," cursed Lieutenant Martin. "That's right in the path of the bloody plane."

Appleyard continued, "After the tank turned down the road, the command car and a motorcycle returned. Thankfully, the troop truck didn't turn back."

"How long until the plane arrives?" asked Donalds.

Martin checked his watch. "Two hours, give or take."

Donalds sat back. Martin was also silent, eyes as big as saucers. They just couldn't catch a break, it seemed. *What else could possibly happen?* the Sergeant thought.

"What are we going to do?" asked Lintz.

Lieutenant Martin looked straight up at Donalds. "Sergeant, what are your thoughts?"

Donalds sighed. This mission was just one obstacle after another, but Donalds knew he had to rally his men. "Lieutenant, place the flares as we had originally planned. My men and I will take care of the tank."

"Sergeant, that is an extremely tall order, do you think you and your men can handle it?" asked the Lieutenant.

"What other choice do we have, LT? It's that or we don't make it out of here alive."

"I know, but it's something that may be a bit beyond..."

Donalds held up his right first finger and shook his head. "We're Black Devils, Lieutenant. We'll do what Major Webb wanted us to do on this mission, but we're going to do it for us now."

As Appleyard, Lintz, and Lieutenant Martin huddled around, Donalds laid out his plan. After he was done, each man nodded their agreement and set about their preparations. About an hour later, Donalds pulled the tin of boot polish from his bag and began to touch up his face. The sun had set low enough in the sky now that it would safely conceal their approach towards the tank. Wiping his hands of the excess, he passed the tin over to Appleyard and checked his watch. The time to act was now.

"Private Lintz, it's time. When you hear me whistle, you know what to do. Lieutenant, be ready with those flares. Private Appleyard, are you ready?"

The young private looked up from the mirror he held in front of his face. "Can I say no, Sarge?"

"No. Grab Corporal Mills's machine gun and both clips and let's move."

Donalds and Appleyard exited from the truck and crawled into the field. The early evening breeze drifted through the grass and wheat. With the height of the grass and position of the truck near the tree line, they were practically invisible in the fading light. Donalds waved his hand forward and both he and Appleyard crawled along on their bellies, inching their way towards the tank. Behind them, the truck started up, which meant Lieutenant Martin and Lintz had carefully unloaded Corporal

Mills. *Good*, thought Donalds, checking his watch. *They're right on schedule.* Digging his elbows into the ground, his gun splayed across his arms, he slowly crawled forward, periodically making sure Appleyard wasn't too far behind. He estimated it would take them about twenty minutes to cross the field. *Lintz will just have to stall until they arrive*, Donalds thought.

Not far away, Private Lintz had driven the truck back towards the main road. He looked out into the field, thinking that he might spot his comrades slowly making their way towards the Germans, but of course, he couldn't; they were too well camouflaged. He eased the lumbering vehicle around the corner of the second access road, bringing it to a halt just a few meters from the command car. He checked to see that his pistol was secure in its holster, and stepped out from the cab. The noise had brought the attention of the commanding officer and a few of the other soldiers. The tank crew seemed to take no notice.

"*Guten abend. [Good evening.]*" I saw your vehicles from the road, do you need any assistance?" Lintz said, approaching the men, saluting curtly.

"Good evening, Private. Thank you for stopping to check on us, but we have everything in hand," said the Sergeant. A lanky man, his right eyebrow was permanently arched up, like he was constantly asking a question. His cheekbones were non-existent and along with a nose bridge that looked like it had been broken, gave the picture of a. An auburn pencil thin mustache traced across his top lip. When he opened his mouth to speak, Lintz could see the tobacco stained mustard color of his teeth. Doing his best to brush off the dismissal in stride, Lintz knew that one way or another, he had to get close to that tank. He needed an opening, and fast.

Behind the German Sergeant, the clattering of tools rang out, and Lintz could hear some cursing in German. One of the tank crew was gesticulating feverishly at the other. This might just work to his advantage.

"Begging the Sergeant's pardon, but I have done some work in the motor pool, I might be able to help."

The Sergeant, checking his watch and no doubt realizing he was behind schedule, looked at the tank crew and then back at Lintz.

"Looks like we could use your help after all, Private. Know anything about tanks?"

"A little, I used to work on them in my spare time," Lintz lied, starting to walk with the Sergeant over to the hulking vehicle. Lintz took a quick look to his right into the field. He could see a few pieces of grass rustling. Was that his comrades getting ready? Donalds had laid out a bold plan, and he had made it clear it was critical that Lintz was ready when he whistled.

They walked up to the tank, and Lintz could now see that the crew had the engine cover off and were digging inside the large, armored vehicle. He said a silent prayer to himself that the vehicle could still move. If the crew had taken apart the engine in any way, they were more than likely going to be captured, or worse. One of the tank crew interrupted his thoughts, jabbing a spanner into his hand.

"Sergeant tells me you know how to use this thing. We need all the help we can get." The tank crewman rubbed his hands together on a dirty rag.

"What's the problem?" asked Lintz, bending over to look at the engine. He pretended to listen as the crewman droned on—in reality, checking to make sure the engine was still intact.

Thankfully, they hadn't gotten far; the engine seemed to have all its parts in the right spots. He hoped.

The crewman had stopped talking, and Lintz realized he had asked him a question. "Sorry, I didn't catch that, what did you say?"

"I said, I think it's the seals. That's why she is running slow and belching smoke." the crewman repeated.

"Yeah, you could be right. You know, I almost joined the tank corps. All that power at your fingertips. I assume you're the driver of this unit?"

The man shook his head and pointed to one of the other crewmen sitting on the back of the tank. "No, I'm the loader. That's Johann, he's the driver."

During a lull in the conversation, a shrill whistle rang out. That was the first one, giving Lintz just two minutes. The Germans looked around quizzically but went back to their conversations.

"Johann, do you have a cigarette?" Lintz asked, putting two fingers to his lips to mime it. He nodded and reached into his pocket, pulling out a crumpled pack. Lintz stepped up on the tank to grab one and waited for Johann to pull out his lighter.

As he did, Lintz made his move.

With his right hand, he pulled his pistol from the holster. At the same time, he moved forward and wrapped his left arm around the man's collar. Lintz watched as a surprised look came over Johann's face and the cigarette dropped from his mouth. Using his body weight, he pulled Johann down backward and both men fell off the bank of the tank. They were now shielded from the rest of the Germans, and more importantly, the road. In the field, Sergeant Donalds put his fingers to his lips and whistled a second time.

"OPEN FIRE, PRIVATE APPLEYARD!" Donalds shouted, moving into a crouched position.

BAM... BAM... BAM... BAM BAM BAM!

The machine gun bucked in Appleyard's hands as he unloaded at the Germans standing along the road. The crewman Lintz had spoken to instantly received two shots to the chest and collapsed. The German Sergeant and two of the other soldiers ran towards the car, but Donalds stood up and leveled his Thompson at them and squeezed off two bursts. One burst clipped the soldier's leg and back, dropping him to the ground. The second rattled off the front of the car, missing the other two men completely. Appleyard continued to fire towards the tank, the bullets pinging off the armor like lead raindrops. One of the crewmen had attempted to fire back with his pistol, but the bullets from the light machine gun ripped him apart, his body slumping across the side of the tank.

Behind the large Panzer, Lintz wrestled with Johann, keeping a tight hold on the German while the bullets ricocheted around them. As the man jostled in his grip, Lintz put the pistol to the side of his head and said, "Be calm, Johann, be very calm and you'll live through this."

Leaning against the tank with his back, Lintz saw a blur of movement to his right. One of the crewmen had come around the side of the tank. Lintz stretched his arm out, aimed the pistol, and fired two quick shots. They rattled off the side of the tank, just missing the ducking German. The crewman crouched down and went to the front of the tank, hiding now from Lintz.

Out front, as Appleyard continued to lay down suppressing fire against any movement he saw, Sergeant Donalds held his Thompson up and moved laterally towards the right side of the tank, where the long barrel of the main gun was pointed. Gun at the ready, beads of sweat dripping down his face, he stepped slowly, inching his way forward.

Suddenly, the crewman jumped out, aimed his pistol, and fired a shot. Donalds instinctively ducked, lucky that the shot missed. He didn't wait for the man to fire again. He raised his gun and fired off a burst. The man fell forward, dead. Donalds quickly climbed the small embankment to the road and pressed himself against the side of the tank.

"LINTZ, YOU ALIVE BACK THERE?" shouted Donalds, removing the clip from his gun and replacing it with a fresh one.

"YES, SIR, BOTH OF US ARE HERE," replied Lintz, struggling to be heard over the rapid-fire of Appleyard's machine gun. *Good*, Donalds thought, Lintz had succeeded in preventing the driver from being caught in the crossfire, exactly as he had planned. Off to his right, Appleyard had ceased firing and he could now hear the unmistakable sounds of the German language, followed by some muzzle flashes near the car. Donalds looked on as Appleyard flattened himself to the ground and a hail of bullets chewed up the farmland near his position. Donalds knew he had to act quickly before Appleyard was killed. Crouching low, he made his way around the front of the tank, passing the dead crewman he had killed earlier. At the edge, he did a quick shoulder check, saw Lintz and the driver only, and continued down the length of the tank. As he passed his subordinate, the German got a good look at Donalds.

"*Der Teufel... [The Devil...]*" the driver whispered, his eyes widening at the sight of the Canadian Sergeant.

Donalds didn't know much German, but that phrase he did know; he had heard it before. The Germans had started to call the Canadian and American unit *Die Schwarzen Teufel*, or The Black Devils, after their confrontation at Anzio. They had earned their nickname after the invasion by spreading fear amongst the Germans, and by the tank driver's look of panic, his boot polish had done the trick tonight too. Donalds smirked a little at the man's visible fear as he moved past them to the other corner of the tank. Searching the road and the field, he looked for the origin of the muzzle flashes that had fired at Appleyard. The car was a few yards away, but Donalds couldn't see anyone inside or crouched behind it. *Had the rest of the Germans fled*?

Further down the road, a smattering of gunfire gave Donalds his answer. It seemed they were sticking around, and Donalds watched on as Appleyard fired back. Once he was done, Donalds caught his eye and made a hand signal for both of them to advance on either side of the road. Appleyard nodded, and both men moved forward. Crossing the open ground, each man advanced on the recently aerated *Kubelwagen*, watching for any sign of movement. Donalds ducked his head out and saw one of the soldiers quickly take cover behind one of the motorcycles.

"Appleyard, on three, I'll give cover fire. I want you to flank them and we'll flush them out."

"You got it, Sarge."

"Wait for my command...1...2...3!" shouted Donalds, popping up above the car and laying down a stream of fire towards the Germans.

At the same time, Appleyard stood up and dashed to his left through the field, trying to gain the angle. In his haste, he didn't notice the stick-like object fly out from behind the motorcycle and hurl itself towards the *Kubelwagen*.

Donalds, however, saw exactly what the object was. It was a 'Potato Masher', a German hand grenade. It clattered against the side of the truck, and Donalds barely had time to dive behind the car before a large explosion ripped through the ground where he had been crouching.

From the field, Appleyard saw the explosion and immediately thought the worst. "SARGE!" he cried out, looking for any signs of movement from his superior officer.

There were none.

Flush with anger, Appleyard raised the Johnson Light Machine Gun and pressed the trigger down as he jogged forward towards the motorcycle. The bullets rattled off the bike and seemed to catch one of the Germans. He cried out in pain and fell over sideways. Appleyard saw him clutching his thigh. Just before he reached the road, his machine gun fell silent. *Damn*, he thought, *the clip must be empty. That was my last one.* He flung the gun down and had just pulled out the pistol from his waistband when he saw it.

A single muzzle flashed.

The bullet caught him in the right shoulder, knocking him off his feet and forcing him to drop his pistol. The pain was excruciating, radiating into his chest and arm. He looked down and briefly glanced at the gaping hole oozing blood, before turning away. He propped himself up and began to feel for the pistol when he heard footsteps closing in on him. He looked up just in time to see a black leather boot kick him hard in the stomach and put him flat on his back. Woozy, he rolled around on the ground. A German soldier, an officer of some kind by the look of his uniform, stood there looking down over him. "*Kommando...*" Appleyard heard the man utter. The pain in his arm was throbbing. Oh, how he wished he had that pistol still in his hand. The soldier quickly looked around and then aimed his pistol down at him.

Appleyard, for the first time in his life, truly feared that he would die. The Canadian looked the man square in the eyes. If he was going to go out, he was going to make damn sure that this German remembered him.

The soldier pulled the trigger, and Appleyard instinctively closed his eyes, waiting for the inevitable.

But it didn't come. All Appleyard heard was a simple, metallic click.

"*Nein!*" said the German, checking his gun, pulling the slide back and forth. Appleyard opened his eyes and watched as the soldier frantically pulled the slide and depressed the trigger, shaking the pistol furiously as no bullets came out. Seeing his chance, Appleyard quickly tried to feel for the gun he had dropped earlier, but the German, who had by now thrown his pistol away in anger, saw what was about to happen. He put his boot on top of Appleyard, close to the wound, and pressed down. Appleyard writhed in pain, and let out a whimper. The soldier then bent down and found what Appleyard had been reaching for, pointing the pistol squarely at the injured Canadian.

The fight that he had, that had gotten him through this war so far, started to leave Appleyard's body. He was out of options now. Surely, these would be his last moments.

Images of his mother, father, and baby sister at their home in Regina flooded Appleyard's mind, and how he wished he could see them one last time... one last Christmas Day dinner, one last summer fishing at Old Wives Lake... training with the guys at Fort Harrison. And finally Sergeant Donalds and Corporal Mills. Appleyard couldn't help feeling a little guilty that he had somehow let them down...

As he stared at the barrel, a little of the fight returned to him. "DO IT, DO IT YA GERMAN BASTARD!" Appleyard shouted at the German through the pain, but he just smiled back and placed the boot on his wound again. Then he said something in German that Appleyard could not understand, almost taunting the Canadian. Appleyard closed his eyes again, and the moments ticked by agonizingly so. The German was making him squirm.

The gentle whistle of a breeze through the grass was the only thing that could be heard. Appleyard felt as if time had stood still.

Suddenly, he heard an odd sound... like a gurgle.

He opened his eyes. The German's body had gone slightly limp. Blood started to dribble from the man's mouth, and he pitched over, landing face down next to Appleyard. Incredulously, he looked up to see a familiar face staring back at him, bloodied combat knife in his hand.

Sergeant Donalds.

"Sarge! You're alive?" Appleyard said excitedly.

Donalds coughed, wiping the knife on his tunic. There were visible cuts all over his arms and legs, and his uniform was tattered and burnt slightly in places, like the edge of a paper that had caught fire.

"Of course, I'm alive, Private. If I die, who's going to make you run all those miles?"

Donalds sheathed his knife and bent down to grab Appleyard. Slinging his arm around his shoulders, Donalds lifted him and they started walking towards the truck. He shouted in the direction of the tank.

"LINTZ! WE'RE ALL CLEAR. GET THAT DRIVER UP AND MOVING THE TANK!"

Meanwhile, Donalds helped Appleyard into the tailgate of the truck.

Over by the tank, Lintz had held onto Johann and slowly got to his feet. "Into the tank, Johann. You do as we say, you walk away alive. You have my word," Lintz said in German. Johann slowly nodded, and Lintz let him go, keeping the pistol trained on him. "Now, get up in that tank and start the engine."

The crewman, free of Lintz's grip, dusted himself off. He turned around for a second, looking at the tank. It was then that he did something that shocked Lintz. The man turned on his feet and ran straight at him, lowering his head for a tackle. The swiftness of the driver's movement caught Lintz off-guard; by the time he lowered his pistol, the German had tackled him to the ground. Lintz felt the air rush out of his lungs, and he could feel the weight of Johann on top of him. The German took both his hands and grabbed at Lintz's arm and the gun. With his arm pinned to the ground, Lintz had to improvise. He thought back to his close-quarters training at Fort Harrison. Summoning what strength he could, he rolled himself and the German so that he was now on top of Johann. The men jostled back and forth; Lintz could see the strain on the German's face, and he was pretty sure his own was twisted in the same fashion. In the midst of wrestling for a dominant position and a mixture of grappling limbs, a loud sound echoed between them.

BANG!

The gun went off, and for a solitary moment, Lintz feared he had been shot.

But when the Germans's grip on him slackened, he knew what had happened. He fell flat on his back, exhausted from the struggle. The German lay next to him, dead. Grateful that he was unharmed, the knot in Lintz's stomach didn't go away. Johann was the driver of the tank, and now he was dead. If they couldn't move the tank, there was no way the plane could land. This field was the only adequate one around for miles. There was no way to contact the plane and get them to re-route to somewhere else. It had to be here and now.

Donalds, hearing the shot, rushed over to Lintz and helped the young Austrian-Canadian to his feet. "Well, isn't this just great, Private. The only guy that knows how to drive that tank, and he's dead."

Lintz was doubled over, still breathing heavily from the struggle. "Sorry sir, he rushed me and caught me off-guard."

Donalds looked down at Lintz, now aware that the man had fought for his life. "Well, the important thing is you're alive. Now, how do you feel about driving that tank?" Both men took a long look up at the hulking piece of machinery.

"How hard could it be?" offered Lintz. They made their way towards the top hatch and eased their way down into the tank. Lintz spotted the driver's chair and contorted his body to sit in it. Donalds hovered above him, trying to discern what everything did.

"Okay, now let's see if we can start this thing," Lintz said out loud, talking mostly to himself. He peered over the console and found the button to start the tank. "Here goes nothing," he said, as the tank's engine spluttered, then failed to turn over. He tried again, and this time the engine caught. The massive steel beast roared to life. Sergeant Donalds clapped him on the shoulder in excitement. Now Lintz just had to figure out how to drive the damn thing. Taking a chance, he depressed one of the large levers on his left. Easing it down gently, the tank lurched forward slightly. Okay, so that was forward and backward movement. There was a second lever to his left, and he moved that forward as well. The top part of the tank began to swivel. Okay, so that was the turret moving. Now, to put it all together—that was the hard part. Lintz felt sweat bead his forehead.

"I don't mean to rush you, Private, but there is a very large plane that will be touching down on this strip of land awfully soon," said Donalds, bending down into the tank from his perch outside the hatch.

Lintz rubbed his hands together. *It's now or never*, he told himself. Using both his hands he moved the levers back and forth. The tank engine began to whine higher, but the machine itself only moved an inch. Lintz tried again, but it had the same effect. Frustrated, he slammed his hands down on the console. He even said a few curse words in German.

Donalds ducked his head back into the tank. "Private, everything okay down there?"

"Sarge... I don't know if I can do this."

Donalds, checking his watch, knew time was short. He didn't have time for the usual speech, so he had to shorten it up. "Private, I need you to do something for me, right now. I need you to think of your brothers. We're all hurting...and we need this to get home. You can do this, Private. I know you can."

Lintz, his head between his hands, looked up at his Sergeant. "Sarge... I..."

"I don't want to hear it, Private. GET. IT. DONE."

Lintz silently nodded his head. Adjusting himself in the seat, he gripped the levers again. "Move... you Nazi piece of junk." Lintz realized he said his thought out loud, but it didn't matter. Giving it some guess, he worked the levers. The massive tank began to splutter and lurch forward.

"KEEP IT UP PRIVATE, WE'RE GETTING THERE," shouted Donalds from outside the hatch. The sound of the engine was deafening, and black smoke belched periodically from the engine. It had even started to fill the inside of the tank. Lintz coughed profusely. The tank slowly moved forward, its engine grinding and whirring. Lintz didn't want to push it beyond more than a crawl in case the engine gave out.

Up top, Donalds stood watching from the hatch. They were moving away from the main road, albeit at a snail's pace. He took a quick look back again, roughly judging the distance. *Just a few more feet*, he thought, a*nd then the plane can land.*

Suddenly, there was a loud bang from behind Donalds. The engine made a high pitch squeal for a few seconds, then ceased to make any noise at all. The tank rolled for a few more feet and then stopped.

"Sarge, what happened?" said Lintz.

"The engine crapped out. Don't think it's going to move anymore."

"Did we move it far enough?"

Donalds looked out into the field and then back to the main road. "It's going to have to be. Come on, let's move Private."

Lintz climbed up out of the tank and headed back down the road, following Donalds. He moved the motorcycles one by one onto the main road. As he walked back, he spotted the Sergeant tending to Private Appleyard in the back of their truck.

"You okay, John?" said Lintz, staring at the blood that had stained the man's jacket. Appleyard, always quick with a comment, was taken aback a little. Probably because Lintz used his first name. Nobody called him John.

"I'll live, thanks to the Sarge here," he croaked out.

Donalds, doing his best to put pressure on the Appleyard's wound, brought the man's hands up to hold the bandage. He looked around the truck and spoke to Lintz. "Alright, Private Lintz, let's get back in position."

Martin would be lighting the flares by now, Donalds hoped. The plane must be close to arriving. They piled back into the truck and headed back to their original spot. Gently, they loaded Corporal Mills into the tailgate, then backed the truck onto the main road. Martin soon joined them as they waited. "Gentlemen... I think we are good to... oh my, what happened? Are you alright?"

Donalds gingerly touched his forehead, where a decent gash was still slightly oozing blood. "Well sir, we asked those Germans nicely if they wanted to move their tank... but sadly, they didn't want to."

"Yep, had to do it the hard way, as per usual with them," Appleyard chimed in, wincing as he squeezed the bandage against his shoulder.

Martin was visibly shocked by the injuries. "You know, Sergeant, I just wanted to..."

"Not the time, Lieutenant. We're fine, just a little tired is all. I think we all are just wanting this mission to be done," Donalds said.

Martin nodded, and all the men sat in silence, save for the winces of pain coming from Appleyard, and some incoherent mumblings from Mills. After what seemed like two lifetimes, they heard the noise they had been waiting to hear. A low drone—far away but quickly approaching them. Donalds was the first to see it, and he nearly jumped in the air like a schoolboy on the last day of classes. He checked his watch. Right on time. Damn those flyboys couldn't drink worth a damn, but they sure could keep a schedule.

"Here she comes," said Martin, stating the obvious. Nobody seemed to notice or care. The C-47 descended rapidly. The men watched as it approached the field, praying for it to land safely. The pilot, who must've seen the tank by now, had turned the plane to the left side of the field. As it landed, the wing narrowly missed the broken hunk of metal and came to a stop near where Martin had dropped the flares. Rolling to a halt, the door swung open and an aircrewman waved his hand.

Martin and Donalds picked up the stretcher with Mills on it and Lintz put Appleyard under his arm and the group slowly made their way to the plane, battered and bruised. A Flight Sergeant greeted them warmly, doing his best to urge them along—they had to avoid German fighter patrols, or something like that. Donalds had stopped listening, as he strained to get the stretcher through the door. Finally, they were all inside. The Flight Sergeant shut the door, radioed up to the cockpit that they had retrieved everyone, and the idling plane began to move forward. As it rumbled across the uneven farm field, and then eventually rose into the air, Donalds found a seat on the bench. It was time to truly reflect on the night's events. They had done it, they had beaten the odds, survived the Germans and their crazed commanding officer. But, as he looked at his injured men, he couldn't help but ask, at what cost?

When he left North America and came to Europe, he thought he knew who the enemy was. They had told him when he joined up, "You're going to fight the Germans, liberate Europe, fight for liberty and freedom" and on and on. We were the good guys; they were the bad guys. But tonight had shown him that those notions were only partially true. He had nearly lost two of his men, not to mention his own life. He looked up at Appleyard, clutching his shoulder and grimacing in pain. He looked down at Mills, fighting for his life.

Thinking of all of this, he wondered, *if the Germans hadn't shot Major Webb, should I have, for what he did?*

"Sergeant?" a muffled voice said.

Each man was subject to his fate, Donalds truly believed that. *But what if I had been the one in that farmhouse, helpless as the Germans butchered everyone in sight. Would I have reacted any differently? Would I have tracked down Vahlen with such vigor, tortured, and then killed him?* The line between justice and vengeance was very narrow.

"Sergeant?" There was that voice again, but Donalds was too lost in his thoughts to pay any attention to it. *Would I have been able to live with myself if I had said yes? Would I have actually killed Vahlen?* Donalds liked to think he was a moral man, but this war had changed him. It had changed everyone he knew. Revenge was a concept that he well understood.

"Sergeant, are you okay?" the voice said a third time. Donalds broke out of his thoughts and looked up to see that it was Lieutenant Martin speaking to him.

"Lieutenant... yeah, just thinking through some things is all."

Lieutenant Martin clapped him on the shoulder and took out something from inside his jacket. Donalds looked up and recognized it as Webb's flask. Martin unscrewed the top and handed it to the Canadian. "Picked it up as I was leaving the house. Figured the original owner wasn't going to need it anymore."

Donalds could hear the lament in Martin's voice, but he took a swig, and the sharp sting of whiskey tinged his lips. The liquid instantly relaxed him.

Martin took back the flask and raised it into the air. "To Major Webb."

Donalds quickly grabbed the man's arm. "No... No... No! I will not cheers to that bastard." Taking a moment, Donalds searched the floor and found the words: "To Anne, and her father, may they rest in peace."

Martin nodded approvingly, then finished his sip. The men sat in silence for a few moments, Martin fingering the cap of the flask while Donalds clasped his hands tightly.

"Do you mind if I ask you a question, Lieutenant?"

"Of course, Sergeant. Ask away."

Donalds paused for a moment, searching for the right words. "Major Webb, how... how long did you know him?"

"Approximately two and half years. A troubled man, as we have seen, but an officer who attempted to do his duty to the best of his ability."

"Huh, how 'bout that." Donalds shook his head, sitting back against the wall of the plane.

"Let me guess, you are wondering how someone like that could do something like this?"

"Pretty close, Lieutenant. The way you described the Major, sounds a bit like me."

"Me as well. And it could extend to everyone on this plane. But everyone on this plane didn't put men at risk for their own personal vendetta. So, we just have to live with the knowledge that we have superior morals, I suppose."

"I wouldn't be so sure about that, Lieutenant, considering I almost shot the man in cold blood." Donalds extended his hand for the flask. Martin obliged.

"Don't beat yourself up, Sergeant. I strongly considered it myself. Webb was my commanding officer, and to some extent, my friend. But his actions were inexcusable."

Martin took back the flask, and the men shared another moment of pleasant silence. It was Martin that broke it first.

"I'm putting you in for a promotion Sergeant and a commendation for the rest of your men. You and your team acquitted yourselves with honor. I'll make sure your commanding officer hears all about the valor shown here today."

Donalds sighed. "Thank you, Lieutenant. But between you and me, I'd settle for you making sure the Corporal and Private Appleyard are well taken care of. They've earned it."

"As you wish, Sergeant. I know you have no reason to trust us, but we could use a man of your talents in the SOE. What I'm saying is, you don't have to go back to Italy if you don't want to. We could do some good if you decided to stick around."

"I appreciate the offer, LT. But after tonight, you'll understand if I'm skeptical of the British and the SOE. Gonna need some time to process it all," Donalds said, folding his arms across his chest and drifting off for some much-needed rest.

Donalds woke sometime later, thanks to some jostling by Private Lintz. He was exhausted and had slept through the landing. As he exited the plane, he saw Lieutenant Martin directing some men to help load Corporal Mills and Private Appleyard into a truck. *A good man,* thought Sergeant Donalds, as he slung his pack on his shoulder and made his way to the truck. Once everyone was loaded up, Donalds smacked the back, and the vehicle took off.

The truck bounced and jostled about down the road and Sergeant Donalds lit a cigarette. The hills and grassland of Bedfordshire sprawled out behind him. He sat that way, in complete silence. He finished his cigarette and flicked it from the side. No sooner had he done so than he spotted Private Appleyard awkwardly making his way to the back. "You should be resting, Private..."

Appleyard sat down with a large sigh. His injured arm hung in front of him, wrapped in a crude sling. "Sarge, when have you known me to stop doing... anything?" Appleyard asked.

Donalds chuckled, nodding his head. "You got me there Private. How's the arm?"

"Just a scratch, sir." Appleyard looked away at the rapidly passing countryside before speaking next. "So, back to Italy then for us?"

Donalds held up his hand. "Us? With that arm, you got there? You'll be on the boat home I'm sure... and Mills, once he's healthy enough to travel again. How is he, by the way?"

"Lieutenant Martin gave him some more morphine. I think he'll be fine till we get to the hospital. That Doctor we met in France did a bang-up job."

"He certainly did. You know, Private, Lieutenant Martin offered to take us into the SOE. I think he still feels guilty that his commanding officer almost got us all killed."

Appleyard looked slightly taken aback. "You're telling me we'd get to do messed up missions like we just came back from regularly? Lieutenant Martin must have been a bit hurt when you said no?"

Donalds sat in silence.

"Wait a minute, you didn't tell him no?"

Donalds's face was stoic. "I didn't say anything. Got a lot to figure out over the next few days."

Appleyard opened his mouth to speak, but stopped himself. He swung his good arm around, making sure his jacket didn't fall off.

"Nobody tells you when you become an officer about the burden...the burden you take on guiding your men. I'm responsible for Mills, I forced him to go when he didn't want to. All for this lofty cause of mine...changing the course of the war." Donalds opined, staring out the back. He held out his hands, looking down longingly at them. "His blood is on my hands. And the decisions I've made will probably haunt me for the rest of my life."

"Sarge...I'm going to say something that you may not like, but I think you need to hear."

Donalds nodded slowly.

"I can say with confidence that the reason Lintz and I chose to volunteer for this mission was because of you. Hell, we would've died more than once if it wasn't for you. If anyone is going to get us through this mess, it's you. Because of those decisions your talking about is the reason we follow you into danger without a second thought."

Donalds looked as if he might shed a tear. But his gruff exterior quickly returned. "Thank you, Private. Thank you."

"Seems like your turning into a philosopher, Sarge." Appleyard shook his head in disbelief. "There's no way I can go home now."

Donalds laughed out loud. It felt good to be in the mood to laugh again. Truth be told, he did like Appleyard, even over the rest of his other men. He admired the man's attitude, even in the most unending horrors, and every unit should be as lucky to have a man such as him.

The two Canadians shared a few more laughs until the truck finally reached its destination. As the rest of the men were piling out, Donalds caught Appleyard by his good arm.

"John, I say we grab a drink. I think we've earned it."

EPILOGUE

THE HORN OF AN INCOMING ship blared in the distance, announcing its arrival into the port. In the shadow of the magnificent polished grey and white stone exterior of the *Cathedrale La Major*—it's gothic windows and doorways glinting in the midday Mediterranean sun—the ocean-side promenade of Marseille was bustling. Couples in love walked arm in arm, children ran and played. She looked on at those were trying to absorb some type of joy into their lives. A walk by the ocean was a perfect way to accomplish that, she reckoned.

Placing her cup back on its saucer, she took a deep, nose-flaring breath. The brine of the air filled her lungs, and she briefly forgot the reason she was there, if only for a small moment. Her café latte had been exquisite; the scenery was just a pleasant addition. Although it wasn't her first time in Marseille, it had been her first time down near the promenade. The café, situated right next to the boardwalk, offered the right kind of anonymity she was looking for; it didn't hurt that the coffee was also good. Two tables away, the waiter was speaking with another customer. She checked her watch. It was almost time.

Gently raising her gloved hand in the air, she waved at the man to get his attention. Once he was finished, he made his way down the row of tables and approached her. "Everything satisfactory, *mademoiselle*?"

"Yes, I believe I am finished. Just the bill, if you please." Her reply was followed by a quick check of her makeup. Touching up a few spots, she used the mirror to look directly behind her. She was hoping to see... ah, there he was. A man, dressed in a dark grey suit and a brown fedora was hurrying towards her. Under his right arm, he carried a brown paper package. As he got close to the table, he removed the package and set it casually on the table. Not stopping, he tipped his fedora in her direction and continued walking as if nothing had happened.

Quickly checking her surroundings, she pulled the brown paper package closer. It was tied loosely with string, and there was a small card attached to the top of it. Removing it, she unfolded the paper, and read the small set of words:

Your target is at General Hospital
Something to help you blend in. Bonne chance!

She smiled at the card, placing it in her clutch. Peeling back a bit of the paper, she nodded her head in agreement at what she found there. With her eyes focused on the package, she barely noticed the waiter arrive with her bill. He placed the small metal tray on the table. "Is there anything else you need?"

Tossing some money on the table and patting the package now in her possession, she said, "No, I think I have everything."

THE FIRST THING MAJOR Vahlen felt was blinding, excruciating pain. He groggily opened his eyes but found that still only one of them could see, and it was blurry. He looked down. Both his hands were covered in bandages, and he tried putting them to his face, which he also found was bandaged. His memory was foggy and he didn't immediately recognize where he was or what exactly had happened in the last day or so. The last thing he remembered was lying on the ground outside that house in

Serronelle. There had been gunfire... and the rest was a little hazy. He was pretty sure he had passed out. He saw the white curtain in front of him, and some shapes just beyond it.

A hospital.

I must be in a hospital, he said to himself.

Vahlen could hardly believe it. He had made it. Despite the Resistance's best efforts, even the surprise appearance of a vengeful British Major, Vahlen was alive. He tried to wave down a passing nurse but was unsuccessful. Finally, Vahlen managed to get one's attention and she came over and checked on him, promising to return with more morphine. As she left, she passed by a blond German Army officer and his men. "Captain, he's awake now, but he is still recovering. Don't keep him up too long, he needs his rest."

Captain Sommer nodded back at her; his arms folded across his chest. He was standing quietly speaking with a few of his men.

While Colonel Grassl may have said the matter in Serronelle was resolved, Sommer was determined to find out exactly what had happened. Sommer smiled back at her, and dragged a nearby chair past the curtain, closer to the bed. He had been to this hospital in Marseille before to visit one of his men, but he was always wary of staying too long. The French may seem like they wanted to help, but deep-down Sommer knew they mostly despised the Germans. He had picked his timing perfectly; Vahlen would have been sent back to Germany, but his condition was too weak to travel. He had to make the most of this moment.

The man before him was a bit better compared to what Sommer had seen a couple of days ago. His face was completely wrapped in bandages, with a large one covering his right eye.

His breathing was shallow, which indicated some type of chest injury, and both his hands were splinted and wrapped tight. "I would ask how you are feeling, but I can guess just by looking at you, *Herr* Vahlen. I feel I must tell you, both *Hauptsturmführer* Teicher and *Obersturmführer* Weiss are dead."

Vahlen stared straight ahead.

"The doctor told me they had to wire your jaw shut, so I will keep my questions to a simple yes or no. Can you manage this?"

Vahlen nodded slowly.

"Good," said Sommer, pulling the chair a bit closer to the bed, and removing a small notebook from his shirt pocket. "I will try to be brief. Colonel Grassl has made his full report to Berlin on your behalf. I have seen it, but there are a couple of facts... that seem not quite right. I wanted to check them with you personally."

Vahlen nodded again.

"In the report, he stated that the Resistance member in the captured German uniform killed *Hauptsturmführer* Kampfer and then was killed himself. It also states that he was killed alongside his British handler, a Major. We found both of them dead in the house not far from where we found you. Is this accurate, *Sturmbannführer*?"

Vahlen's uncovered eye narrowed, and he shook his head to signal no.

"I knew it!" Sommer hissed, writing furiously in his notebook, "I knew we should have investigated more. Grassl is a fool."

Vahlen lifted one of his legs to tap Captain Sommer on the thigh and tried to point to the notebook with his hand. Sommer looked up and handed the pen and paper over to him. For the next five minutes, Sommer watched as Vahlen attempted to write something in the notebook, finally passing it back to Sommer and collapsing back down on the bed from exhaustion. Looking down, Sommer made out the words *killer, girl,* and *commandos.*

"I don't understand, *Herr* Vahlen. Are you saying the 'killer' of *Hauptsturmführer* Kampfer was a girl? Wait... was she from Serronelle?"

Vahlen nodded yes.

"And that there were commandos also there?"

Again, he nodded yes.

Captain Sommer sat back in his chair, closing the notebook. "Thank you, *Herr* Vahlen. I will make sure Berlin hears of this. You can rest assured that I will follow up." Replacing his notebook in his shirt pocket, he stood from the chair. "They tell me that you are to go by train back to Germany tonight and that Himmler himself has personally arranged care for you. I wish you a speedy recovery, *Sturmbannführer*. Now I will leave you be. *Heil* Hitler." Captain Sommer saluted and returned to speak with the two soldiers he had been talking to earlier.

Soon they left, and Vahlen eased back down onto the bed. The pain on his left side was throbbing again now; he was sure he had a cracked rib or something. He had asked the nurse for more morphine and was hoping that she would return soon. He sat there thinking that he couldn't wait to be on that train back to Germany.

After what seemed an eternity, the nurse he had seen earlier approached his bed, pulling the curtain around. She set the tray on the bedside table and checked his pulse. "Ready for some more morphine, *monsieur*?" She propped up his pillow and tucked in his blanket.

Vahlen nodded and held out his right arm. She was just out of sight on his left side, but there was something about her perfume that was familiar. He couldn't quite put his finger on it. She came around the bed, syringe at the ready. After gently finding his vein, she injected the needle and depressed the plunger. Vahlen closed his one uncovered eye and waited patiently for the wave of euphoria to wash over him.

But it never came.

His arm started to burn, and the pain started to radiate up and down his left side. He reached across and started to claw at the skin. This wasn't morphine...

"Starting to hurt, *Herr* Vahlen? I should think so. Tell me, do you recognize this?"

Vahlen looked down as the nurse tossed a bloody handkerchief on his lap. He remembered seeing it... but from where...

"I injected you with a fast-acting poison. We don't have long," said the nurse, coming into view now. Her face was covered by a mask, and Vahlen strained to see anything that might give away who she was.

Then, it suddenly dawned on him.

The girl from Serronelle. The one who had killed *Hauptsturmführer* Kampfer.

So, she's still alive. The little bitch is still alive.

She came around the bed and grabbed his right arm, holding it against his body. The pain was growing larger now, flowing into his shoulder and down into his chest.

"It will only take a few minutes more, Maxi, before the poison will have made its way through you."

He tried to sit up, but she put her body weight into it now, and with his injuries, he could barely move a muscle. His muffled scream was barely audible through the bandages. The pain from the poison was starting to overwhelm him now. The girl was now in front of him and removed her mask. Vahlen's eye widened at the sight of her. Still holding onto his arm, she gestured at her face.

"Take a good look, *Herr* Vahlen. Take a look at your handiwork." The nurse grabbed Vahlen's collar and held him close. She started to point at the small scars that were visible on her face. "But... I survived. You, however, should have died in that house in Serronelle. If not for what you did to that girl all those years, ago, or even to me, then for that innocent little boy you shot."

Vahlen struggled to do anything. His insides felt on fire.

"Imagine my surprise, when I found out from my friends in Marseille that a large Major in the *SS* was brought to the hospital. So, I just had to wait until the right moment to get close to you. Just like Kampfer." She checked her watch and put the mask back onto her face. She leaned in close so that her mouth was no more than a few inches from his ear.

"Remember the name of Martine Cuvier, Major. Remember this face... when the devil greets you in hell."

With that, Martine patted his shoulder and sauntered toward the curtain. Vahlen, fury pulsating through him, attempted to get out of bed, but his breathing had started to become shallow and sparse. Gasping for air, his body went numb and he couldn't feel his hands or feet anymore. As his periphery vision blurred, he cursed out in German.

Cursed that he had come to Marseille. Cursed that he had ever gone to Serronelle in the first place.

———◆———

DONALDS SAT UNEASILY in the chair. *Damn hospital chairs, do they have to make them so uncomfortable?* He'd been sitting there for the better part of an hour. Since they'd arrived back from France, he had barely left Mills's side, only to sleep and sometimes eat. The doctors had managed to stabilize him, but he was in and out of consciousness.

All the guilt and pain and regret were there, swimming around in his head; he still felt guilty that he had put Mills in this position. Of course, the anger, ever-present since Serronelle, bubbled below the surface as well. More and more, Donalds felt himself drowning in anger all the time. He shifted again uncomfortably in the chair when he heard a familiar voice behind him.

"How is he, Sergeant?"

Donalds turned and saw Lieutenant Martin standing behind him, a look of concern on his face. He gave a curt salute, receiving one in turn.

"Hello, Lieutenant," Donalds turned back towards Mills. "They told me this morning that he will be permanently paralyzed... from the waist down. Seems the bullet missed all his organs but nicked his spine. But, he's still alive... that's something, I guess."

"I'm sorry to hear that. A bloody shame. This is the price of someone else's agenda, it seems."

Donalds stood up, throwing his hands in the air, and began to pace. "That kind of talk doesn't do anything, Lieutenant. Sure, I can blame the Germans. It's their fault for starting the war, right?"

Martin shifted uneasily. "Sergeant, I don't think that..."

"I know!" Donalds interrupted Martin, stepping closer to him. "I've got a real good idea who to blame."

With his hand, he outstretched a finger towards Martin. "The British, Lieutenant. The goddamn British."

Donalds had raised his voice enough that other people in the hospital began to take notice of their conversation. Realizing this, he turned away, resting his hands on the chair.

"Look, Sergeant... You're right. You're absolutely right. Webb duped us all, but in the end, he paid for it with his life. Mills, Private Appleyard, Private Lintz... even yourself almost died for a cause that ultimately wasn't your own. I must take some blame for that—perhaps if I was more attentive, you chaps wouldn't be in this position. I will have to live with the events of last night for the rest of my life. But, as we Brits like to say, it's time to carry on."

Donalds snorted, standing up and folding his arms across his chest. "I've tried. Right now, I'm not sure if I can, Lieutenant."

"And that is your right, Sergeant, which is why I am here."

"Official business, then. So, this isn't just a social call?" Donalds asked.

"I'm afraid not, although I was concerned about the Corporal here. But, to the matter at hand. I've come to offer you two choices, Sergeant."

"Oh, and what would those be?"

Martin rubbed the back of his head with his hand and shifted his feet. Donalds thought it must have been a nervous tick of some sort.

"I've spoken to your commanding officer, a Colonel Frederick. He's said that in light of recent events, he's happy with whatever decision you choose."

Donalds sighed. The last few days were starting to catch up to him and he suddenly felt weary. Grasping the chair, he sunk back down.

"Those options. What are they?"

"I've arranged that you and your men can get that boat home back to Canada, as soon as you'd like. Mills of course will stay here in our care, but will follow on once he's able to be moved."

Donalds nodded his head. "And the second?"

"Well, I've just come from a meeting with command and they've seen fit to promote me, in light of Major Webb's untimely demise. Further to that, the second option would be that you would be promoted and seconded to me, under a new team I'm setting up."

Donalds sat silent. One question tugged at his mind. "And what about Webb? Will the record show what he's done?"

Martin hesitated. "Yes and no. Command is aware of what Webb has done, but in the interests of morale, the record will be sealed. I have no say in the matter, I'm afraid."

Donalds guffawed, slapping his thigh. Of course, they would cover it all up. Truth be told, Donalds hadn't expected anything less.

"Fine, Lieutenant, cover up your dirty little secret. I don't care. It's not like people's lives matter." He pointed at a prostrate Mills, emphasizing his point.

Martin approached Donalds, putting his hand on the man's shoulder. "You mustn't think like that, Sergeant. All of you matter, I know that. And you saved lives back there in France, mine included. For that, I will always be grateful."

"Well, I'm glad you're still able to be grateful, Lieutenant." Donalds turned back, leaning over the end of the bed, his eyes staring down at Mills. "You don't understand. I forced Corporal Mills to come on this mission. He thought I would put him in danger...and he was right."

"If I may, Peter— can I call you Peter?"

Donalds nodded slowly.

"Good. Now, Peter, while it may seem that you indeed needlessly put your men in danger, your intentions were noble, like mine surely were as well. We were going to capture the bad guy, get some magic intelligence that would've saved hundreds of thousands of lives, and be hailed as heroes. Sadly, that was not the case, and Major Webb hoodwinked us all, but... well what I'm trying to say is that, as an officer, you put your men into danger every day. Don't let this messed up situation paralyze you and prevent you from doing your bloody job, which is helping us win this war and saving innocent lives."

Donalds tilted his head up. The man made a good point; his quarrel wasn't with Lieutenant Martin, it was with Webb, and that bastard was dead.

"If I can say, Sergeant, the invasion of continental Europe is imminent. Our boys will be starting the second front sometime in the next couple of months. Soldiers with the skills of you and your men will be in high demand as we try to liberate France. You can still make a difference. I know that's what you really want, isn't it? Damn, I know I'd feel better with you at my side."

"Well, Lieutenant, when you put it like that, I guess there is only really one choice to make." Donalds stood and outstretched his hand. "Looks like I'm your man."

"Good," Martin replied, grasping the man's hand and shaking vigorously. "Take your time with Mills. When you're ready, come see me and we'll get you set up."

Martin turned to leave when Donalds piped up. "Oh, Lieutenant, what about my other men?"

Martin turned at the doorway to the hospital room. "Well, Appleyard and Lintz have already signed up, so you were the last piece." A sheepish grin crossed his face.

Bloody Brits, Donalds thought. *The nerve of these guys.* Donalds shook his head. "I should've known." He stood, and put his right arm forehead, saluting the SOE man.

"Carry on Sergeant, carry on," Martin stated, leaving the room.

Donalds sat back down, wondering what would come next. It was clear now, in his mind, that some fight and fire had returned to him. Instead of wanting to make a difference, to be the man that single-handedly won the war on his own, he knew that his real goal was helping as many as he could.

And he would use the inspiration of Mills to keep his mind focused from this day onward.

Don't miss out!

Visit the website below and you can sign up to receive emails whenever Ethan Watts publishes a new book. There's no charge and no obligation.

https://books2read.com/r/B-A-MKQP-MQTQB

BOOKS 2 READ

Connecting independent readers to independent writers.

Printed in Great Britain
by Amazon

22512473R00185